Life after the Tribulation

GOD'S PLAN FOR THE MILLENNIAL KINGDOM

By: D. L. Curwick

Life After The Tribulation
GOD'S PLAN FOR THE MILLENNIAL KINGDOM

Table of Contents

PREFACE

Reading and studying the Bible has always been one of my favorite things I do in my life and the prophetic future has always held for me an attraction of its own. Naturally, I have read a handful of books on the subject of the "End Times" and even though I appreciated these stories, I always felt sure critical components to the story were missing; something wasn't right about the story, but I could not put my finger on it. So, I felt compelled to begin my own studies of the Scriptures and research what God is telling us about the future.

As my studies continued to develop, three things began to surface that I hadn't really questioned before but should have. First, there are hundreds of books or so it seems, written about the Tribulation period of which most Christian scholars seem to agree, occurs over a seven-year period before Christ returns to the Earth. However, there are very few writings specifically about the Millennial Age, that 1000-year period when Jesus reigns over the Kingdom of God on Earth. I asked myself, "Why is it that there can be volumes written about 7 years of the future and often only paragraphs written about the following 1,000 years?"

It cannot be because there is very little said in the Bible about the Millennium Age. On the contrary, Jesus and the Prophets say much about the Millennial Kingdom to come and about Messiah, its king, found in prophecies scattered throughout the Scriptures like so many pieces to a grand puzzle. When I began to piece together the messianic kingdom messages a fascinating story emerged out of the Great Tribulation, about the Messiah King and His Kingdom and what He will accomplish in order to bring Humanity to its destiny. But how could I be sure this story portrays God's Plan for the Millennium?

The second thing I never really questioned before was, "What is the purpose behind all of the various plans of God revealed to us in the Bible, especially the plan for the Millennial Kingdom, what is the point, and why would it take 1,000 years to achieve?" Many of the common explanations given especially those about the Millennium, created more questions than gave answers, and many of those seemed unrealistic. "God has a plan" we often say and it is true. He has a plan for you and me, but He also has many other plans that are still in play for His creation. To complicate matters, God has attached many promises to these plans that are written in black and white in the Scriptures, promises that have been made to many, many people over many thousands of years.

This led me to the third thing I never really gave much thought to; How will Jesus Christ fulfill all these plans and keep all the promises that God made? But He will, the Scriptures tell us, *"For all the promises of God in Him are Yes, and in Him Amen, to the glory of God through us."* 2 Corinthians, 1:20 We cannot say that all of the promises of God have been fulfilled, but we can say that there is a plan in place for completing them and a person in place who has the authority of God to fulfill them all to the glory of God. I came away with an understanding that many of these multiple plans of God are intentionally connected to one another and I began to see a master plan of God's making. Of course, God would have a Master Plan, A master plan that is intended to achieve a master outcome of His will, one that He has also revealed in the Scriptures. I saw that His plans moved towards their completion through the Millennial Age and beyond and that a realistic story about the Kingdom of God emerges out of His Master Plan. A story that guides our commonsense thinking beyond the fulfillment of all of God's plans, into a New Heaven and New Earth, and a life with God. I encourage the reader to join me in discovering God's Master Plan for the Millennial Kingdom.

INTRODUCTION

In those days when Jesus walked on this Earth, many people in Israel had preconceived expectations taken from the Scriptures about the coming Kingdom of God. They had in mind the glory of Israel to return and a Messiah King who would come to usher it all in. As things turned out, many of those Jews were mistaken about Jesus and His Kingdom and wrong about Israel and the Messiah. So, it needs to be asked, "Could it be that many people in the Church today, are as mistaken in their expectations about the second coming of Messiah and the Kingdom of God, as those Jews were back then about His first coming?" It is reasonable to think that this is the case.

The thought-provoking question just posed usually comes to mind when I read or hear about the coming "end-times." The comments that come from people or literature often tell an end-times story that is more in line with what we want to believe, rather than tell a story about what God has already planned to happen. This is not unlike what many Jews did in Jesus' day when they so badly wanted to see Israel glorified among the nations.

What many Christians believe about the return of Jesus, why He is coming back to set up a kingdom, who is coming with Him, and what He will do here on Earth, reveals a huge disparity from what the Scriptures already reveal, often without our realizing it. Disparities that create misunderstandings about God's character and His Master Plan. It is this disparity about the return of Jesus that became the spark that put this writing into motion.

Our God is not a God of confusion but rather a God who reveals Himself and His plans through His Holy Scriptures to people like you and me. He doesn't always speak the way we would like Him to but when He does speak to us, He expects you and me to take Him at His very word. We will do well to listen to what God has to say about His plans. In this writing, we will look at those plans of God that lead us to a better understanding of the purpose behind an age that will last for 1,000 years. We will come to understand that all of His various plans are components of a Master Plan of God that has an ultimate objective to be achieved when His Plan is completed.

We will come to understand what God will accomplish through the execution of His Master Plan and why those accomplishments are necessary before there can be a New Heaven and New Earth. We will also see which plans will come to their fulfillment by the end of the Millennium Age.

For some readers, this writing will be a departure from a common "end times" diet, of fast-food stories about the latest in scary technology, evil nations, and the current world crisis that will take us into the Tribulation. Readers will take in a thoughtful examination of what the Scriptures say about Tribulation events and also how a judged world transitions into the Kingdom of God and advances the Master Plan of God. Readers should be prepared to have their understanding of the Millennial Kingdom and its purpose in God's plans challenged by the words of Scripture, reason, and a bit of logical conjecture. Discover a story told from the Scriptures and how this story brings into view the fulfillment of God's Master Plan. Come away with a newfound appreciation for "The Prophets" who experienced the earthly Kingdom of God and spoke of its glorious return. Walk away with a richer adoration for Jesus Christ as King of kings and Lord of lords, and for the God who has planned it all for His glory!

The purpose of this writing is to identify the Master Plan of God and to articulate that portion of the Plan starting at the Tribulation, into the Millennium and on to the New Heavens and New Earth. The reader will come to understand God's purpose behind His plans for the Kingdom of God and the forms of the Kingdom, from the physical to the supernatural. The reader will be presented with a realistic account of the Millennium Kingdom story and beyond, to that time when God brings an end to the temporary Heavens and Earth and begins the new.

The work of this writing is intended to be presented as a simple, easy-to-understand composition and has intentionally omitted the use of many theological terms. Yet the intent is to remain theologically accurate and proper in its use of the Scriptures and to present a Millennial Kingdom storyline that is faithful to the Word of God and satisfies the Master Plan of God, at least as much as writing about the future can be. The reader will not find any charts, graphs, illustrations, spreadsheet data, or any such types of information to accompany the simple writings, but there will be numerous references to Bible verses.

In **Part One**, there will be an extensive review of Christian doctrine needed to correct common misconceptions about the Millennial Age and the Kingdom of God and to set a scriptural context for the Millennial story and beyond that is told in **Parts Two and Three.**

The hope for this writing is that those who embrace the Millennial story and how it fits into God's Master Plan, will grow in their knowledge and understanding of God and the nature of God's glory. Also, to grow in their relationship with the Lord Jesus Christ, and to honor Him wherever they are in their spiritual journey.

Why should anyone consider what this writer has to say about this subject, what credentials does he hold? That is a good question that deserves an answer, why should people give any thought to what is said here in this writing? I am not a Theologian or a formally trained Bible Scholar, a Pastor of some mega-church, a known Christian who has become a motivational speaker, nor am I the Director of a large Evangelical outreach ministry. I have never written a book either. I have this to say:

1. I am just an average Christian man who loves the Lord and believes unapologetically that the Bible is the revealed Word of God and that God gave us His Words of Scripture not to confuse us but to reveal Himself to us. But also, He desires to let us in on His plans for us so that we can cooperate with Him in their execution and worship Him for whom He shows Himself to be. I also believe that the Word of God shows us who we are and what God thinks about us, both the good and the bad. Words of truth are given to us so that we might align our opinions about ourselves with those of God.

2. I believe that every Christian is indwelt with the power of the Holy Spirit and that I am capable, possibly gifted, with the ability to share the Word of God with anyone who seeks to grow in their knowledge and relationship with the Lord and be built up in their faith. I don't need a formal degree of some kind to do that.

3. I can think logically, and creatively as well, and can effectively convey my thoughts and understanding about God and His revealed Word and do so without harm to the truth that is revealed in the Scriptures. I endeavor to make sure I understand what the writer of the Scripture said and what he meant by it, using tried and true practices. I am committed to expressing my thoughts without adding to the prophetic Word of God or taking away from it as we are warned not to do in Revelation 22:18,19.

Points of clarification to take note of when reading this writing.

1. The New King James Version (NKJV) of the Bible has been selected for all Scripture quoted and referenced.

2. The Book of Revelation is to be read much like any of the historical books found in the Scriptures. To be read as a story being told from start to finish, without attempts to jump back and forward through times and events mixing its messages at will. The book is a progressive, supernatural revelation from Jesus, and within it, there are some visions with symbolism that do occur but they are manageable. Revelation is also like many historical stories, it has secondary stories within the main story that are needed in order to bring the reader up to speed with the different characters, their history, and their place in the main story. Unique to Revelation is that in the first three chapters, Jesus Christ gives His last exhortations to His Church and their place in the future. Then He proceeds to give them God's plan for the end of His physical creation, the beginning of a new supernatural realm, and end to His revealed Master Plan.

3. The title given to Jesus as "Christ" is also translated as "Messiah" both of which are used throughout this writing. The word "Christ" is used when speaking in a Christian context, topic, or about the church, and the word "Messiah" is used when speaking in a Jewish context, topic, or about Israel. Where neither of the above conditions apply or when both titles could apply, I simply choose either one since they refer to the same person bearing that title.

4. In this writing, the word "God" is used in most instances with the understanding that it could refer to God the Father, God the Son, or God the Holy Spirit because there is only one God. The individual references to the three persons of God are made only when it is necessary to make a distinction that otherwise may not be clear.

5. I tried to express where I see the logic in something, but I limited my logical deductions to using the words, "possible, plausible, and probable." Often without explaining why I think the statement made is logical; letting what has been said speak for itself.

6. Finally, it is my desire for the reader to consider asking themselves, "What are proper responses for Christians today, assuming that a Rapture is soon and that the return of Jesus Christ is imminent? How do we see ourselves preparing for a Church departure? Can we make any provision for those who are not taken, to help them come to terms with their predicament? Do we realize that those who are left behind at the Rapture could be no more than seven years and a day away from living in the Millennial Kingdom days? How will this change our thoughts about the Jews, our witness to them, and our response to growing antisemitism? The writer has his thoughts about these questions, hopefully, you will have yours soon.

PART ONE:
THE MASTER PLAN

CHAPTER 1:
What Is A Master Plan And Does God Have One?

Those of us who are familiar with the Bible can easily see numerous plans written out in various details that God has either completed or is expected to complete sometime in the future. We do not see the term "Master Plan" used anywhere on the pages of God's Word. For those who may get a bit hung up on that little tidbit, I remind you that we do not find the terms "Trinity" or "Rapture" in the Bible either, yet that does not negate that there is a Trinity or a Rapture, and not finding the term Master Plan does not negate its reality either. In the Bible, we do find other words used in combination with still more words that turn the concepts of the Trinity or the Rapture into dogmas, truths of the faith. But what about the idea of a Master Plan?

A master plan is simply an overall "Big Picture" that is to be completed with a big-picture outcome to be expected. It is an all-encompassing plan that brings order and consistency to all the individual plans that fall within the set boundaries of the Planner's authority. When a master plan is completed, all of the individual plans will have been completed as well. The independent plans are not completed all at once or in one duration of time. These plans and their objectives are completed in some kind of logical or reasonable sequence, each with its timeframe and accomplishments which its Planner has determined. Conforming to the master plan is the process of completing multiple subordinate projects or plans that eventually complete the overall plan. Cities and large construction development enterprises have master plans that they use to manage the direction and progress made over time. Their planner oversees various projects and improvements to be sure that they are compliant with the overall master plan. Master plans dictate order and expectations upon individual project plans that will be or are currently being performed so they will support the master plan objective.

A master plan will consist of multiple individual plans that are separate from one another in their goal, execution, and time frame, but are connected within the whole and serve to play their part in the success of the completed master plan. The master plan will have at least one high-level master outcome that threads through each of the individual plans and their respective goals, connecting all the individual goals together in ways that will satisfy the master outcome. A master plan reflects the vision, and values of its planners, it reveals what planners believe is missing, what needs replacing, what requires restoration, and what needs to be permanently removed in order to fulfill the master objective. A master plan is a means by which the planners can do what is best for all of the participants who are affected by the changes made in a city, or in a development, or in God's case, His creation.

A master plan is not only a tool for the planner to document all that is to be done, but it also communicates with others who have not taken part in the planning. The master plan brings understanding to other people as to what the Planner intends to do in various parts of the plan and as a whole. Once the plan is understood by others then it will ideally cause people who grasp its vision to be inspired to enter into the plan for themselves; believing that the plan and its outcome are worth their personal investment. When this happens, the vision of the Planner becomes their vision, they see how they can fit in and they become excited at the prospect of making their contributions to its goals in ways that are meaningful to them and to others.

Why would God have a Master Plan? He can achieve His purposes without one. He is God, He can do things when He wants and how He wants, and when it is done, it's all good! Right? If God wanted it so, He could instantly fulfill all that He wills to be done. If God wants the New Heaven and Earth that He talks about at the end of the Bible, in Revelation, chapter 21, He can move it up in the schedule and skip all of the stuff in between. It is true, God doesn't need a Master Plan. Unlike some City Planners who can't remember everything, God can. God will always do all things perfectly, with or without a Master Plan that documents the way to His desired outcome, His final objective.

There are two very good reasons why God might want a Master Plan. First: It gives various instructions on how we are to live and work with one another within the community. The behaviors and expectations that have been established by God found within His Plan are agreed to by all who want to belong. Ancient Israel was such a community and so is the Church today.

Second: It establishes communication between God and humanity. If God wants people to understand what He plans to do and how He will do it, then for our sake, He has His plans written down, including their purposes. God can certainly execute all that He wants to complete without anybody having a clue as to why, how, or in what way. But He does not do that; He reveals His plans to us in the Scriptures.

Imagine for just a moment that God did not communicate any of His plans to us concerning the Rapture. We may be standing around one day doing our own thing. We could be sitting on a bus or sleeping in bed, and then in a twinkling of an eye, something incredible changed. You and I are no longer like we were a moment ago. God has just executed one of His plan's objectives, but we didn't know about that objective. However, from what has just happened to us in that moment, we suddenly find ourselves present with Jesus and instantly taken into Heaven. Once we understand that we have been raptured, we would praise God and give Him the glory for what He has done. No action on our part was called for because God did not share His plans with us beforehand.

God shares His plans with us for a purpose. God wants us to know and to take part in what He is doing, even to partake in the glory of it all. In the example given, God has promised that there will be a rapture, "a taking away" of the Church on the Earth to join those whom Jesus comes to raise from the dead in a glorious, long-awaited resurrection. Those who have died in Christ in faith will be resurrected, and those who are living at this time will be changed instantly, in the twinkling of an eye. Changed from mortal to immortal and changed from corruptible to incorruptible. To be found anew in Christlikeness.

Because God has told us this plan of His, we can do many things in response before it all happens. We can live by faith that God will be faithful to us and that He will see it all through, just as He has said in the Scriptures. We can also tell others about it and live as though it could happen today, even sing about it, write about it, and pray that it will happen soon. Unfortunately, some may even choose not to believe God's revealed plan about the rapture at all, instead choosing to believe it is a misunderstanding of some kind, or wishful thinking for weak people.

The point to make here is this: When God shares His plan with us, we should, in response, bring praise and glory to Him and trust in His plan. We have the free will to recognize its execution, as well as celebrate its outcome. However, we will often do the opposite because we also have the free will to choose to ignore what God has shared or to reject what He has told us. When we understand aspects of God's plans that include us, our ability to know Him grows. How we react to another person's plans is a matter of our free will. We don't have to accept another person's plans, but if we respond with cooperation and agree to their plans, the relationship between these two people grows stronger because the plans that are now shared have become a greater priority to both of them. The commitment to see it all happen and the anticipation of the plan's fulfillment grows. This is true in our relationships with people, and it is true in our relationship with God, He wants us to know about His plans.

It is amazing to realize when the God of all creation shares His plans with us, as He has done through the Scriptures, we can understand what He has in mind for us and the world we live in.

When we understand any plan of God that He has shared with us, we have the potential to bring Him glory and become a reflection of His glory. God's glory and our ability to reflect it are common to all plans of God. When we interact with God's plans with purpose, we bring God glory. Therefore, it is logical to conclude that there will be no greater glory that we can be a part of than in the fulfillment of God's Master Plan.

We know that God has many plans that He has shared with humanity over the years, having spoken through a variety of people who were given God's word. The Bible tells us that God has a great and awesome plan to redeem people and reconcile with them. And the Bible's narratives never stray very far from this monumental plan. But it isn't the only plan; He will also bring about final justice and put an end to all evil. He has a plan to stop the tears and pain forever and put an end to Death. God has a plan to raise up the dead to life and ultimately bring them into a New Heaven and Earth to live with Him there. He also has a plan to be in a personal relationship with every redeemed person who has ever lived. We can see that there are many great and varied plans that God has yet to complete in the future. Some of His plans have already been completed, His physical creation for one and His plan to build Israel into a nation while in Egypt for another. God's plan to bring Israel out of Egypt to possess the Promised Land and create a Kingdom of God on Earth is still another completed plan of God.

One major outcome in the Master Plan that God wants us to know is that He will make everything new again. Speaking in the context of the New Heavens and New Earth, God declares to all who will hear it, *"Behold I make all things new."* (Revelation 21:5) This does not mean that He will destroy everything and start over with only new things. If that were the case, then all people would perish and new people would be made without any remnant of the old, but that is not what the Scriptures are telling us happens when God creates a New Heaven and a New Earth. (Revelation 21:1) It helps us to see that in Revelation 21:4, that God will wipe away every tear from our eyes and take away all the things that plague humanity. In light of this, there would be no tears or any concern for past things if we "old" Earth people perished completely and were replaced by "new" Earth people to be with Him. Also, the idea of redeeming people and bringing them to Heaven would be meaningless if what God means by "making all things new" includes a new us in a total start-over, emptied of everything that we are now.

We are clearly told, *"Therefore, if anyone is in Christ, he is a new creation; old things have passed away; behold, all things have become new"* (.2 Corinthians 5:17) Yes, old (former) things have passed away, but not everything has passed away. Whatever "all things" may be, it will certainly include a restoration of those remaining things to a like-new condition, not a complete replacement of all its parts. In this restoring work, God the planner, will determine what will be preserved, what will be destroyed, and what will be added. His Plan tells us that He will do such things, and He gives us some specifics on what is destroyed and what isn't, what is added new, and what is restored like new. But He doesn't give us specifics on everything.

The actions God takes in the working out of His Master Plan are made up of combinations of what is preserved, what is destroyed, and what is added. It is like a restoration, but in doing so, making all things better and leaving nothing untouched, this is believed to be the meaning of the words, "I make all things new." We see in the Bible that God has continued to reveal portions of His Master Plan with us as recorded in Scriptures that have taken over 1600 years to write and be compiled into one complete volume of writings. In all of this, we see a pattern form in His revelation where God shares His plans with us in portions, when He is revealing Himself to humanity over time. An example of what is meant here is this, that generally speaking, those people who live in these days of the Church, have a better understanding of who God is, and what His plans are for people in the future, than those people who lived before the Church during the days of the Law and the Prophets.

If we continue with this line of thought and look backward in time, those people who knew only the Law and the Prophets had a better understanding of who God is and a better understanding of God's Master Plan than those who lived in Abraham's day. If we continue to recede backward in time to Cain and Abel, we see in the Scriptures that people knew much less about God and even less about His Master Plan. As far as we know, God did not create Adam and Eve and then give them His Master Plan complete with a New Heavens and New Earth concept. He doesn't call on Abraham and explain to him the details about how all the families of the Earth will be blessed; or tell Moses that the Law that he has been given, is to be made obsolete by a new and better covenant. No, God reveals His plan in a progression that would make some sense to its recipients based on what they already know about God; What we see in God's words and activities over time as recorded in the Scriptures is another step in the Master Plan, not a Plan B or a change to a new idea altogether.

This fact is so obvious but needs to be stated: God has shared many of His plans, but not all of His plans. God will always remain a God of mystery to us in some way. For example, we know that the angelic realm is intertwined with humanity and that God has revealed that He intends to put an end to all evil, including angelic evil. Satan couldn't wait to get in between God and Adam and we do not know why. God has not said why Satan and so many angels have become our enemies. We have been told that there is to be a war in the Heavenly realm where Satan is defeated and he is cast out of Heaven and bound to the Earth, but we are not told what causes that war to break out because God does not tell us. We know a little more about Satan and his aspirations and a great deal less about those angels that follow him into war with God or why they assault human beings. We should not expect specific plans such as this one, to provide answers to all our questions because He is a sovereign God who wills what He wills. However, it is reasonable to think that we have enough on our plate trying to understand the problems we have with our physical realm, without trying to understand the spiritual realm. He is a God of mystery, to be sure.

We should expect that at the fulfillment of the Master Plan, God will have nothing less than a perfect relationship with His creatures, both angels and humans, without taking away their free will. Just as the Father and His Son Jesus demonstrated for us in their relationship. To take away free will would take away the ability to be perfectly relational with Him. However, our relationship with God is far from perfect and from what we have seen in the angelic realm, their relationship with God is not perfect either. Many people question what God has done with His creation; sin abounds, justice is rare, evil exists, nature is barbaric, and people are threatened with a place called hell, which He made for angels who reject a God that they probably know better than we do. Without understanding some things about God's Master Plan, human and angelic experiences with God's creation call into question both His character and His attributes.

How can a God with the attributes of being all-powerful, all-knowing, and all-present lose control of His creation and allow it to become the mess that it is, both in the physical realm and in the spiritual realm? If this all-powerful God hates sin and evil as much as He says He does, why haven't we seen good things such as Justice, Righteousness, Love, Truth, Mercy, and Grace in their perfect forms? This dilemma that we face is exactly what the Master Plan of God is going to resolve. People throughout history struggle with the nagging questions that ask," Why doesn't God just put an end to sin now and all of its evil effects?" Once sin is eradicated, all will be good to go forward, right? Not likely. God knows us better than we know ourselves, and it seems reasonable to suspect that our knowledge of good and evil, which we picked up along with our sinful nature (Genesis 3:22), leads us to form moral opinions about what we understand to be good or to be evil. Being limited in our ability to perfectly determine good from evil in all matters we fail to get it right at times by believing wrongly, often in cases where things are not so black and white. The day will come when the saints will be capable of judging the things of this world in complete righteousness, but not while we live in the flesh. (1 Corinthians 6:2)

In the Master Plan that He has given to us, God will validate all of His claims about Himself. Not because of any obligation on His part to angels, or people, or because He is concerned about their opinion of Him, but for His Holy name's sake. The following simple example shows a particular plan of God that has been executed completely and then how God validates that plan.

It was in God's plan to create a physical realm complete with a planet Earth teeming with plant and animal life, and He did just that. When He rested on the seventh day and ceased all creative activities, we can say that God's plan for creating the physical realm was completed. In response to what God has done with creation, people recognized that God Almighty, which they referred to Him as, is the "creator of the Heavens and the Earth" and that there is no other. God has made all things both in the physical realm and spiritual just as He says in the Scriptures as in John 1:1,2; resulting in many people throughout history believing this about God. Yet, it is obvious that there are plenty of people who challenge that there is a God who is the creator of all things. They propose other answers, other possibilities other than a divinely created realm. Humanity over the ages has sought out other answers, sincerely believing that there are other powerful forces at work in this physical realm. Still, others reject any notion that there is such a thing as a spiritual realm altogether. God will validate that He is the creator of all things when he puts an end to the existing physical realm and creates the New Heaven and Earth. Below are four examples of God validating His claims on all things.

#1 GOD IS THE GOD OF THE SCRIPTURES

God's plan to validate that He alone is the "Almighty Creator" is revealed in the Scriptures. God will have given all those who have stood opposed to this claim, all the time in the world to present their case against Him with an alternate claim, whether it be a belief in some worldly religion, naturalism, or unrevealed power. The opposed, will have had all of human history up until that day when Jesus, the Lamb of God breaks that sixth seal during the Tribulation. (Revelation 6:12-17)

He alone is the creator of all things, (John 1:1-3) with all of the unseen witnesses in Heaven testifying to the validity of that claim. (Revelation 10:5, 6)

#2 GOD ALONE IS BOTH JUST AND THE JUSTIFIER

God reveals in His plan that He will execute final justice and validate that He alone is the Just One. Some people and even some angels would challenge the claim that God is just. They challenge what God's justice should look like, and they rebel against any claims that God alone should decide what is just and what isn't. God has, in the Master Plan, given both the angels and people all the time in the world to deny any validation from God that He alone is both, "Just and the Justifier;" the only judge over the Heavens and the Earth, who is validated by a great host of Heavenly witnesses that testify God alone is Just. (Revelation 15:3-4, 19:1-5)

#3 GOD IS LOVE, PERFECT AND ETERNAL

Unlike our love, God will demonstrate that His love is perfect and eternal. It is in God's plan to make known to people that He loves them and wants to be with them forever. In response to His love for us, He desires that we act upon our free will and love Him in return. God will validate that He is "Love." The truth in God's word states clearly that, *"God so loved the world that He gave his only begotten Son, that whosoever believes in Him should not perish but have eternal life."* (John 3:16) This plan of God is to provide for all people who have ever lived in this world with a Savior. A Savior who demonstrated God's love for us even while we were His enemies. Even though we lived lives rejecting God, He sought us out as one of His own. His love for each of us moves Him to reconcile with us, to pay the just penalty for our sins, and to make us right in His sight. Because God loves us, it is in His Master Plan to come as God the Son into the world, born in the flesh of a man, for the purpose of dying in our place. He chose to be our stand-in for condemnation, our proxy in judgment, for all people, for all time because He loves us.

We find in the Scriptures that, in God's plan, He will allow these ongoing deceptions and rejections of His love to continue up until that "Day," when Christ returns to make love's claim with all Godly power and authority, Christ returns to receive both the living and the dead to

Himself and brings them into the Kingdom of God to be with Him there. Then, at that time the lies, and deception of the world's religions will be broken permanently by the indisputable fact of God's powerful presence. His truth is validated in the redeemed who trusted in His love, and His love is the motivator for His plan of redemption that He has revealed to humanity.

Although this is not revealed to us about God in His plan. We can confidently say that if God is love then He must love the angels as well. How could He not love these servants of His if God is love? However, the love of God cannot be achieved without the free will to choose to love. Satan and the angels who rebelled against God, it would seem to us, have already chosen to no longer accept God's love for them, and have chosen to not love God either. We are shown in the Master Plan that, in the New Heaven and New Earth, those who are there, will be loved by God and that we will be with Him and His angels forever. Validating for all beings that God is eternal love.

#4 GOD THE SOVEREIGN RULER OVER ALL THINGS

There is one last validation example of another plan of God, with obvious ties to other plans within God's Master Plan. This particular plan of God holds a prominent place among plans and is a theme that runs through most of Scripture. This plan declares that God is the absolute authority and ruler (King is the thought here), and His Kingdom is forever. God will reign over all the created order, both in the Heavens and on Earth. The plan is that God will unite all things under His sovereign control. Angels and humanity will both take their place within the kingdom of God. When all angels and people have willfully subjected themselves to God's rule and this plan is completed, then the "Sovereign" God will be validated.

God will validate that He alone is the sovereign King over the Heavens and the Earth. Witnesses in Heaven will testify that God the Son is King and validate Him as "King of kings and Lord of lords." (Revelation 19:16) In all things pertaining to government, authority, power, and order, are His alone.

There are several more plans of God easily found in the Scriptures that, in their own way, will be validated. God is Omniscient,

Omnipresent, Omnipotent, Mercy, Salvation, Wisdom, Truth, Good, Faith, and Holy. The validations by God will be done in the presence of humanity, the angelic realm, and all the other beings found in the throne room of Heaven and in the presence of God. Those present are to be witnesses to His validations and will give God all honor, praise, and glory for who He is. We see a pattern of these events validating who God is and what He has done, recorded for us in Revelation 5:1-14, 7:9-17, 10:1-7, 11:15-19, 15:1-8, 18:4-8, and 19:1-5.

In summation, when God has completed every plan that He has ever shared with us, He will have validated that God alone is "all things." That our creation, our time, our life and its quality, our relationships, our soul, our eternal destiny, and our place with Him are found to be only in Him and by Him. We have no control over any of these things, only God does. "God is all things to us." Truly, He is our only way in all things, and all things find their source in Him. This understanding reveals for us the common tie that connects all the various plans of God into forming the Master Plan of God. It is here that we find the master objective of the Master Plan of God, **"that God may be all in all."**

The Apostle Paul states this in a letter he has written to the Church in Corinth, explaining that Jesus who rose from the dead, will have those who are His, resurrected at His coming, and then He will bring everything into submission under His authority, then He will destroy death itself, and then when everything is subject to His rule, submit Himself to God so, *"that God may be all in all."* (1 Corinthians 15: 28) In Paul's words, the outcome of this Plan has become clear, and that Jesus Christ will be the person who fulfills the Master Plan of God.

There is not another scriptural statement in the Bible that better serves to express the ultimate outcome of all that God intends to make happen. This is the ultimate result of His executed Master Plan. It is the one thing that God will be, the one thing we should expect Him to be, and He wants us to know it. Paul's simple statement may sound strange to us at first if you have never thought much about what God wants to ultimately achieve with His creation. We live in a sinful, rebellious world with many who refuse to even consider willfully submitting their will to God. People attempt to rationally argue and live life against this idea that God is all in all. Some people claim that we live in an unintended creation without a god of any kind. Others claim that there is truth, power, and authority that should not belong to the god of the Bible. In any case, there is not now nor in the Millennium, any shortage of people who refuse to *"bring every thought into captivity to the obedience of Christ."* (2 Corinthians 10:5) At the completion of His Master Plan, all of the redeemed have freely aligned their will to God's will and accept, "that God is all, in all."

In the following chapter, we will look at how this statement has an extremely deep reach into all the other purposes of God. This statement, "that God may be all in all," is a perfectly profound claim that belongs solely to the great "I AM." If the claim "I AM who I AM" identifies for us the depth of who God is, then it is reasonable to say that "God may be all in all" identifies the profound depth of what God is doing. We will take time to look at what God is doing now and during the Millennium to come, and how the Master Plan and all that it entails are satisfied when this simple statement reaches its fulfillment.

CHAPTER 2:
God May Be All In All

The simple statement "that God may be all in all" is the master objective of God that He will achieve with His creation. We can see that this becomes evident in a review of the many individual objectives that God has willed to accomplish, that we find in the Bible. Every plan, or as some say, every purpose of God has a connection to this master outcome. We find this master outcome coming out of a statement from the words of the Apostle Paul in 1 Corinthians 15:20-28. In these verses, Paul is describing the resurrection of Jesus Christ and a progression of future events that eventually will lead to this master outcome of God's Master Plan. Paul writes, *"But now Christ is risen from the dead and has become the first fruits of those who have fallen asleep. For since by man came death, by man also came the resurrection of the dead. For as in Adam all die, even so in Christ, all shall be made alive. But each one in his own order: Christ the first fruits, afterward those who are Christ's at His coming. Then comes the end, when He delivers the kingdom of God to the Father when He puts an end to all rule and all authority and power. For He must reign till He has put all enemies under His feet. The last enemy that will be destroyed is death. For He has put all things under His feet. But when He says "all things are put under Him," it is evident that He who put all things under Him is excepted. Now when all things are made subject to Him, then, the Son Himself will also be subject to Him who put all things under Him, that God may be all in all."* There it is, the revealed outcome of God's Master Plan.

What exactly does the statement "that God may be all in all" mean? How should we understand it? First, let's look at what it does not mean. It does not mean that all things are God. A tree, or that squirrel sitting in it is not God. Or to say God is found in everything. This would suggest that God is common, nothing other than the varied parts of His creation, and that God is not distinct from the physical realm and makes no distinctions about what His presence glorifies. That is not the personal God of the Scriptures. What the statement, "God may be all in all" claims is that all things, meaning everything, has its purpose for existence in the personal willful choices made by the creator, God. It claims that the existence of a creation, both physical and spiritual, rests in the will of

God alone. God determines how each thing is as it should be, and when all things become exactly as they should be, then God will be all in all. As Paul has pointed out to us, everything is not as it should be. This statement and its outcome are true whether something is animate or inanimate, seen or unseen. All the beings who have free will cannot change the reality of the statement, only their submission to it and acceptance of it. For the one who accepts what God has determined for them to be, their existence is found in God. Those who do not accept what God has determined for them to be, are claiming that their existence is found outside of God. The person or angel who rejects God's will for them, is also rejecting their purpose for existing. That person will eventually come to realize, apart from God, they serve no purpose and are suitable for nothing.

When achieved, the master outcome, "that God may be all in all" will result in perfect relationships between God, angels, and His people, and bring them into a glorious state of existence before He creates a New Heaven and a New Earth. And in that new creation, the inanimate, and animate things will be made new as well by the will of God and take their appropriate places in the new creation for eternity. We saw God do a very similar thing with the environment and life in the Garden of Eden when He made the physical Heavens and the Earth. We also saw that God changed that environment and all life when sin entered it. And we will see it change once more to its final supernatural state when sin is removed. Paul shares this truth about God being all in all with the men at the Areopagus saying, *"For in Him we live and move and have our being,"* (Acts 17:28a)

In the 1 Corinthians, 15:20-28 text, the Apostle Paul identifies several problems God wants us to recognize and to believe that He has a plan for dealing with them. In God's plan, Adam and the race of humans die for their sins just as He said would happen. All human kingdoms reject God's authority and are willing to use their power to resist their creator's rule over them. That the sinful acts of kings and their subjects, who are in rebellion, are actually identified as enemies of God. Paul also tells us that there are spiritual powers at work, which are opposed to God's rule. Paul reveals that the last enemy of God's creation is death itself. In Paul's statements, there is much wrong with God's creation and there are enemies that will need to be overcome. Paul tells us the outcome will be that God will have corrected each of these things that are wrong with His creation, so that God may be all in all.

For the Master Plan to be fulfilled, someone will need to step into the mess all of Adam's race has gotten itself into. Someone needs to take control over everything, end the rebellion in every person's heart, and create a means of achieving heartfelt reconciliation with God. For those enemies who refuse to reconcile peace with God, there needs to be someone who will deal with them permanently. Someone needs to consolidate all physical and spiritual authority and power in a just and righteous way. After the hostilities have ended, someone needs to rebuild relationships with each other and with God. New hearts and minds freed from sin will need to take total control of our free will and permanently align it with God's will.

Someone will have to put an end to the dying and put Death itself out of its misery. Someone will need to end all angelic rebellion and hostilities toward humanity, and someone will need to free the animate and inanimate natures of creation in preparation for a New Heaven and a New Earth. Finally, when that someone can claim that *"all things are put under His subjection"* and *"all things are made subject to Him,"* then that someone, who we know to be Messiah, will also be subject to Him, (that is to say that God the Son will subject Himself to God the Father) that "God may be all in all." Praise God in Jesus Christ, the very name that is above all names. Our Savior and Lord had to become one of us, who had to die, and rise from death to a resurrected life and execute to the fullest extent God's Master Plan all to the glory of God, Amen!

There are additional things about God's Master Plan in general that should be understood. With man-made master plans, there is a beginning and an end. However, just because the physical realm in which we live has a beginning and end does not mean that God's Master Plan does. God has no beginning or end, and neither does His Master Plan.

When speaking about the summation of all that God has planned to result in the outcome," that God may be all in all," we need to limit that understanding to only God's physical creation now, the New Heavens and New Earth, and our stepping into an existence that will have no end.

Our access to God's Master Plan is limited to only what He has shared with us in His word and in His Creation, nothing more.

It would be neglectful not to bring into this writing another angelic connection to mankind besides the dark forces of Satan. In all probability, the angels of Heaven have much greater involvement in the Master Plan than we could ever know in this life. Angels are servants of God who are called to bring messages to people. They assist people in understanding God's will to be done and help people understand what God plans to do in the future. Angels share only those things that God wants us to know. Angels are looking out for the good of mankind, but they are also God's executioners in times of judgment. They seem to know much more about the Master Plan than we do, but not all of it. It may be that humanity is a bit of a mystery to the angels as well. They may know more about God's Master Plan than we do, but like people, they may also find God to be a mystery.

We all know that angels are either on the side of God's will or they seek their own will. There is a dark side in the angelic realm where evil resides in the demonic. It would seem very probable, logically speaking, that Satan and the other fallen angels are opposed to the Master Plan of God. The demonic opposition does not appear to be against the creation of a temporary physical realm because we do not see any aggression towards the created things of the world, with the exception being humanity, which is not temporary. It is humanity that Satan and the principalities and powers of spiritual darkness are opposed to. We don't know what the specific details are, but we see Satan actively and intensely, corrupting human affairs throughout our existence. He seeks to inflict us with emotional and mental misery and move us to cause physical pain and death upon one another. He is the devil, whom Jesus called a murderer and the father of lies.

It is highly probable that angels have taken issue with God in that mankind was to be made into the image of God, to be both a physical and a spiritual being that has been given free will, and for each to have their own personal relationship with God. These angels probably stand in opposition to God's expectation that the angels accept these creatures, these images of God that He has made out of dirt. It is likely they reject the fact that God is calling many of these dirt people "sons of glory" and that the Son of God would actually become one of them and is not ashamed to call them His "brethren." We can reasonably speculate that this was the likely cause of the angelic rebellion that sided with Lucifer (Satan), whom we are told in the Scriptures desired to rule over the angels like a god himself. Regardless of the cause of the angelic rebellion, their sin resulted in a Heavenly conflict in which we have no details, and we do not have any word from God for the reason why they fell from God's grace, which He has offered to us. What we do understand from the Scriptures is that there has been no reconciliation between the dark forces of the Heavenly realm and God and that there never will be. We see again the negative side of free will, this time it is in the spiritual realm.

For "God to be all and in all" and fulfill that final outcome of the Master Plan, Satan and the demonic principalities and powers of evil will need to be separated and dealt with, in finality. We are shown in the Scriptures that God will do that very thing. We are told that it is in the plan of God to remove Satan from the spiritual and physical realms and cast the angel into the eternal Lake of Fire. Satan will not go willingly; there will be hell to pay. He will make an all-out push to corrupt humanity in every way possible, and there will be a war in Heaven that is very likely to precede the Great Tribulation period of God's judgments. (Revelation 12:7) We know very little about the spiritual realm of God's creation, and that is the way God would have it to be. But we do know it is in the Master Plan of God to once and for all bring all spiritual opposition and hostilities to an end, both in Heaven and on Earth.

As a side note, when a master plan is first proposed, whether it be a city plan, land development plan, or a planned outcome from God, there is always someone who opposes the plan in its entirety or in part. We must not forget that there are angelic beings, and people from all times in history who are opposed to God's Master Plan in part, or in whole. The opposition will do everything possible to stop it or delay God's Plan even at the risk of having God's wrath come upon them. They do not want God to be "all in all." We will see this played out in a number of events before, during, and after the Millennial Age.

We touched on this just briefly earlier, but now we will want to review how God's will and our free will interact in relation to one another. God could easily command instant change to make His creation into the desired outcome of His will, so "that God is all in all." If God should want a New Heaven and New Earth, one that is occupied with supernatural people and angels who sinlessly submit to His will, then there is nothing stopping Him from just speaking the word, and it would be so. But God doesn't do that; the last thing that God wants to do with us is end our relationship with Him and start over. Rather, God has a plan. He has chosen a better way, a more glorious way! A glorious way to execute a Master Plan is not always the easiest or most simplistic way to get the job done, but this plan is relational to its core. His plan required the death of His Son in order to allow our relationship with Him to turn from rejection to redemption. God intentionally complicated the Master Plan's execution, most of the objectives, and the validations of who He is, by giving men and women "free will." Having free will allows people to sin, but, free will also invites each of us to choose to come alongside God on a journey toward humanity's destiny, and to dwell in the light of His glory. Free will allows us to discover for ourselves, both individually and collectively, what God wants to do with us and, more to the point, what He is to be to us.

As much as we would like to and as much as we try to do this, we cannot participate in His planning. However, He insists that we take part in the execution of the Master Plan because He is relational. We can picture what this looks like if we see ourselves being like a little eight-year-old grandchild who wants to help Papa build a deck. Papa encourages the child to help, and the child is thrilled to join in. In return, Papa is delighted to have the child be with him while it is being built. When that deck is done, both Papa and the grandchild will agree that they built it together. However, it will have required that Papa give more of his attention to what the grandchild is attempting to do and less to the actual building. He will say," It's only time, so what if it takes a longer time to finish the job!" He'd rather be nurturing this relationship, not wanting it any other way, and neither does God. The redeemed are to take part in achieving some of God's plans but not all. We join in on the work to be done by embracing God's plan as our plan. And He is willing to let us do our childlike work for Him. Papa doesn't tell the child to figure out what should be done or to go fetch their own tools, not at all. Papa gives the child everything he needs to be successful, and so does

God with us. He directs the believer by the Holy Spirit and equips them with the spiritual tools needed for their assigned tasks according to the plan.

God wants our participation individually but also as a community, so that we can experience and glorify Him personally but also with others, who are going through the same experiences. We can recognize that we have a role in God's plan and willfully think and act in alignment with His will. We can contribute to the advancement of the Master Plan which reveals spiritual maturity, But the opposite is equally true as well.

In God's creation which includes the spiritual and physical realms, we can identify four parts of it that will need to be restored, destroyed, or reconstructed, according to God's Master Plan, in order "that God may be all in all." These four parts would be the "Inanimate Things" found in the physical realm. "Living Things" which entails all plants and animals, "Angels", and then "Mankind". We cannot comment on any type of inanimate thing in the spiritual realm because we have no experiences with them, and know very little about them, things such as walls made of jewels, glassy seas, and heavenly thunder with lightning. The same is true for any plant or animal life in the spiritual realm. We have a picture in mind that has all of these things found in "Paradise" an Eden-like place; Jesus spoke well of it to the thief on the cross.

#1 THE INANIMATE CREATION

There are a great number and variety of inanimate creations, such as stars, gasses, liquids, planets, mountains, and weather events, all made out of the basic building blocks that we identify in a table of elements, gravity, subatomic energy, and time. In the hands of God, these creations should reveal a functional design that works in perfect coexistence with all other things. The inanimate exists for a purpose. It is to be a foundational support for life to exist and should never take the life it was created to support. The inanimate creation also reveals that the power of its creator is eternal and unlimited. God has created what appears to be an infinite number of inanimate things that serve a higher purpose, even to support life should He desire to do so. Amazingly, all the things in the physical realm (universe) He made out of nothing.

This would be true of the inanimate things found in the spiritual realm as well. God is the sustainer of the physical and spiritual realms and all things supernatural and natural, both terrestrial, celestial, and supernatural. God's invisible attributes are clearly seen in those things that are made manifest to us. In them, we see His perfection, beauty, and majesty; awesome power; a sense of infinity; and timelessness that clearly and magnificently glorify God. *"The heavens declare the glory of the Lord!"* (Psalms 19:1) The inanimate creation is amazing just as it is, but it is not in perfect harmony with the rest of creation. As beautiful or inspiring as it may be, it remains imperfect; it has natural aspects to it that are life-threatening. Terrestrial things such as earthquakes, multiple weather-related threats, and volcanoes. There are celestial things such as rogue asteroids, solar flares, black holes, and comets that threaten life. The cosmos itself has very little tolerance for any kind of life. It is probable that all these imperfections in creation are the results of the curse that God placed on creation along with all living things. The perfection of God will require that what He has deemed to be flaws in creation be corrected or replaced. We see at this present time that there is something wrong with the "Inanimate Things" in the physical realm. That everything is not what it needs to be for an eternity with God. The Scriptures tell us that this physical realm is a temporary reality that must be given over to a new, eternal reality. God has in His Master Plan the solutions and is currently working on His plan and purposes so that, "God may be all in all."

#2 LIVING THINGS, THE PLANT AND ANIMAL CREATION

A second part of God's creation that will need to be restored, destroyed, or reconstructed according to God's Master Plan, in order "that God may be all in all" is the animate world of "Living Things," all plant and animal life. Everything that lives or has ever lived finds its life in God as His created work. He alone is the sole life-giver. It is observed that the science community has, for the most part, lost its zeal in attempts to create life out of non-life, not even a mold. The work of science continues to prove that there is no combination of known elements and energy that are suitable hosts to turn on a life switch of any kind. Humans are unable to cause or witness even the simplest of life forms to emerge out of a cosmic power drink made from elements, chemicals, energy, and time. Rather, science is finding that even simple single-cell life forms are not so simple after all. God is uniquely the one and only one who can give life, let that life perish, and bring it back to life again if He chooses to do so. God is sovereign over all the living. No life at any stage is an accident, but each is uniquely designed and created according to their kind and to the environment God has placed them in, and they glorify God in their unique ways.

As incredibly wonderous as it all is to us, the animal and plant life in this physical realm is not perfect. We understand this is due to the sin of Adam and Eve and the Fall. God has cursed the world we live in, as recorded in Genesis chapter 3, because of sin. Mankind deserves an environment that is equally corrupted as we are, and that is what we have. What we lightly refer to as the actions of "Mother Nature" is the product of the fallen environment that we live in. One that does not naturally cooperate with us, and has all the appearance of acting randomly, even brutally. An environment of corruption and death, a so-called "circle of life" where life is dependent upon death for survival, where life is short, and death is forever.

Mankind has always had to struggle with plant life to feed themselves by forcing the Earth to produce food by the sweat of our brow. Mankind struggles to contend with the animal, bird, and insect worlds for the sources of food that the Earth produces. Many plants are often of no value to people or they produce toxins and poisons. Animal life also battles for survival against each other as well and with other species in a world gone corrupt, that runs on an eat-or-be-eaten system, where life is a slave to death in what we call the food chain. So amazing and complex is this brutal environment that many species have failed to survive for one reason or another. Science has shown that God has created more species of animals that have become extinct, than what exists today. As amazing as nature is to us, it suffers immensely from diminished glory compared to what it is intended to be. We are told in God's word *"For the earnest expectation of the creation eagerly awaits the revealing of the sons of God"* (Romans 8:19).

God is telling us the environment in which we will one day live will be better when the people who live in it are better. Also, we are told, *"For the whole creation has been subjected to futility, not willingly, but because of Him who subjected it in hope."* (Romans 8:20) We also know that creation groans and labors in a growing distress that is increasingly like labor pains. As humanity's corruption multiplies in volume, it seems so does nature's pain. It is God who has done this, but not without giving us hope that one day the curse will be removed and all nature will become as it is supposed to be. Although we do not know specific details of all that has happened to the living things of the Earth, we can find nature's condition written in Romans 8:19-25 and Genesis 3:17-19.

We see at this present time there is something wrong with plant and animal life in the physical realm. Everything is not what it needs to be for an eternity with God to come. But God has in His Master Plan the solution to fill the gap and is currently executing His plans so that "God may be all in all."

#3 THE ANGELIC REALM

A third part of God's creation that will need to be restored, destroyed, or reconstructed according to God's Master Plan, in order "that God may be all in all" is in the angelic realm. Angels are uniquely created spiritual beings that are a great mystery to all people throughout time. Angels were created by God, but their beginning has not been revealed to us. Their beginning would have likely occurred outside of time and space. Angels are confusing to us and are part of the mystery of God that remains unknown. Do angels love God? Angels do have free will and seem to have been created with the capacity to choose to or at least understand love. (Daniel 10:11,19) There is much that has not been revealed to humanity about these spectacular beings. These spirits are observed by people only when the angel or God deems it appropriate for the occasion. We are told in God's word that they are acting in service to God and glorifying Him in these works and Angels are in numbers that exceed ten thousand, thousand.

We know very little about any of this, and we have more questions than answers. God has shown us that the angels of Heaven are His faithful servants who have interceded on our behalf throughout history to bring us protection, deliverance, understanding, and guidance. The Scriptures reveal angels to also be God's agents of death, deliver judgments, and contend with evil forces that seek to destroy God's chosen people or change God's plan for you and me or humanity as a whole. The angels of Heaven have a track record throughout human history as our spiritual defenders against wickedness, both physical and spiritual. Many individuals have given accounts of amazing interventions performed by angels when a life is in peril, or offering comfort and tenderness that children can relate to. We are aware of the names of some angels and their dealings with people, especially the wicked angel Lucifer, known better as Satan.

Satan is not censored from speaking his mind in heaven, he is allowed to come into God's presence even today, to make accusations against us all, most of which are probably true by the way. He has been doing this since before the days of Job, the angelic story is entwined with humanity's story from the beginning of creation. Satan is the ruling prince of darkness over this world and he will do everything in his power to retain authority over every society and its culture. Satan's work can be observed in his attempts to destroy the image of God in humanity. Satan and the demons have taken dominion over the world away from humanity, they rule the affairs of mankind through world systems of power and worldly religions that seize control and take advantage of the majority of mankind. Those who have been freed from Satan's domain find themselves in a spiritual war while living in enemy territory. It is very reasonable to think that Satan's primary goal is to prevent the horrible destiny that waits for him when this world ends. (Revelation 20:7-10)

Satan is acting upon schemes that are intended to cause God to change His Master Plan in ways that will work to his advantage. Satan and the forces of darkness are likely in frequent skirmishes with the Heavenly forces; of which we are not even aware but will climax with a war in the Heavens, if we understand Revelation 12:7-12 correctly. For now, we see the effects of supernatural evil at work in this world every day. There is something permanently corrupted about the fallen angels of the spiritual realm, but we lack the details as to why, which God will likely reveal to us one day.

The angelic realm is far from perfect at this time. From a human perspective, the supernatural influences of evil are winning the day in God's physical creation.

The spiritual war and skirmishes between the holy and evil angels will need to end and the angelic hostility towards mankind as well. For "God to be all in all," the angelic realm in the Heavens, and on Earth will need to be in total subjection to God, their self-will aligned in perfect submission to His will.

#4 HUMANITY ON THE EARTH

The fourth part of God's creation that will need to be restored, destroyed, or reconstructed according to God's Master Plan in order "that God may be all in all" is that of humanity. Mankind is uniquely created to function in the role of the image bearer of God and possesses all the qualities needed to execute all that God commands people to do in ways that imitate and glorify their Lord. God has given all people, some God-like attributes and character to be manifested in each person. People have been given not only physical life but also a soul, making them uniquely different from any other creature which likely includes angels. People have been created to be in a relationship with their creator, and they have been created with a conscience that is to work harmoniously with God in all aspects of their relationship. Humanity was created to know God personally, obey God absolutely, and do the will of God without question or compromise.

Should we believe that the sole purpose of God's Master Plan is simply to bring His created order into a perfect submission that results in God being all, and in all, then we miss a critical part of what God intends to make happen. He wants something more than that. He wants something he refuses to take; God wants our love. It is not that God feels incomplete without our love; it is rather, in His nature to love. And He has created us with the potential to love one another and to love Him too, with a genuine love that flows naturally out of our own free will, free from conditions, and with a pure heart. We were created to love the Lord our God with all of our heart, mind, and strength and be holy imitators of God's love, however, the gap is wide and shows that we are not able to love like He does.

The desire of God, that we fully love Him has not been met by any member of mankind ever but with one exception, Jesus Christ, the one and only, born without a sinful nature. We are not to God's satisfaction; we are corrupted by sin. We cannot love Him with all our heart, mind, and strength and we cannot love one another as He loves us. Our ability to love as God loves went out the window with the first bite into the forbidden fruit. In truth, much of humanity has moved so far out from the presence of God that it does not know much about Him and does not know Him personally, certainly not enough to claim they love Him.

If He willed to do so, God-like responses could have been built into the minds of every person so that their actions would result in God's will being done just as He expects it to be. But God has in mind a different kind of relationship with us; He has given each of us free will to choose to obey Him when there is an option not to. God also added to us along with free will, His attribute of love; God is love. Even with this attribute, the gap reveals that love for God and love for one another does not come easily. When God gave us ten simple-to-understand commandments that tell us what loving God and loving people should look like, humanity in return does its best to confuse their applications, deny their authority, pretend to keep them or redefine them to satisfy preferences. The value God places on His love for us is ultimately expressed by the cost God the Father paid with the life of His own son, Jesus Christ. This love is for all, and when we are confronted with Jesus, it is within our own free will to either accept God's love or to reject it, to share His love for us with others, or withhold it from whomever we will. We are not blackmailed into a relationship with God, it is quite the opposite, we are offered a gift that brings life and allows us to align our free will with God's will if we so choose it.

In our world today, humanity is nowhere near meeting these expectations; the gap is wide. Our free will combined with a sinful nature has bred corruption in all generations of people from the days of Adam and Eve until now, and with that twisted nature comes several forms of corrupted behaviors involving love, which are unacceptable to God. In addition to man's natural-born corruption, Satan and the dark forces of evil continually work to deface the image of God in humanity. Keeping people in bondage and under his domain without them even knowing it, until they are eventually taken by death. The evil forces strive to stop God's love and its influence on redeeming people. This has resulted in a spiritual war that is waging today for the hearts and minds of all people. A war that you and I are participants in, whether we believe it or not, a war we choose sides in daily. War, not love dominates God's creation and the gap will continue to widen on into the days of the Tribulation when judgments come.

For "God to be all in all." The war must end in a victory according to God's will. Those freed by the Savior will find themselves overcomers of their world and the "Evil One", as spoken of by Jesus to His Church in Revelation, chapters 2 and 3. The overcomer will enter into a perfect relationship with God and with all others who are also in a perfect relationship with God, just as Jesus said in His prayers to the Father. (John 17:17-26) All people will be in harmony with all the angels of Heaven, but not while we live in the physical realm. All people will be in complete subjection to His will and purposes, as stated in 1 Corinthians 15:28. All people found in His love will also bring God glory. By faith, the redeemed are assured that God has a place for them when their part in the war has ended. The redeemed know that they are not yet everything they need to be to spend eternity with God, but know that one day, *"He who has begun a good work in you, will complete it until the day of Jesus Christ."* (Philippians 1:6) God has in His Master Plan a solution in play so that "God may be all in all."

When we look at these four parts of God's creation collectively, we see that a massive gap exists in each of the physical and spiritual realms as they exist now and where they will be when God creates the New Heavens and the New Earth. What is meant by this "massive gap" does not mean a gap in time, or a gap existing between two objects like some kind of void. It is not a circumstance where something is missing. The gap that exists between God's master outcome for His creation and its present condition today is a gap in quality, measured in terms of what is good, and bad according to what God values. Said another way, this is a gap of imperfections resulting from sin. You could say this gap violates His holy nature and the desire that God has for His creation is to become holy with Him. The gap greatly diminishes the glory due to Him. This gap has broken God's heart and has caused Him to grieve so strongly that His anger towards humanity can barely be contained, He is longsuffering even now because of this gap.

When we look at these four parts of God's creation, we find that rebellion and chaos exist both in the spiritual realm and in the physical realm. Any advancements that we can see in God's plan to achieve a creation where "God may be all in all" appear to have made little progress here in the physical realm and may have even taken steps backward from reaching that goal. An example of a backward step is found with the Kingdom of Israel, which never really made much of a positive spiritual impact over its neighboring nations and kingdoms under the domain of Satan. As a nation of His "priests," Israel eventually failed. And so, it was spoken by some of the Prophets of God, that Israel actually caused these nations to despise God and to move further away from Him and His Kingdom, rather than be drawn towards it.

Another example of a backward step is the Church body in the world today, which is often found willing to imitate the world more than it imitates God. The jury is still out as to whether or not the Church has learned from its past corruptions and losses and in its attempts to create a physical Kingdom of God of its own, only to see its' kingdom succumb to Satan like all other kingdoms of man.

Surely the Church has made an impact on the gaps. Christ's Church has made an unstoppable impact on the world over time, impacting the world's cultures and values and bringing Christian virtues into much of the world. The gates of hell barring the way into Satan's domain have not stopped the Church from being the shining witness of God's light when it enters into the darkness. The result we continue to see today in the Church of Jesus Christ is this. *"He has delivered us from the power of darkness and conveyed us into the kingdom of the Son of His love, in whom we have redemption through His blood."* Colossians 1:13,14) The fruits of redemption produced In Israel and in the Church are never intended to be for a temporary kingdom in a temporary world but for the eternal Kingdom of God, where there are no gaps to fill.

The "Gap" between God's fulfillment of His master objective and our present-day situation appears to be getting larger, not smaller. The rebellion against God grows in numbers and intensity. Mankind looks for new ways to distance itself from His light with every new generation. Love for God is diminishing, while love of the darkness grows in people. *"And this is the condemnation, that the light has come into the world, and men loved darkness rather than light because their deeds were evil."* (John 3:19) With a growing world population, more, not less people are acting like Cain did, who willfully choose to leave the presence of God. Mankind continues to grow in numbers that outpace the growth of the Kingdom of God and the physical realm of God's creation continues to grow as a breeding ground for sin and Satanic activity. However, while this is occurring on Earth, the spiritual Kingdom of God also continues to grow in number daily, all to the glory of God. This gives us cause to pause here for a moment to ask, "How then will God's creation ever achieve the level of goodness and glory that it was created for?" "What actions will God use to eliminate the gaps in the four parts of creation, to change the quality of creation today" and "What will have changed between man, angels, and God to assure that their free will never again be used in opposition to God?"

CHAPTER 3:
Filling The Gaps

When we consider what was said previously about the four parts of His creation and look at each part objectively, using the Scriptures as our reference point for truth, we easily see the gap in each of these four parts when we compare them to the ultimate outcome in the Master Plan, "that God may be all in all." In our way of thinking, we see that a reaction from God is in order because that would be our response. To be clear, God had his Master Plan long before these gaps ever came to be. He did not form a plan because he was forced to react to events and activities that challenged his sovereignty as the creator or his power as God. His Master Plan is as timeless as He is, it is, an eternal will that manifests itself to us as God's Master Plan. He has allowed the activities and events against Him to occur so that He may make Himself known to all of creation, "That they may know I am the Lord God" is a basic requirement to understand, before we can grasp that, "God will be all in all."

In His Master Plan, there are to be no wasted activities of any kind, and every action of God is a valid one even if there is redundancy. We read from Scriptures stories such as the Flood account, where God destroys all of wicked mankind except for one family only to see that the wickedness returns. We see God repeatedly punish Israel for their unfaithfulness and then save them from their foes. We can be mistaken to think redundancy is without purpose.

We may tend to think God is getting nowhere with His plan, and we start to look in the Scriptures for changes in God's plans because much of what we see happening in the Biblical accounts does not seem to eliminate the gaps at all; rather, we see redundancy and a widening in the gaps. However, a God with the attributes of the great "I AM" would not be troubled by what we perceive as getting nowhere. Nor does He ever act out of character in executing His Plan. From the Scriptures, we can identify the actions God has taken or will take, and we can see the results of those actions. Once we have a good understanding of what God is going to do to eliminate the gaps in the four parts of creation, we are better able to understand how "God may be all in all" when all is accomplished.

The intent for the remaining chapter is not to identify a comprehensive "Master Plan" that shows how every activity found in the Scriptures fits into His plan, and where it serves to aid in the ultimate outcome, "that God may be all in all." The remainder of this chapter will use the Scriptures to identify those aspects of the Master Plan that tell us, what God will do about the gaps found in the four parts of His creation.

We will start with the "Inanimate Things" of the physical realm. What we know about the existing physical realm is that God made everything in the universe out of nothing. There were no resources and none were needed. We are told that God simply spoke it into existence. Suddenly there was a fully functional, complex universe operating in something we call time as if it had always done so, as if time always existed. As observers of the physical realm, we have little difficulty accepting that it had a beginning. But we do have more difficulty accepting how it could ever have an end, but it will. We are told in the Scriptures that the Heavens and the Earth are passing away and will one day be dissolved in some kind of supernatural fire that will bring an end to it all. That thought alone is amazing when you consider the billions upon billions of cosmic bodies spread out in galaxies that are multiple trillions of miles away from one another. Truly, the Heavens do declare the glory of the Lord, and there is much we have come to marvel about our God, from our observations of His cosmic work.

In response to the gaps found in the physical realm, we are told that God will create a New Heaven and a New Earth that will come into existence to replace a creation that was not made to last forever. It is plausible to think the new matter God will use will not be like the matter used for the old physical realm; it will have to be some kind of supernatural matter that is not subject to change or to the law of physics. The thought here is that a sun could burn eternally yet not be consumed. God gave us a little foretaste of this very thing by not consuming the burning bush which fascinated Moses. This new matter mentioned in the Scriptures is not clearly understood because what the Apostle John is describing for us in Revelation, chapters, 21 and 22, are supernatural things that He is seeing in the spiritual realm. We don't know what is imagery or what will actually be observable to the eyes as He described them. In any case, John is tasked with the job of trying to tell us about some things we already know about that are made out of things we have never seen before. It is like trying to describe a never-before-seen primary color. We know all about colors but we cannot even imagine a new primary color and how it would change the entire color prism as we know it. John is describing streets of gold that are clear as glass. Walls made of jasper, sapphire, and a whole assortment of precious stones. Gates made from pearl and a massive three-dimensional city that floats out of Heaven and rests upon a mountain, what is described is almost too hard to believe. He describes an out with the old and in with the New Heavens and Earth without the limitations of the laws of physics and that is likely just for starters, a realm where all things are possible.

Our exposure to this supernatural realm in these chapters is very limited to only what the Apostle John sees and hears when spoken to. There is nothing else to consider, no touch, taste, or smell to stimulate his other senses which would very likely blow his mind. What we can know is that God, speaking from His throne said, **"Behold, I make all things new."** We need to consider this: If this temporary realm in all its amazing ways declares God's glory, how much more will this eternal New Heaven and the New Earth declare the glory of the Lord! A new creation supernaturally suited to support all other created things in perfect harmony with its environment; No gaps, no threats to life at any level of place.

The second part of creation, the "Animate Things" the plants and animals. When Adam and Eve were in the Garden of Eden, we are told they were to eat freely of the fruit given for food, with that one exception, of course, and to plant and till the Earth. They were given dominion over the animal world, in which they named every creature. In the New Heaven and New Earth, we do not yet know what the relationship will be between humanity and the animal world. Will people rule over it, or will that not be necessary? We know next to nothing about the plant and animal world in the new supernatural realm. We are also told of a "Tree of Life" that will bear twelve kinds of fruits, one for each month, and that the leaves of this tree are for the healing of people, supernatural trees planted all along the sides of the "River of Life" that flows out from the throne of God. (Revelation 22:1-2)

We can understand from these images and other language in the Scriptures that we will eat bread, have feasts, and drink wine in the new

Kingdom. Animals are also mentioned in connection with the New Heaven and New Earth; the wolf and lamb shall feed together, not upon one another. The lion shall eat straw like the ox, and dust will be the food for serpents; they shall not hurt or destroy (Isaiah 65:25). In Isaiah 11:6-9, these verses use similar language in regards to goats, cows, bears, oxen, and vipers, but it isn't clear for certain that this text refers to the New Heaven and New Earth or if it applies to transcendence of the Millennium Kingdom. It is certain to be expected that the futility that afflicts all of the creation described in Romans 8:20,21 including the plant and animal worlds and the corruption that keeps them both in bondage, will not transfer into the New Heaven and Earth.

In the Master Plan of God, it is reasonable to believe there will be plant and animal life that we are familiar with, but as with all things that God restores, He will also make better and prepare them for an eternity in the supernatural realm. The fact that Death will end and eternal life will likely extend to all living things is certain. As a result of a renewal of nature, we can expect the plant and animal world will be very different from what is experienced today. To fill the gaps in God's creation the plant and animal worlds of the "New Earth" to come, will interact in perfect harmony according to their maker's intent, within their own kind, and with all other kinds found within their environment. Life, wherever it is found, will serve God in all the ways it was created to do so and with a supernatural nature. One day, all life will be revealed in Godly perfection, beauty, and majesty, bring Him surpassing glory. All animate things have a role in the plans and purposes of God and they have a place in the Master Plan because God has promised with an everlasting covenant. (Genesis 9.9-12) A place in a supernatural realm, in a New Heaven and a New Earth where the "Living Things" will flourish. What this will look like, we can only speculate. We do not know how this will all work, but we do know that this new nature of plants and animals will bring God greater glory than the Garden of Eden ever could.

The third part of God's creation is the "Angelic Realm. In the Master Plan, there is no probable reason to think that the service of the heavenly angels will change dramatically. They will likely assist God in filling the gaps of creation. The Scriptures tell us these spirit beings will act for God and attend to people through the Tribulation period and it is very likely that their roles will continue throughout the Millennium age as well.

These angels will remain true to God, sinless in their being, and give full submission of their will to Him. It is highly probable that they will serve the Son of God routinely in the Millennial Kingdom, doing His bidding as King and High Priest of both the Earthly and Heavenly realms.

Unfortunately, many people can say they have had experiences with the angels of darkness. These would be those fallen, angels who rebelled against God before the creation of the world. The gaps in God's creation caused by these angels will be permanently closed. They will have been removed from God's presence, condemned, and their sentences carried out. They will be joined by those angels who had left their proper domain and abode and who are now in the everlasting chains of the judgment of God (Genesis 6:1 and Jude 6). None will escape God's judgment.

In the Master Plan, God allows the dark angels to assault humanity in nearly every way possible in their attempts to separate them from God, causing fear and destruction among the human race. These demons terrorize some people but also enlist others into their service, enticing them with supernatural activities including, possession of a person, hauntings, occultic activities, sorceries, and divinations. Their end on Earth is not clearly identified in a foretold event, but it is a very plausible supposition to think that their final end comes in reference to a supernatural flood sent by Satan (the dragon) to destroy the remnant of Israel in the wilderness. (Revelation 12:15,16) Believing even now, that he can cause a change in the Master Plan by means of bringing genocide upon those who will be subjects of the King, the Son of David. There is more to say on this in the story to come.

The end of the realm of demons and their final judgment are not shared with us in detail but we are assured that Jesus will end their contributions to the gap. When Jesus encountered demons during his earthly ministry, it always ended badly for them. They knew Him by sight and they feared the Son of God. A fear that He was coming for them to torment them, before the foreordained time that God had chosen for their destruction. (Matthew 8:28,29)

Satan, that is, the angel Lucifer, had previously made a failed attempt to be a god over the angelic realm and the dark angels appear to have followed Him into a rebellion against God. Defeated in the angelic realm, Satan has taken control over the kingdoms of humanity and rules over the world now as his dark domain. But rather than rule over mankind, Satan's preference would be for God to destroy all signs of humanity's existence. Satan remains to this day the relentless enemy of all people everywhere and has very likely opposed humanity since before the creation of the physical realm. Now he seeks to corrupt the image of God in people.

The Master Plan of God allows Satan to tempt and deceive Adam and Eve into sinning. This deceiver may have had the expectation that God would eventually destroy Adam and Eve and put an end to humanity, but that was not in the plan and God wasn't about to change it. Satan's plan to destroy humanity did not stop with Adam and Eve. He pursues our destruction, and with all the power of a great angelic being at his fingertips, Satan fills people's hearts with rebellion and darkens their minds with lies; he is not one to tangle with. He is the power behind false religions and the wickedness that filled the people of the Earth, and God allows this as well.

Before their end comes, there will be a war in Heaven occurring before the Great Tribulation period starts, possibly a war over the Church rapture or possibly the resurrection of the dead in Messiah, its cause is not known. (Revelation 12:7) It will result in Satan and his horde being thrown out of the spiritual realm permanently and cast to the Earth. Here on Earth, he will unleash his plans to drive humanity into worshiping him directly. He will also do everything in His power to prevent the Kingdom of God from coming to Earth and put an end to his dominion over mankind. (Revelation 12:7-17) Satan will lose his demonic army in that flood in the wilderness and then fail again with the Antichrist at Armageddon. His Antichrist will be captured and thrown into the Lake of Fire and the armies he brought with him will be destroyed. Satan himself will be incarcerated in the abyss for the duration of the Millennial Kingdom of God, where Messiah will reign on the Earth as King of kings and Lord of lords. Then as stated in the Master Plan of God, after the one-thousand-year incarceration, Satan is released from his imprisonment and returns once again to deceive sinful humanity, leading them in a final rebellion against God and against His plan to bring an end to the Earth.

In a final act of judgment, God will close the angelic gap of hostility and rebellion. Satan will be cast into the Lake of Fire eternally. (Revelation 20:10) All of Satan's efforts to destroy humanity and force God into changing His Master Plan will fail before the end of the physical realm occurs. Even though Satan has control over all the kingdoms that mankind has ever formed and was able to employ his supernatural powers in the myriads of false religions of the world, the deceptions will end and the gap permanently closed. Satan at his end will bring eternal glory to God, by becoming the recipient of His holy wrath which will display His power, truth, righteousness, and justice eternally. Unbridled holy wrath that brings glory to Him and reveals to all creation, that God is all in all.

The fourth part of God's creation is humanity. Humanity has become a different creature from what God originally created it to be, and we see it in ourselves today. The manifestation of the image of God has sadly become a disfigured "has-been" of what it once was. The attributes of godliness are marred by the natural corruption of sin. His characteristics that were extended into mankind have been glazed over with sweet perversions, and the conscience has been seared and scarred often beyond feeling. Sin has caused a permanent separation in every person's relationship with God. A relationship once personal and intimate, now as distant enemies.

God took action against those in the Garden of Eden that day. He brings curses upon all three parties for their crimes. (Genesis 3) He extends the tragedy to include all of mankind's environment subjecting all of creation to man's fall. Refusing to allow sinful people to exist in an ideal world that was made good for them in every way. Through these events, we witness and have become participants ourselves in a world where God is no longer recognized as "He is all in all." In the minds and hearts of people, a choice was made that does not include Him. It did not matter if they did not know the full consequences of their actions; we seldom do. People became vulnerable to the influences of the serpent (Satan), who deceives them. Blinded to the things of God, and in rebellion against His will. People have become broken creatures knowing good from evil but unable to abolish the very evil that works within themselves. Every person ever born is born into this tragedy that befell humanity, and the sin flowing through our veins, so to speak, will eventually cause not only our death but also a death of a second kind. Mankind's catastrophic disaster will require an impossible deliverance coming from an impossible deliverer that can only come from God, in order to close this gap.

Immediately after the fall of mankind, God continued to implement His Master Plan. Not a plan to replace mankind with a better version, but a plan to restore people, and save them from what they have become. It is not a worldwide inoculation of sorts that blocks sin's effects like some sort of vaccine. It is not a plan to save people by association with certain groups who are given special favor from God and it is not a plan to save people by inheritance through a favored family status. It is a plan that will require every person to act on their own free will in response to what God does for them. That same free will that opened up the door for sin to enter into us is now an open door for our salvation. In God's plan, we can enter into salvation by faith, confessing to God that we are sinful law-breakers and there is nothing we can do about it. Because we cannot stop the sin in us, we admit that we have no righteousness in God's eyes. In other words, we have no righteousness of our own creation. We come to God with nothing to offer Him, and we ask Him to save us from our sin and judgment. Only trusting in His tender mercies and loving-kindness (having faith in His grace) that God has promised to all who have this faith in Him. Believing He will impute His righteousness upon us through the substitute payment of death for our sins, a payment made by God himself. This does not change when people enter into the Millennial Kingdom.

As said previously, it is in the Master Plan for God to progressively reveal Himself and His plans to people over great periods of time, improving our understanding of His plans for humanity and His plan for our redemption. In the early days of humanity, we understand that the plan of redemption was shared with people through the activity of the Holy Spirit of God, who convicts the world of sin, righteousness, and judgment. In those early days, there were no written laws of God or Scriptures to guide the believers. Starting with Abel, the son of Adam and Eve, it is very probable that his conscience convicted him of breaking God's moral laws. It is very probable through the work of the Holy Spirit, that Abel turned to God in an act of repentance and asks God for redemption. Either Abel learns from his father Adam or through the direction of the Holy Spirit, that he must offer up a lamb to be sacrificed as a substitute death for his sins. We understand this act of worship as an earthly copy of what God has done for us in the spirit through the Lamb of God, the Lord Jesus Christ. Abel doesn't know about Jesus, but he trusts (has faith) that God will make the true sacrifice that delivers him from his sins and imputes to him God's own righteousness. The writer of Hebrews refers to the faith Abel had, stating, "That he was righteous." (Hebrews 11:4)

Over time, God continues to reveal more of Himself to mankind and also reveals more about His work of redemption as He expands the pattern of the saving power of faith. Over the centuries in the land of Canaan, we see another progression in God's revelation of Himself and the pattern for redemption. In a test of faith, when Abraham is called by God to sacrifice his beloved son Isaac, we see a first-time connection between faith and the resurrection of the body from the dead in the act of a sacrificial offering for sins. The writer of Hebrews speaks about Abraham's faith, *"concluding that God was able to raise him up (that Isaac), even from the dead, from which he received him in a figurative sense."* (Hebrews 11:19) Abraham believed that God would raise the dead if His promise required it, Abraham was righteous by faith. Four centuries later, after Abraham, every household of Israel in the land of Egypt, sacrificed a lamb and spread its blood over their door lintels to cause death to "Passover" all those protected by the blood of the lamb; a lamb of God, sacrificed to save each family. A lamb who would be their deliverer from death.

Once again, the salvation pattern expands outward when the High Priest in Israel, at the temple altar, offers up a single sacrificial lamb for the sins of an entire nation. A lamb of God who delivers all Israel from the law of sin and death. Many centuries after that, God's revelation of salvation by faith, fulfills this pattern when God offers up His Son, Jesus Christ, the last and eternal Lamb of God, to take away the sins of the world. Jesus, the righteous payment for sin by death. The substitute Lamb of God is for all who by faith, place their trust in this imputed righteousness of God.

This is the offering of God that He brings to humanity that will put an end to the gap, starting with Adam and continuing through all the ages past, into the present, and through the Millennial age to come. Righteousness in Jesus for all who have faith in the "Deliverer" from God. It is the plan of God to redeem from every generation, nation, people, and tongue, a people of God, taken from the corruption of sinful humanity. This plan is being played out today across the pages of world history and will reach those who will live in the Millennial Age. It is this plan that brings all the redeemed into the Heavenly Kingdom of God to dwell with Jesus in His Father's house. There in Heaven, He will be their God, and they will be His people. However, the plan of redemption does not end here with the redeeming Savior taking our spirit into Heaven to be with Him, leaving our bodies to return to the dust that they were created from, His redemption plan expands once more to claim the bodies of every person who ever lived as well.

It is in the Master Plan of God that at the Father's appointed time, the Lord Himself will descend from Heaven with a shout, with the voice of an archangel, and the sounding of the trumpet of God. And Jesus Messiah will gather up all those who will rise from their graves. He will raise up bodily, only those who He has redeemed throughout all human history at their appointed time, in a resurrection of the dead to be united with their spirits once again. (John 5:25-29) Only the righteous will experience a bodily resurrection to life in the eternal Kingdom of God; this is the first of the two types of resurrections in the Scriptures.

Those who are alive who are His Church, will also be caught up to the Lord Jesus in a Rapture, the redeemed are snatched away from the Earth alive, to be with their Savior who comes for them. All who are redeemed will experience a glorious transformation free from the effects of sin. The dead who were buried in corruption will be raised incorruptible. Those planted in the ground to turn back to dust in dishonor will be raised in glory. Those sown into the earth powerless are raised up in power. And those who are alive and who are His at His coming will be changed in a moment, in a twinkling of an eye, delivered from their sinful nature bound in human flesh. (1 Corinthians 15:42-54, 1 Thessalonians 4:16,17, John 5:28,29)

All the redeemed of God will be changed back into the likeness of bearing the image of the first man, Adam, but also of their "Redeemer"

Jesus. We will have not only a restored body but a body made better, a body in the likeness of Jesus, who is the first fruits of the resurrection. A supernatural body prepared for a new supernatural Heaven and Earth. To think that our body would only be physical as it was in Adam's day would be mistaken; those bodies are temporary and made for the physical realm. Those kinds of bodies made of flesh and blood cannot enter the Kingdom of God. (1 Corinthians 15:50) These new glorious bodies will emerge bearing the image of the Heavenly Man, who is our Lord and Savior. (1 Corinthians 15:49) What these bodies can and cannot do is not revealed to us in detail, but they will be immortal, with our redemption complete, we will be made new! Will we be able to come and go in an instant, go through physical barriers, and yet be touched? These are likely so, but we can only speculate about that now, but one day we will be as the Psalmist claims,*" As for me, I will see your face in righteousness; I shall be satisfied when I awake in your likeness."* (Psalm 17:15)

In the Master Plan of God, the redeemed will be changed into the likeness of their "Deliverer" and be forever freed from sin and yet, retain our free will in a new supernatural nature like Jesus and we will be able to love others like He does. But what about the unredeemed, what is their destiny?

On the opposing side of redemption is God's plan for judgment that will close the gap. There we find that sin is the unchallenged slave master over every generation, from Adam to the very last person to be born at the end of the Millennial Age. Death is the wages they will receive at the end of their captivity to sin. The rebellion against God fills the hearts of all who reject God's moral law, that part of the image of God that lives within each of us. Having a conscience and being aware of their sins, the rebellious reject God's forgiveness and willfully walk away from His righteous deliverance. Many more people simply remain content in their place in life, never desiring to seek the truth of God for themselves or long for a relationship with Him, seeking rather, the things of the world.

It is the Master Plan of God that all who remain unredeemed will be allowed to walk a path that leads away from the presence of God and right through the doorway into spiritual hell. But spiritual hell is just a temporary stop, a greater separation from God awaits them. With the destruction of the old Heavens and the Earth, there will no longer be a place for the dead, both physically and spiritually. The dead face a judgment day before God and are cast into the Lake of Fire, which is called the second death. (Revelation 20:11-15) This also has a part in the Master Plan of God.

When God finally makes us and all things new, the gap will be filled and humanity will function perfectly in a relationship with God. Each person will always love God and love one another. The gap will be permanently closed with a bond that causes oneness in the heart and eternal spirit, just as Jesus told us in John 17:20-26. Love is to be the underlying attribute of God that defines this relationship, and that love will be mutual. All will glorify God in their relationships with Him and each other and God will be all in all to His creatures forever.

CHAPTER 4:
Advancing The Master Plan

In the example of the grandchild who wants to help Papa build a deck, there will be certain work in the progression of the deck that only Papa can do by himself, alone. We see the same thing in the execution of the Master Plan. God's plans for filling the gaps found in the Inanimate and Animate parts of His creation are God's alone to do, we have nothing to contribute. He will fill these gaps in their proper sequence which will come after He has filled the gaps in the Angelic and Human parts of creation. Of the Angelic part, only where angels have intertwined with humanity do we get to experience how God will fill the gaps in the angelic realm, otherwise we are not involved directly. For the rest of God's work in the angelic part, we have nothing to contribute or participate in.

Naturally, it is in the Human part of God's creation that we find multiple plans that God carries out throughout history. Some plans are directly targeted to fill the "gaps" that move towards the master outcome. Other plans of God, act to set up the necessary conditions before God moves forward to fill the gaps.

Of all the activities found in the Scriptures, we will focus on the actions of God that are key to the Master Plan. Actions that must be completed before there will be a New Heaven and a New Earth. For each item, there is a brief summary explaining why it is a key plan. It is important to note that each item on the list below will have a direct impact on the situations and outcomes that define the Millennial Kingdom and the time to come that follows it. This awareness will help the reader to understand the time of the Great Tribulation and its transition into the Millennial Age that eventually leads to the creation of the New Heaven and New Earth.

The Abrahamic Covenant

Forms of the Kingdom of God

High Priests and their Laws

The Davidic Covenant

The Prophets of the Messiah

God with Us

The Church

The Triune Judgments of God

The Millennial Age

The Final Rebellion

These summaries are not intended to be an exhaustive account of what the Scriptures have to say about the subject but are intended to provide the reader with a reasonable understanding of how the Master Plan will advance to that time when God creates a New Heaven and Earth.

The Abrahamic Covenant

We find the promises God made to Abram in Genesis 12 when he is told by God to leave his country and family behind and go to a land that He will show him. Abram, by faith, agrees to do what God asks of him, and he goes to Canaan. This is where his father Terah had intended to take the family but he died in Haran. God promises Abram the following: 1. To make from you a great people. 2. To be blessed and have a great name come from the blessing. 3. God will bless those who bless Abram and curse those who curse Abram. 4. In Abram, all the families of the Earth shall be blessed.

Years later, when Abraham is old, he does not see much hope in having any descendants whatsoever, but in a vision from God, he is told that he will have descendants in number like the stars in the night sky. Abram trusted God, and his faith was accounted to him as righteousness. (Genesis 15:5, 6)

When Abram is 99 years old, God expands on the covenant promises to Abram by adding that he will be a father to many people groups in exceedingly fruitful numbers. People groups and kings will come from the blessed line of Abram, whom God renames "Abraham" to mark the occasion. (Genesis 17:1-8) This expansion in the covenant promise is not an afterthought on God's part but an intentional act to make distinctions between the children that would come from the line of Isaac and Jacob, (later named Israel) and the offspring (seeds) of Abraham that will come out of the exceedingly fruitful nations of the Gentiles. This distinction between the two lines will be expanded again by God with signs such as circumcision, laws, and a community relationship with God, as well as the possession of the promised land. Distinctions that take the promises of God generationally through the chosen line of Israel directly to Jesus Messiah; the One who will execute these plans and fulfill the promises God made to Abram and to all his descendants. (Psalms 105:6-12) The Scriptures tell us that Jesus is the "Seed" of Abraham where all the promises of God given to Abraham are fulfilled. That the blessings of Abraham come to all the families of the Earth, those who receive the blessing, receive it through faith in the "Seed" of the promise of God, "who is Christ." (Galatians 3:14-16)

This covenant of faith is a critical piece of the Master Plan of God for the redemption of humanity from condemnation. Righteousness by faith alone; Abraham believed in God and it was accounted to Him as righteousness. When Abraham offered up a sacrifice to God, he believed that God would redeem him and keep His promises. It is a truth for both Jews and Gentiles, slave or free, male or female, for all those who have ever put their trust in God's righteousness. *"And if you are Christ's then you are Abraham's seed and heirs to the promise."* (Galatians 3:28,29) This is part of the revealed Plan of God; the promises that God made to one man who was righteous by faith, have been extended down through all time to all people who have faith in a righteous God who saves. A promise of God that will be kept by the One who makes righteousness possible, for all who trust in Him. Jesus Christ is the "One Seed" who by faith makes it possible for the families of the Earth to be blessed, to inherit the New Heaven and New Earth. This blessing to all the families of the Earth and the fulfillment of the promise of God remains an active promise of God today and will continue until the end of the Millennial Kingdom. (Psalm 22:27-31)

Forms of The Kingdom of God

One critical theme found in the Scriptures that is difficult to understand is the concept of the Kingdom of God. It is common misunderstandings about the Kingdom of God, that throw many people off the path to understanding the purpose for the Kingdom of God during the Millennial Age. In the Scriptures and so far in this writing, as well, much is said about the various forms of the Kingdom of God. We understand that there is a spiritual form of the Kingdom of God that Jesus spoke so much about, a Kingdom that continues to grow with each new arrival into heaven. Israel was a temporary physical form of the Kingdom of God; the Millennial Kingdom is also in a temporary physical and spiritual form of the Kingdom that transcends from the physical realm into the supernatural; and lastly, there is the final Kingdom form, which is supernatural and eternal. Each of these forms represents the Kingdom of God. The following is intended to show how each of these kingdom forms has a place in the Master Plan of God and provides us with a progression of revelation that takes the Kingdom of God into its final form in the New Heaven and New Earth.

The Kingdom of (Heaven) God:

Pre-existent before time, the Kingdom of (Heaven) God is inclusive of what Jesus called Paradise, the angelic realm, the throne room of God, our Father's house, and what people generally refer to as "Heaven," or the Kingdom of Heaven. It is no surprise to any of us that this makes up the entire spiritual realm of God's creation. The Master Plan of God will have all people who have been redeemed by God throughout the ages of time be with Him in this Kingdom of God when they leave their physical lives behind. To be clear, there is nothing physical in this Kingdom. It is this spiritual Kingdom of God that Jesus came to preach about: "Seek first the Kingdom of God and His righteousness." When God finally makes "all things new," this form of the Kingdom will, in ways not revealed to us, become one with the transcendent Millennial Kingdom. Together they become the eternal form of the Supernatural Kingdom of God, within the realm of the New Heaven and New Earth expressed in Revelation, chapters 21 and 22.

The Kingdom of Israel:

The Kingdom of Israel is the one and only physical Kingdom of God to have ever existed on Earth. God founded this Kingdom and He is its King just as He has said in Scripture. (Exodus 19:6) Israel is a physical kingdom bound to God. This Kingdom has its place in God's plan as a physical copy of the spiritual Kingdom of God. The Kingdom of Israel is like a shadow cast from what can be expected in the spiritual realm. It has been furnished with a copy of the City of God, Temple of God, High Priest of God, and Laws and Prophets of God. Also, there are angelic interactions with people both inside and outside of the Kingdom and plenty of God-directed providential activity. This Earthly Kingdom is temporary. Another truth about its citizens is that they are not naturalized citizens by birthright in the spiritual Kingdom of God. A fact that many of the Jewish people had difficulty accepting as God's truth. This earthly Kingdom is intended to be God's witness to the nations of the world and to cause the nations to fear the Lord.

The Kingdom of Israel always struggled in vain to be the proper representation of the Kingdom of God to the world and to itself as well. This was due to the nation's rejection of God as their king and the rebellious sinful nature of its people. Israel's people intentionally rejected the God who made Israel His Kingdom; Rather, they desired that His Kingdom become their own kingdom to be run in their own way. We will see similarities to this at the end of the Millennium. Outright false worship in the Kingdom of God brought the Northern Kingdom to ruin and religious syncretism to the Southern Kingdom, which caused the nations around Israel to despise Israel and their God. The fear of the God of Israel became but a hiss and a curse among the people of the nations. Eventually, after much time and after redundant warnings from God, He has the physical Kingdom rendered powerless when its people failed to be priests of God's Kingdom causing the final curtain to fall on Israel's sovereignty, only to be renewed once again at the start of the Millennial Age as the Millennial Kingdom.

The Millennial Kingdom:

The Millennial Kingdom is certainly the least understood kingdom type that is found in the Scriptures. It is certainly not a transference of the spiritual Kingdom of Heaven to the Earth at Christ's return. It is rather a physical Kingdom that Jesus Messiah builds out of the ashes of a judged world. He will begin to build the Kingdom of God starting with His chosen people who are the ancestors of the first physical Kingdom of God, Israel. Those people who find their legacy in Abraham, Moses, Jacob their father, and a nation of people who struggled to live righteously with God. A people desiring the ways of the world rather than the ways of God. As a result of their father's failures, none of the nations of the world ever came to the knowledge or experienced the glorious Kingdom of God on Earth. This world has never had the experience of participating in kingdom life with the King of Glory as their Lord and High Priest, someone who would rule over them in true righteousness and bring prosperity to all who submit to His will, but that will change.

The Millennial Kingdom begins with the whole House of Israel being raised up physically through the power of Jesus Messiah. A fulfillment of the prophecy is found in Ezekiel 37:1-14, which is a dramatic vision of a valley of dry bones coming to life. More about how Jesus renews Israel will be shared in the Millennial story.

Consistent with the pattern of God's character, Israel becomes more than just a restored physical Kingdom of Israel and another copy of the heavenly realm; it becomes better than its people ever believed possible. It is a kingdom that will complete transcendence from the physical into the supernatural because its builder is King over both the physical and spiritual Kingdoms. Starting with Israel, the Kingdom of God comes to Earth to rule over all the kingdoms of the world. Jesus Messiah reigns as King of kings and Lord of lords, consolidating all power and authority over the Earth under His rule, just as required in the Master Plan.

A renewed Kingdom of Israel is a better kingdom, not because Israel is better, far from it. It is because when God restores, He makes better, in order to bring Him greater glory. This renewed kingdom is referred to as the restoration of Israel in Acts 1:6, 7 and Acts 3:20, 21. It will be quite different from what it was previously, it will have the rightful King of the Jews on the throne of David. It will have an everlasting final High Priest and his Law to lead the people in faith. This kingdom will have the final "Prophet," in Messiah as well, the revealer of God's will and word, who will fulfill every promise of God that remains to be honored. This Millennial Kingdom will bring about the conclusion of the covenants and close the gaps of quality in God's creation that are needed before there is a final transcendence into the eternal Supernatural Kingdom to come.

High Priests and Their Laws

When we think of High Priests and God's laws we think of the Levitical laws, we think of Moses, Aaron, and his sons, who were called into their roles as priests whether they wanted to or not, where they served God in the tabernacle. This was a temporary priesthood that administered a temporary "Law" in a temporary kingdom. It was never in the Master Plan of God to be the covenant for the Church, or for living in God's Kingdom during the Millennium Age, or in the New Heaven and Earth. Its laws, ordinances, and worship practices served as copies of the Heavenly things that were of Christ, the High Priest of God.

The Mosaic Law was to be the covenant practice for Israel in the Kingdom of God on Earth. God's chosen people were to be set apart from all other nations to be a holy people before Him, their "Redeemer King." It was in the plan of God to reveal to humanity God's righteous demands for holy perfection from His people. In doing so, all the High Priests from the line of Aaron proved to be weak flesh, and their Law against sin brought death to them and all the people under it.

God's purpose for that Law and its High Priest was to show for all to see that every man is spiritually bankrupt and in need of a High Priest who can offer life to the sinner and impute a righteousness acceptable to God. The sinless God/man (Jesus Christ) who knows our sins and offers up to God what is required for our salvation has become our High Priest and the Redeemer King, whom Israel came to know as the Messiah, after the order of Melchizedek. Also, in the Master Plan of God.

The first "High Priest" in the scriptural accounts was Melchizedek, who was the priest to God Most High and was also a king. Melchizedek lived in the days of Abraham, and Abraham honored him. The writer of the book of Hebrews reveals several significant facts about this man Melchizedek who comes and goes in three short verses in Genesis chapter 14; we do not know anything more about this priest. We don't know what law or laws of commandment he officiated, and we don't know what observances and priestly duties he performed in the name of God Most High. He was also a king, so he probably had worshippers of God in the city of Salem, which he ruled over. There is no mention of any priestly order that is connected to Melchizedek; he remains a mystery of a man who was made in the likeness of the Son of God. (Genesis 14:18 and Hebrews 7:1-9)

We know that there were redeemed people living in the days before the Kingdom of Israel came into being. People in those days practiced the act of making sacrificial offerings to God and called upon the name of the Lord God Almighty. They would have to respond to the moral law built into their conscience and respond to the Holy Spirit, who moves people to confession, repentance, and salvation. But how Melchizedek, as a priest, brought God to the people and the people to God is a mystery. We are told that Jesus became High Priest forever according to the priestly order of Melchizedek.

The Lord announces in a sworn statement given to King David: that the Messiah will be a king whose strength comes out of Zion to rule in the midst of His enemies. But also, the Messiah will be a priest forever. Not the last priest in a long line of Levitical priests since the days of Moses and Aaron, but a priest according to the order of Melchizedek. (Psalms 110:1-4)

When Jesus returns to set up His Kingdom, He will return as both the King and High Priest of Heaven and Earth. Both roles will endure beyond His millennial reign on Earth and into eternity.

It is in the Master Plan of God to replace the priesthood and obsolete covenant law with a new and better covenant with Israel and those of the Millennium Kingdom, as He did with His Church. Quoting Jeremiah 31:31-34, the writer of Hebrews says, *"Behold the days are coming, says the Lord, when I will make a new covenant with the house of Israel and with the house of Judah"* (Hebrews 8:8), and*" For this is the covenant that I will make with the house of Israel after those days, says the Lord: I will put My laws in their minds and write them on their hearts; and I will be their God, and they shall be my people"* (Hebrews 8:10-12).

With a change in the High Priest, the law changes from that of Moses to the law of Christ. We can see that in the progression of God's Master Plan being executed, the two offices of the High Priest and King are merging together into one person, which is Messiah, our Lord (Zechariah 6:12,13). As High Priest, Jesus will restore Israel as a holy priesthood among the nations of the world and make both of them better. Many, very many will likely become citizens of a growing spiritual Kingdom of God, and in doing so, God will be glorified.

The Davidic Covenant

At times when the ancient superpowers to the north and south of the Promised Land were not at war with one another, other wars were fought among the smaller kingdoms in the region: Israel, Moab, Edom, Syria, Philistia, and Ammon. King David's reign was at such a time as this.

As Israel conquered several of the regional kings and their kingdoms, King David turned many of his resources and attention to fulfilling his desire to build a house for the Lord, a temple for God. However, when God was approached by the prophet Nathan with David's idea, He was less than enthusiastic and turned the tables on David, telling the king that God would make him a house and that David's seed (son) would build a house for His name. *"And your house and your kingdom shall be established forever before you. Your throne shall be established forever."* (2 Samuel 7:16) Of this son of David who will build God's house, God will establish the throne of his Kingdom forever. God will be His Father, and he shall be God's son (2 Samuel 7:12-14). All these words should sound familiar to readers of the New Testament because we understand now that God is expressing to David more about His plans than what David may have initially understood. Yes, David's son, King Solomon, was to build a physical temple, be king over the physical Kingdom of God, and carry on the name of the House of David, but God meant so much more than that.

The significance of what the Scriptures say about the House of David, and the everlasting Kingdom of God and its King should not be misunderstood if we are to make sense of the events that occur in the Millennial Kingdom. It is this covenant promise that God made to David that intentionally links Israel, the physical Kingdom of God, to the physical Millennial Kingdom of God to come. The covenant also reveals that the Son of David and this Kingdom will carry over into the final state of the Kingdom of God, which will be in the New Heaven and New Earth.

The full impact of what the Davidic Covenant meant to the Plan of God was not revealed to David or the Prophets all at once. God revealed His Kingdom plan progressively. He revealed to David and then His prophets that this son of David would also be God's son (Isaiah 9:6,7; Luke 1:32,33). That this king would not only be the King of the Jews but the King of kings and Lord of lords over all the Earth, as stated by a prophet. (Daniel 7:13,14). It is God's Plan to show how the physical Kingdom that failed God under the rule and authority of men will prosper and bring honor and glory to God when it is placed under the rule of the Messiah King. (Psalm 45:1-7).

This Kingdom will commence with the end of Satan's rule and dominion and Messiah's claim over the kingdoms of this world. Through the execution of God's Kingdom plan and the fulfillment of the Davidic Covenant, the chosen people, who are at odds with God and all the Gentile nations around them, will become the Kingdom of Priests God has called Israel to be.

No longer fighting for their survival with their surrounding neighbors, they will bring God to the people and the people to God, just as the prophets had foretold. Israel will take the gospel message of faith to the nations. The number of people who will find a saving faith in their Lord and King will likely grow with each generation through the mission work of Israel. This too is in the Master Plan of God.

It is during this Kingdom of the Messiah, that all the relational promises God ever made to the people of Israel will come true. It is during the time of the Millennial Kingdom that Israel will show unwavering commitment to their King. It is a time when the whole of Israel will be redeemed, raised up out of its dead bones, just as Ezekiel had prophesied. They will walk as an army of priests with the Son of David as the King of Israel and of the eternal Kingdom of God. All powers and authorities throughout the world will become subject to His authority. Messiah will fulfill the Master Plan of God for a Millennial Kingdom and prepare all things to be ready for the New Heaven and New Earth "that God may be all in all."

The Prophets of the Messiah

In the Scriptures, we find that most of the prophets who spoke on behalf of God lived during the same period as the physical Kingdom of God. Those prophets had direct ties to the kings and the priesthood, and could speak concerning the Levitical laws. Many of the messages that the prophets declared to both Israel and Judah and their respective kings, was about their faithlessness. in breaking God's laws, civil laws, moral laws, and all the covenant laws that carry consequences of blessings and cursing according to God's promises. The prophet's messages to Israel and Judah would condemn their behavior, even logically arguing points raised against their willingness to break their relationship with God.

Prophets could reveal ahead of time what will transpire in their time if the rebellion or unfaithfulness continues. They not only warned the people of their day but also how badly things will end for them and for the future generations of the children of Jacob. The prophets also extended God's warnings and assured judgments to come to the nations of the region as well as to the superpowers who invaded the Promised Land, plundered the temple, and eventually ended the sovereignty of both Israel and Judah. But the Prophets also spoke of how God would bless all who would be faithful to Him.

When reading their letters, the prophets took issue with the sins of Jacob's children, their faithlessness to God, their lust for other gods, and the pagan ways of life that insulted God and rejected His truth. They rejected the covenant that made them unlike any other people on Earth. Like many people today, they did not want to stand out and do life differently, they preferred the things of this world, *" the lust of the flesh, the lust of the eyes, and the pride of life."* (1 John 2:16) Yet, these same people held on to the form of their faith, keeping with the festivals, ceremonies, and traditions. They like many people today convince themselves that they are satisfying the requirements that God had for them. The prophets spoke against this kind of phony faith and behavior, which led one such prophet to rename God's people "Sodom" after that infamously wicked city He obliterated in brimstone and sulfur.

It would be in error for us today to think that the entirety of the messages given by the prophets are now obsolete or completed in fulfillment with the Messiah's first coming into the world. It would be in error to think that the prophets who speak God's eternal words, no longer have any impact in a world of new covenant believers. Those in error will miss out on much of what God's word says will come to pass in the execution of His Master Plan.

Every prophet who spoke words of extreme judgment aimed at Israel and Judah also spoke words from God about a time to follow of future blessings, righteousness, and salvation from God that will come to Israel through the Messiah, and His Kingdom. (Jeremiah 23:5-8). The

Messiah will bring a new covenant to replace the old for all the house of Israel (Jeremiah 31:31-34). There are promises of a better day for the children of Israel. Days with great times of peace that will come to a people who have scarcely known peace. And in those latter days, the Gentiles will seek out the people of Israel and their king, not for war, but for a blessing and to come to know the God of Israel as their God. (Isaiah 2:2-4; Zechariah 8:20-23).

It will be a day when the Lord gives the children of Israel new hearts to replace their hearts of stone and also a new spirit to be in them (Ezekiel 36:26). It is important to understand what the prophets say, but also what they do not say. These messages are not for the Church to claim today, but for Israel in the latter days to come. What the prophets tell us is that in the latter days Gentiles who desire to know the Lord will seek after Messiah's Jews, not Christians (Zechariah 8:20-23).

The prophets deliver God's messages about reconciliation, peace with the Lord, and a promise of a day when the Promised Land will remain in Israel's possession forever. These latter-day messages and those like them are clearly for a time to come in the Millennial age after the Church has left this Earth. The prophets revealed these plans of God to the faithful Jewish people of God and documented them in the Scriptures along with all the promises that He gave to them.

Hear what the prophets have said, and we will see in the Master Plan of God, an ancient love story that will play out on the pages of a not-so-far-off future. An amazing story of pain, sorrow, and hopelessness, among the Jewish people. A story that continues long after the prophets are gone, leaving behind God's plan.

After many years, God sends the "One" whom the prophetess Anna speaks of, for all who *"looked to the redemption in Jerusalem."* (Luke 2:38) But when He came to His own people, they refused him. He was despised and rejected by men, and the iniquity of us all was laid upon him. Then they led him as a lamb to the slaughter. Just as foretold by the prophets, there in the city of Jerusalem, people delivered death to the only one who would have delivered them from it. Now, Jesus desires to return to Jerusalem and to His people Israel once again. When He does return, He will do something totally unbelievable if it were not prophesied in the Scriptures.

The prophets have a story to be told in the Master Plan of God. Although some may choose to reject this story, it would be wise to never doubt that the covenant promises God made to Israel will be kept by Father God, because our faith requires us to take God at His word. *"Thus says the Lord: "If you can break My covenant with the day and My covenant with the night so that there will not be day and night in their season, then My covenant may also be broken with David My servant, so that he shall not have a son to reign on his throne, and with the Levites, the priests, My ministers, "* (Jeremiah 33:20,21).

We see in the Scriptures that God did not break the Davidic covenant but only rendered it inoperable by removing His presence from the physical Kingdom of God because of their disobedience. This was done in a way that is much like a parent taking possession of the car keys, the car is not broken, it is only rendered powerless to the disobedience of the child. God's presence in the temple is the key to the physical Kingdom and His removal was manifested when He left Solomon's Temple. This is as recorded in Ezekiel, chapter, 10. With God's departure from the kingdom, there was given prophetic promises that He will scatter the Kingdom's people throughout the world, and then in the later days, return them to the land and give them the keys to His Kingdom once again by giving His people a new heart and spirit; the departure from the Kingdom was not to be permanent.

To summarize, we have looked at these four parts of God's creation: "Inanimate Things, Living Things, Angels, and Mankind," which together make up what God has revealed to us about His creation, both in the physical and spiritual. There are massive gaps that exist in the created order. Failures in the quality of their current condition and where that quality will be when God creates the New Heavens and the New Earth. Although everything in God's creation is good and their condition is exactly what He wanted them to be when He made them, they did not stay that way. Free will and sin changed all of that, sin among angelic beings and the sin of all humanity.

God has revealed to us several plans that when fully executed, will not only restore all things to being good once again but also make them all better than they were originally. He will not only make all things new (Revelation 21:5), but He will make them to last into eternity. These various plans are all part of the one Master Plan of God. The very completion of all His plans will result in a master outcome being: "that God is all in all."

We have also seen and will continue to see, that God continues to progressively reveal Himself to us, and when He does so, He chooses to reveal a part of His Master Plan to us as well. We can understand that God is revealing more of Himself to humanity as time goes on, until that time in the New Heaven and the New Earth when we become intimately bonded relationally to the Father, Son, and Holy Spirit. Another certainty for us to understand is that God does not change His plans. Rather, He brings them to fulfillment not just to keep His promises but because of who He is and because of His character.

God with Us

Before the birth of Jesus Christ, Mary's husband Joseph, is told by the angel that the child Mary is bearing will save His people from their sins, and he is to call His name Jesus, who is *"Immanuel," which means "God with us."* (Matthew 1:23) At the birth of Jesus, we see God taking another step in revealing Himself and His plan. The angel tells Mary, *"The Lord will give Him the throne of His father David. And He will reign over the house of Jacob forever, and of His kingdom there shall be no end."* (Luke 1:33) In these two statements given by the angel, we see the plan of God developing, Jesus is to be the "Deliverer," the redeemer from sin and death. He is the righteousness of God imputed to those of faith since the days of Abel. And that He is the long-awaited Messiah and King of the eternal Kingdom of God that the Prophets spoke of. Jesus does not fail to live up to the call to come down from His glory and be with us. He reveals that He is in fact the Son of God, the King of the Jews, and His message from the start for all people everywhere was to seek the Kingdom of God and His righteousness first. He is the Lamb of God who takes away the sins of the world and does so by His death on the cross, and then He proves to be the "First Fruits" of the resurrection, conquering Death and holding the keys to life for all.

Jesus ratifies the New Covenant with His blood and sits as "High Priest of the Kingdom of God." He will not remove the previous covenants of God but will bring every covenant God has ever made to completion. Jesus brings His people into a deeper relationship with the

Father, and intimacy with the Holy Spirit, our ever-present advocate, who dwells within the redeemed. Because of what He has done, the righteous are now members of the household of God and inheritors of the eternal Kingdom. As He said He would, Jesus has gone to the Father to prepare a place for us in His Father's house, promising to one day take us there to be with Him and the Father.

It was also revealed to us by God, that Jesus demonstrates He alone has power and authority over each of the four parts of God's creation, as well as Death, Hell, and Life itself. He demonstrates that He can change people's hearts, remove sins, and has command over all judgments. Jesus shows us that He will be the one to carry out and fulfill the Master Plan of God. With His return at the end of the Great Tribulation, "God is with Us" will once again to walk upon the Earth. He will eliminate all four gaps in God's creation order according to the plan of God. For the Messiah will rightly claim, *"All authority has been given to Me in Heaven and on earth."* (Matthew 28:19) And when the time comes for the world to end, Jesus Messiah will have put an end to all earthly rule, all authority, and all power by putting His enemies under His feet. The last enemy that will be destroyed is death itself. *"Now when all things are made subject to Him, then the Son Himself will also become subject to the Father, who put all things under the Son, that God may be all in all."* (1 Corinthians 15:24-28) Wow! What a Savior, what a friend we have in Jesus!

The Church

The Church is another revelation of who God is and also, a progression in showing humanity what He will do, following the pattern found in His Master Plan. It would be mistaken of us to think that the Church is God's Plan B. The Scriptures do not say that the Church is a replacement for Israel, or that by default, awarded as the new owners of God's promises that were given to Israel, it isn't. Rather, the Scriptures reveal that the Church manifests the presence of Israel's Messiah on the Earth as His body and has been given its' own promises from God, which we do find in the New Covenant Scriptures. For more than 2000 years, the Universal Church has been Jesus Christ's sole witness to a lost humanity. The birth of the Church and its engagement with Gentiles was something that not only caught the Prophets but also the angels by surprise; a mystery of God having been revealed to the Apostles. (Ephesians 3) To be clear, the Church was built by Jesus Christ and did not exist before that day at Pentecost, when the Holy Spirit came to permanently indwell the righteous by faith under a new covenant. The result of the Holy Spirit's presence is that the believer becomes a spiritual temple of God. Love of God and love for one another are to be the hallmarks of the Church as Jesus commanded it to be.

The Church is the entire collective people of God who were saved by faith under the new covenant of Christ, who are called individually into an eternal fellowship with the Father, our Lord Jesus Christ, with the Holy Spirit, and with one another. Individual churches are to be recognized in the world not as buildings or places but as manifestations of the body of Christ, which functions here on the Earth physically in His absence. This body of Christ is to be under the complete control of its head Jesus Christ and live in the power of the Holy Spirit. The Church manifests Jesus Christ to the world when we live in obedience to the new covenant commandments and serve Him in the "commission" from God. The mission of the Church that Jesus has given it is to, *"Go therefore and make disciples of all nations, baptizing them in the name of the Father, and of the Son, and of the Holy Spirit."* (Matthew 28:18-19) Resulting in new disciples redeemed in Christ and new citizens of the spiritual Kingdom of God, each having been given an inheritance in the new supernatural Heaven and New Earth to come. It is significant to note that although the Church at its beginning was mostly Jewish, the Great Commission and the Holy Spirit's mission has been primarily directed towards the Gentile world and so the vast majority of the Church is made up of Gentiles of every kind from around the world.

This spiritual body of Christ will remain on this Earth until Jesus Messiah removes it and replaces it with His own supernatural presence, when He returns to be the King of kings and Lord of lords over Israel and all of the kingdoms of this world. In the Millennium Age, believers in the Messiah will not form new local churches but will be Kingdom citizens like the Jews will. Like all the redeemed they are inheritors of the spiritual Kingdom of God. This change occurs when the Church is taken in a rapture event, not unlike what Enoch experienced but not exactly like it. While Enoch was simply taken away and was no more. The Church is changed in the twinkling of an eye and joined up with all the resurrected, redeemed saints of the faith who have died. (1 Thessalonians 4:13-17) Another difference between the two raptures is that it is likely that few, people actually saw what happened to Enoch, but with the Rapture of the Church, there will be what is described as an "appearing," a glorious physical manifestation of Jesus at that moment for all on the Earth to see, which is stated so many times in the New Testament letters. Until that day comes, the Church will remain the most influential force for God among mankind on this Earth. Local churches around the world, are empowered by the Holy Spirit, who has the power to raise the dead to life.

The Church is raiding Satan's domain, so it is now and will continue to be, the primary target of Satan's attacks until it is taken up by Jesus. After that event, Satan will shift his evil plans to focus upon Israel once again. As Jesus' hands, feet, and heart, the Church has broken into the domain of darkness that rules over all the kingdoms of this world and brings the light of His domain into the world. The gates of hell cannot prevail against the Church and its work of redemption, which continues to bring people into the Kingdom of God. The commission of the Church will continue until the fullness of the Gentiles has come in, and its time and mission have come to an end, (Romans 11:25) when Jesus Christ comes to take the Church to His Father's house and claim it for His "Bride," preparing her in splendor for the marriage to come. (Revelation 19:7-9)

For over 2000 years, the Church, made up of mostly Gentiles is the royal priesthood of God; it has engaged in warfare with the worldly darkness of men and demons. Armed with the Word of God, equipped with the Holy Spirit, and supported by a Heavenly host of angels, the Church wages a spiritual war for the souls of all people, pulling them from hell's fire that they may enter the Kingdom of God, the redemption of people from every tribe, nation, kingdom and tongue. According to God's Master Plan, the Church will share in the inheritance of the New Heaven and New Earth with all the redeemed.

The Triune Judgments of God

CHAPTER 4: Advancing The Master Plan

The Triune Judgments of God refer to the three judgments that happen during the Tribulation period described in chapters 6 through 19 in the Book of Revelation.

There are a ton of Christian writers who have much to say about this period of time, so this writing will be kept to a minimum. It should be noted that in the Tribulation period, there are three judgments of God that He executes. One: Humanity's rebellion against God's authority is to be judged by God. Two: Satan's rule over the kingdoms of this world will be overthrown, and the demonic realm judged. Three: All the false religions of the world, including the worship of money and wealth, are judged by God. By executing these three judgments, God is preparing His creation, both in the spiritual and physical realms to receive the Millennium Kingdom of God. Three things will happen as a result of these judgments, things that have never happened on Earth in the days since its beginning.

First: Humanity will collectively, and individually come to realize that they are not in control of anything, but that there is a God who is in control of everything. This man-made world it created for itself is a world of kingdoms that have set themselves against God and "His Anointed." It is a world seeking to free itself from the rule of God and His authority, and it will be responded to with Godly wrath. (Psalm 2:1-6) It is a world where people believe they have every right to determine what is justice, what is good, what is evil, and what is righteous. It is a world dominated by humanistic worldviews, worldly religions, and the worship of money that compete for the minds and hearts of the people, and the power that comes with it. It is a world that will soon hide itself in fear; the people of every nation will be terrified by the prospect of judgment when they are supernaturally exposed to the face of Jesus, the Lamb of God. Suddenly, every eye shall see Him as He appears. All people everywhere will be overcome with the prospect of having to suffer the consequences for their evil deeds, that will come from the wrath of the Lamb. (Revelation 6:12-17; Matthew 24:29-31) What God does to the people of the world will change humanity forever.

Second: Before the end of the Tribulation, the demonic realm will be judged and cast into the eternal Lake of Fire, never to deceive, torment, or oppress people again. Satan himself will be bound with chains and incarcerated in the bottomless pit (Revelation 20:1-3). For the next 1000 years, humankind on the Earth will no longer have a supernatural evil to contend with. And peace will finally come to the angelic realm.

Third: All the religions of the world will become spiritually impotent when all of the evil principalities and powers suddenly vanish along with their spiritual activities. Religious people of every kind will see their faith quickly become irrelevant in the face of what God and the Lamb will do during the Tribulation. As in the days of Moses and Pharoah, false gods will be unable to respond to counter the Lamb, but this time it will be worldwide. These false gods and their counterfeit religions that are empowered supernaturally by demonic forces will fall silent around the world forever, becoming voiceless and dead. (Isaiah 41:21-24). The Master Plan of God reveals that He will cause the forces of Satan to destroy," MYSTERY, BABYLON THE GREAT, THE MOTHER OF HARLOTS, AND THE ABOMINATIONS OF THE EARTH" (Revelation 17:5) This "Scarlet Harlot," that symbolically represents the gods of mankind throughout history, including the god of wealth and money, which will be the prominent god at the time of the Tribulation. When the Triune Judgments are completed according to the Master Plan, then the stage will be set for the Messiah to return and restore Israel and the worldwide Kingdom of God.

The Millennial Age

The Millennial Age is that 1000-year period that follows the "Tribulation Judgments" and precedes the "Final Rebellion" against God. Of which all occur before there is a New Heaven and a New Earth. (Revelation 20:7 through 21:1) Before the start of this Millennial Kingdom, the book of Revelation, chapter 19, tells us that the Messiah returns to the Earth to face the armies that have come to Israel to make war against Him. "Armageddon" ends with the "Beast," who is the Antichrist, and his "False Prophet" being thrown into the lake of fire and their armies killed, their bodies left for the birds to eat.

There is nothing in Revelation chapter 19 or elsewhere in Scripture that says, after the Armageddon event, suddenly all will be well on Earth, it won't be. The good news is that the Lamb, that is, Jesus Messiah

(Revelation 17:14, 1 Timothy 6:15), will begin to reign over the Earth for 1000 years as the King of kings and Lord of lords.

When Messiah has completed that 1,000-year reign, great strides in the completion of the Master Plan will have been made. Both the Abrahamic and Davidic covenants will have been completed. All the families of the Earth that are to receive a blessing have received it. Jews and Gentiles still on the Earth will bond together in righteousness and fellowship, all in the name of their King who is High Priest and Prophet, the Lord Jesus Messiah. The redeemed in Heaven and the Earth, both Jews and Gentiles will be in obedient subjection to Messiah. The gaps in the created order that separate the realities of this world from what will be in the New Heavens and New Earth will be substantially closer to reaching the master objective in God's Plan, "that God may be all in all," but it will be a thousand years in the making.

Many other amazing workings occurred during the Millennium Age according to the prophets of old, and we will take a deep dive into their messages about the Millennium and the people who lived during it. The Scriptures tell us that the pathway for the restored physical Kingdom of God (Acts 3:20,21) on Earth will not be without challenges and monstrous-sized obstacles to overcome.

The King returns to rule over a broken world. A world that for the most part, God has decimated. The environment has been severely compromised by the plagues God sent upon the water, land, and air. Pollution will be inescapable and at levels never known to mankind before. As a result of God's judgments, much of the plant and animal life will struggle to survive.

The people who survive and live along every coast line will find the oceans to be filled with the dead of every kind washing in with the tides. The nations who survive and live in cities will live in utter ruin and anarchy. But life will continue as it always has; people will find ways to live and have families, even in survival mode. Generations will come and go, and with them will come, new opportunities for all. The King and His servants will move forward with the plan of God to build the Kingdom of God and nurture its transcendence into the supernatural realm.

Most certainly, the greatest challenge set before the triumphant King of kings and His servants, is that most of the remaining people, Jews and Gentiles alike, who survived all the broken seals, trumpets, and bowls sent by God for judgment, will be in total fear of the Lord God. They will hate the Lamb of God for what He has done to them, to their loved ones, and to their world, this too has a part in the Master Plan of God.

What kind of High Priest of God will it take to be able to cause the remains of humanity to come to love this God that they fear? How long will they dread the thought of having this King rule over them? What kind of Prophet will be able to share words from God that will cause them to listen, trust in His words, and obey His Holiness? What kind of King will it take to rule the nations using a rod of iron and yet be able to convince them that all His use of power and exercise of His authority are done in righteousness, in justice, and for their good?

The King of Glory, that's who; the Alpha and the Omega, the First and the Last (Revelation 22:13). The Root and Offspring of David, the Bright and Morning Star (Revelation 22:16). The "One" who will execute God's Master Plan. We will see more detail on this as we move into the story.

The Last Rebellion

At the end of the Millennial Age when 1000 years have passed, Satan is released from his incarceration to go out and deceive the nations once again, to inspire them to rebel against God and rise up for battle in numbers that certainly will exceed those of Armageddon. This is the final rebellion against God, an end of opposition to God's Master Plan, and control for the Kingdom of God. (Revelation 20:7-10)

Some people look at this event and ask reasonable questions like, why is there going to be another rebellion and threat to the Kingdom? Why does Satan get a second chance to deceive humanity? It does initially appear to be a bit redundant. Why didn't God just end all evil things at the time of the Tribulation? We should understand that the plan of God to put an end to the physical realm could not end with the Tribulation event, but now at the end of the Millennial Age, the time is right and the condition of sinful humanity has prepared itself for a final judgment.

What is shocking about this worldwide rebellion is that it occurred after the whole world just spent 1000 years with no Satanic presence and 1000 years with the King of kings and Lord of lords. All the while living in His Kingdom where justice, truth, righteousness, and worldwide peace will have reigned for generations. According to the prophets, life in the Kingdom will be a time when Gentiles will hunger for the word of God, seek relationships with the Jews, seek the blessings of the King, and worship God in the Spirit. It will be a time of hope and prosperity, a time when the gospel message of salvation is heard by all who live on Earth. A world where God is glorified by so many like never before in human history. However different, it will be, it is also a time just like all other times when people have free will to make choices.

So, we ask, what happened? Could Satan alone change so many hearts and minds when the people know that he has been released and is on the prowl again? What changes will occur that will suddenly cause a worldwide rebellion? A change so powerful that a vast majority of people will turn their backs on what God has done for them and on the generations that have passed before them?

Predictions about the world coming to an end and how people will react have been a part of the human psyche from the beginning. People fear it but also entertain themselves with stories about the end in which almost always, somebody steps up and in the last possible moment to save humanity from certain destruction. In the real world, predictions claiming that the end is near are never taken very seriously by most people because they never become true. Time after time the world survives to see another day. But at the end of the Millennial Age, it is the word of God that is saying the end of the world is near and people worldwide have good reasons to believe it is true. The world will be faced with the realization from the Scriptures that the Kingdom of God was to remain on Earth for 1000 years only and that the countdown began when Messiah returned to reign as King of kings and Lord of lords. When the time for the Kingdom expires, a worldwide rebellion initiated by satanic deception takes place, but only "for a little while," before the Earth is destroyed by God. (Revelation 20:1-11)

It is certain that there will be an end to this physical world (Revelation 21:1) The Apostle Peter, warns those who doubt this that the world which was once judged and destroyed by water, will one day face a judgment and be destroyed by fire. (2 Peter 3:6-13). We can be certain that there will be an end to humanity's rebellion. We can be certain that Satan will experience justice due to him. In this last rebellion, mankind will demonstrate a final rejection of God Himself. Unwilling to be under the subjection of His will, and rejecting this: "that God may be all in all."

When: All things, are brought under the subjection of Jesus Messiah, and the work of the Kingdom of God on Earth has been completed. When: sinful humanity is no longer on the Earth and the physical realm is destroyed by God. When: the last of the spiritual hostilities have been judged and all the promises of God fulfilled. When: all the "Gaps" in the quality of God's creation at the end of the Millennium close completely. When the master outcome of God's Master Plan is achieved, and "God will be all in all," then, a New Heaven and Earth will come into existence.

CHAPTER 5:
God Of The Master Plan

The thing with plans, especially long-range plans, is that they will often have to be changed due to new developments that cause us to take a second look at our plans. Sometimes it is unknown factors that suddenly and inconveniently appear that cause us to lose control over what we are attempting to accomplish. Situations are not what we thought they were, and what we thought we knew, turns out to not be what we expected at all.

Our long-range plans, we say, need to be flexible and nimble enough to make adjustments due to the actions of others. If we do not make the changes to our plan, it may completely fail or cause the outcome to be compromised in some serious way. Another thing that happens with our long-range plans is that we lose interest in them. Remember the plans you made to be more disciplined about losing that twenty pounds and cut way back on fast food. You bought an outfit to workout in and a yoga mat too. Then you started executing your plan, but when you decided not to join that health club near the office…. We drop one plan for another one that will work out better for us, or so we think. Or maybe it's just that we have a new object of interest. You're into skydiving, or pickleball now instead of mountain biking for instance.

There is nothing wrong with changing your plans as long as it doesn't hurt anyone else. When we change our plans, those people who have been working on their own plans alongside you and your plan, become irritated and disappointed in you for abandoning what you once loved for another new passion. They feel abandoned; they feel like they matter less, now that you have another interest and new goals to achieve. Should your change in plans be life-changing, such as a divorce or a change to a new marriage partner, then those impacted negatively by the change cannot help but believe they are being rejected, insignificant, unloved, and treated with cruelty or insensitively. You've changed, and so have your plans.

People do this kind of stuff all the time, but it is safe to say God never does and never will. God does not change. *"God is not a human, that he should lie, not a human being, that He should change His mind.*

Does He speak and then not act? Does He promise and then not fulfill?" (Numbers 23:19) God has gone on record saying, *"I, the Lord, do not change."* (Malachi 3:6) Because God does not change, He does not change any portion of His Master Plan.

Another thing about God and His plans is when He makes a promise to someone, He keeps it. It is right to say that the promises God makes, whether they seem good or bad, become a revealed part of His Master Plan, and He will have actions planned to fulfill them. In the covenant God made with Abraham recorded in Genesis, chapter 15, God tells Abraham that his descendants would serve and be afflicted by strangers in a land that was not theirs for four hundred years. Afterward, that nation will be judged, and Abraham's descendants will come out of that land with great possessions. God kept His word, it happened just as He said it would, with no special prophetic interpretations needed from men.

After those 400 years lapsed, God began to cause to happen everything that was promised to Abraham. The promise was not to Abraham alone, it would extend into the lives of everyone else whom God has included in that promise. God is faithful to keep His promises to Abraham, Isaac, and Jacob and all the generations of Israelites who were in the lineage for those 400 years. They were recipients of the promise, both the good and bad of it. This should tell us that the plan and promises of God always trump our own life situations where we find it, whether we like our lot in life or not. At any single point in time, a person can be an oppressed Israelite who lives and dies as a slave in Egypt. And then the following week, another person following in the slave's footsteps is suddenly free and has the abundance of Egyptian wealth at their disposal; God kept His word to both. Regardless of how they felt about their situation, they are both equally in the will of God. In Moses's day, there should have been Israelites who saw and understood that the 400 years were up and that their generation was the generation to make the Exodus out of Egypt. They should have prepared for God to act. They should have been prepared by those generations before them to be vigilant and ready for their departure, but it doesn't appear to be so.

From the Scriptures, we see no indication that they were ready for God to act on that promise to Abraham. We see this pattern throughout both Israel's history and in church history as well, that people do not respond well to God's promises. Israel worshipped God and prayed for deliverance from their oppression, but there are no indications that they trusted in God to keep His promise to Abraham; rather, the opposite occurred, with no expressions of hope or anticipation of deliverance. By faith, they should have known that deliverance was at their doorstep after the 400 years of the prophecy had passed. They either forgot about the promise or they stopped believing in the power of God's promises. They would need to be reminded of that covenant promise that God had made more than once, the children of Abraham will be reminded again in the Millennial Age. There are three points to be made from what Israel experienced at this time before their deliverance from Egypt.

#1 There is no expiration date on God's promises. God is not moved by time; a day is as 1000 years to the Eternal One, it simply doesn't impact God. It doesn't matter that it has been over 2000 years since Jesus Christ promised the Church His return. And it doesn't matter that promises God made to the faithful in Israel, about a glorious Kingdom of Israel to come are over 2800 years old. God would not make any promise that He would not honor. An example of God as the "Promise Keeper" is given to us by the Apostle Peter, who says this about God's promises. *"We are, according to His promise, looking forward to a New Heaven and a New Earth where righteousness dwells."* (2 Peter 3:13).

Because God made a promise to the righteous that they can count on a New Heaven and a New Earth, it doesn't matter that it has been 2000 years in the making with another 1000 years to go. There isn't a promise God has made that He won't keep!

#2 God will keep His promises even if we forget He ever made them, or if we choose not to believe He will keep it. This is true for the people of Moses' day, and for us today as well.

#3 God's promises will benefit people who do not know Him or His promises. Many of the Israelites in Egypt suddenly came to the realization that they were beneficiaries of something that they had taken no part in claiming for themselves; they were totally unconnected to, or concerned with any plans of God. It is not until they begin to experience the promise unfolding in front of their eyes that hope and understanding begin to grow. They benefit simply because of who God is. This is what people will experience in the early days of the Millennium Kingdom.

It is critical to God and to us as well that He keeps every promise with every single person who has been reached by that promise, just as God intended them to receive it. Regardless of the span of centuries, the number of people, cultures, and languages, or even if those who are affected by God's promise believe God's promise or not. To add clarity, the Church has been given promises that Israel is not entitled to, and there are promises made to the Jews to which the Church is not entitled. And then there are promises that both are entitled to, which is why it is important to know which is which if we are to better understand His Master Plan.

How could we possibly trust in a God who fails to keep all of His promises? We couldn't. It may be hard to see how God can keep every promise He has ever made to every single person affected by that promise but He will keep them because His character requires it. It is difficult for us to see why God would keep a promise that people have forgotten about or dismissed as something that is not going to happen, but He will because of who He is.

We are the ones with the questionable character and the ones who do not come through with what we said we would do. And when all else fails we try to change the expectations of that promise we made and we often think that God is like us.

Unfortunately, there are times when we feel we have to break our promises. When we learn certain facts that we were not aware of before the promise was given, and plans are in motion. We can all relate to this, we like to entertain ourselves with TV, and movies with plots of this nature. But it would not be entertaining for us to think that God would do this to us. Fortunately for us, God does not change, even when we fail Him and prove to be unfaithful to Him. God knows it all, and He will never say, "Sorry, my friend, I didn't know things would come to this!"

It is also important to remember when we consider the Master Plan, we cannot cause God to change His mind. To be clear about this, setting conditions upon our free will actions can result in a different response from God, but that is not an act of changing His mind. It is, however, an act of bringing the proper consequences into play in response to our actions. It is not in God's nature to change because our Lord is

Omniscient; He knows all things, and He has never changed. In order to make a key point, we ask, "Did Israel historically act in ways that caused God to change His mind and break His promises?" Such a thing would be impossible to happen; God would either have known He would be breaking a promise when He made it, or He would not have known he would be breaking a promise, neither option is possible. If people could cause God to withdraw from His promise or compromise the terms of that promise, then all people over all time, including the Church, would have no assurances from God but only His good intentions.

If we apply this line of reasoning to all the promises God gave to Israel about the Messianic Kingdom to come in the future, then we have to conclude that those promises will be kept just as they were given to the people by the prophets, just as He intended them to be kept, and just as He has told them. We cannot honestly distort the prophetic words from God about a coming King and Kingdom of Israel by changing them into something else while remaining assured that the prophet's words of judgment happens to happen just as they were foretold. Such an action to intentionally deceive people is not possible with God. The same can be said for taking issue with the prophet's writing style, Jewish thinking, poetic mannerism, compassionate but false encouragement, or other such nonsense that is used to change what God has intentionally told people into meaning something else altogether.

We humans will at times, have a plan of ours with a highly valued outcome in mind and we will do whatever it takes to get there. When we see problems confronting our plan or difficulty in executing a key step, we often act inconsistently and often with regret for the lengths we have to go to get what we want out of our plan. We may even cheat others, cheat on our taxes, or cheat in some other way to give us the bump we need in order to stay with the plan. People act in these ways because we are unrighteous.

To be right with God, we cannot ever be partially righteous with God. We can never by our own merits, be right before God although we would like to think we can. If you hold onto that line of thinking, believing that one day you will be able to show God that you are righteous, then you are among those whom the Apostle Paul writes here, saying," *For being ignorant of God's righteousness and seeking to establish their own righteousness, they have not submitted to God's righteousness."* (Romans 10:3) Paul's point is that you are ignorant if you think you can ever be righteous before God or if you think both you and God can be independently righteous. Just look at God's standard for righteousness, and you will be quick to understand why he says this. We are just too messed up by our sinful nature to be righteous. We can have His, or our own but we cannot have both.

There are four points to note about God's righteousness that are important factors in the Master Plan.

#1 God does not experience problems executing His plans to their completion because of who He is and because of His character. That nothing can happen to make God act outside of His righteous character.

#2 He alone is righteous; only God can be right with His own standards for righteousness. We would have to be God ourselves in order to achieve God-like righteousness.

#3 It is in God's plan to treat all people and the angels with true righteousness. God alone can and will treat every person who ever existed without partiality, that is, without undue favor or rejection above or below that for which they were created.

#4 We can have faith that His righteousness is Just. That He will treat us in a righteous manner because it is in His nature to do so. That is what God does, and for Him not to do that would be a change in His character, and we already understand that God does not change.

What is God's righteousness, and how should we understand it? It is an attribute of God that by His divine holiness, determines all moral law and how this law is to be governed. The righteous attribute of God by nature determines truth from lies and is the absolute source of justice. It is a dispenser of rewards and punishments and does so in perfect harmony with all of His other Godly attributes. God is righteous always, this is key to understanding God, during the Millennium and afterward at the final rebellion.

The God of the Master Plan is also relational, and He reveals Himself to us in three persons: Father, Son, and Holy Spirit, in relationship as the three persons of the Trinity. Relationships play a big part in the execution of many of His plans because He is relational. God has told us much about what He has done already, what He is doing now, and some things that He is going to do in the future. He tells us many of His plans, but not all.

However, God does not settle for us knowing what His plans are, He also wants us to be involved and to contribute to the execution of His plans. This was previously shared earlier with the example of the grandchild who is helping Papa build a deck. God desires a growing relationship with His people, and to have experiences, even shared bad experiences, that bond us more closely together with Him. We see in the Scriptures that relationship building is a strong driver in the way God has chosen to execute His Master Plan. God could accomplish all that He desires without any kind of personal investment into our individual lives, but He is committing to loving us so that we will respond by loving Him in return. When that time comes when it can be said, "that God is all in all" we will know Him intimately, love Him with such deep affection, and with a sense of oneness with Him, that we would never give thought to ever using our free will to hurt Him or offend Him. That is the kind of relationship John is relaying to us in Revelation, chapter 21, in his efforts to describe the Heavenly City of God. Because of this, we can understand that God is not executing His plans with a focus on getting the job done so "that God may be all in all," but rather in His preparing people for the supernatural bonding with Him that will occur in the New Heaven and New Earth where God will be "all in all."

Scriptures show us that God is also in a relationship with the angels as well as with people. As previously stated, we know very little about the angels and even less about their relationships with God. What we do know about angel relationships with God is revealed most insightfully when Satan speaks with God directly and quite candidly about people in a conversation recorded in Job Chapters 1 and 2. We can expect to understand more about God's relationship with the angels and see our relationship with them develop in the New Heaven and New Earth.

If we are to understand our relationship with God, we need to look at the beginning with Adam and Eve, and the first relationship between the two. In that relationship, the couple knew God personally as being God Almighty, the creator and provider of all things. They very likely understood God to be Omnipotent, Omnipresent, Omniscient. Once

Adam and Eve ate the fruit of the Tree of Knowledge of Good and Evil, they became sinners and knew they would die. Although they knew for a fact that God existed and that He is who He says He is, they most likely became like everyone else who has ever lived since, they wondered if after they died, would God be merciful enough to save them. Would God find a way to restore them in the personal relationship He had with them? Is the relationship they have now with Him worth keeping beyond this life in the flesh and into the future?

And so, faith was born. (Hebrews 11:1) It comes to all who will receive it as a gift from God (Ephesians 2:8) and it is this faith that makes all the difference in our relationship with God. It isn't whether or not someone believes in God or thinks that there is a God. The question to be answered is do we trust God? Faith, and what is done with it, is critically important in our relationship with God and is essential to our redemption. How can we ever bond close enough with God if we do not have faith that He will save us after death? It is by faith that we respond in trust to God as He reveals Himself and His plans. Without this faith, it is impossible to please God.

Demonstrations of faith are very likely what Adam passed on to His children and his grandchildren's children. But there is no guarantee that they will embrace faith and make it their own. Abel, repented of His sins and offered up a sacrificial lamb, in an act of faith in the imputed righteousness of God. His brother Cain, on the other hand, has no faith in God's offer to atone for his sins and prefers a life of sin rather than doing the right thing as God told him to do. (Genesis 4:6,7) After speaking with Abel (likely about God's conditions for atonement for sins) Cain murders his brother for no known reason other than because of Abel's act of faith. Afterward, Cain accepts the consequences of his sin without any repentance. God does not offer Cain protection from the same fate that befell his brother, but will only discourage others from killing him. (Genesis 4: 13-15) Cain never sought out redemption from God and he willfully left God out of his life forever. (Genesis 4:16) From that time forward people will reject faith as God's sole condition for a relationship with Him. Confusing to many people, it is a faith that is not about God's reality but one of trusting and loving Him to the point in which we seek to obey Him. This is true today as it was for Abel and it will continue to be true during the Millennial Age.

Abraham has an experience with God when he is told to sacrifice the life of his son Isaac, up on a mountain. This forced Abraham to reveal his faith in an act of trust and obedience; believing that God would raise his son's dead body and keep His promises. (Hebrews 11:17-19). God shows Abraham, and all who follow, that redemption from sin, and eternal life come by having the righteousness of God imputed to them by faith. Abraham did nothing to merit God's approval other than to trust and obey God in the relationship that he had with Him even onto death. This would become an issue for those alive after the Millennium Age ends, as we will see.

In the Scriptures, we see that God is progressively revealing Himself to individuals and showing them what redemption is. But also, He is connecting with people collectively, in groups of people that have common bonds to one another like families, tribes, kingdoms, and churches. There is also a progression of God connecting with us in deeper and more intimate ways relationally. In the days of Abraham and his descendants, we see that God is revealing to them that He is a promise maker and a promise keeper and what is impossible for man, is possible with God. He reveals that faith is the key that turns hopeful thinking into demonstratable assurance in the promises that God gives to that person. We see that God makes promises to Abraham, that the man will never see fulfilled in his lifetime or those of his children, and his children's children. This results in the faithful followers of God's promises to increase in numbers over time and eventually swell with each generation into an innumerable number of people trusting God to come through and keep all of His promises which includes you and I.

We recognize the progression of intimacy that God is willing to have with us, played out in the pages of Scripture using Israel as His example. That God forms relationships with just your average, everyday sinful, men, and women, and reveals to them who He is, and who they are to Him. In the days before Abraham, God was known as the "Almighty Creator." It was when the descendants of Abraham were slaves in Egypt that they were first referred to by God as "My People." Escalating the relationship, these two parties enter into a life-and-death contract together in the days of Moses and they become "Priests of the Kingdom of God." Entering into their Promised Land, God and Israel enter into another relationship, one of a King and "His Servants." The pattern of God's revealing of Himself and His plans to Israel extends beyond that of Lord and servant, beyond that of a child and parent. The relationship enters into even the most intimate of human relationships, that of husband and wife. This broad range of relationships is in preparation for the New Heaven and New Earth relationship that God is to have with everyone who is going into eternity with Him, where "God is all, in all" in our relationship with Him.

What we can know and trust about the God of the Master Plan is that when it comes to people, it is in His nature to restore and make better those people who are in a relationship with Him rather than replace them. (1 Peter 2:12) God not only prefers to restore people back to what they were originally created to be, but He also makes them better. He restores and renews people in ways that prepare them for the time to come when they join Him in the New Heaven and New Earth. Christians can observe this transformation occurring in their lives. They see by faith that the change God makes in them frees them from sin's bondage and as "new creations in Christ," have the ability to overcome the sins and failures that they went through in their former selves. He does this with us relationally and He has done this throughout biblical history but for only those whom He calls into this relationship. Regardless of our opinions and senses, and for reasons only He knows; the vast majority of people God does not restore and renew, we must trust in His will, His love, and His righteousness even in times of great judgment, He is a God who will judge the world permanently.

The Flood account found in Genesis 6 is one of the two accounts where God resets the four parts of the physical creation. In the Flood account the old Earth passed away and a New Earth emerges and the redeemed people on the Ark make the transition from a judged world to a restored world. A world that is familiar to them yet, new to them, where life could start over again. The "angelic realm" experienced a reset of sorts as well. In a demonic attempt to corrupt the image of God in humanity with their own, demonic angels bred supernatural people from women. Their evil deeds were wiped out from the earth along with all mankind. (Genesis 6:1-4) and those angels were judged, possibly being those angels referred to in Jude, verse 6.

God will do a final reset in the future after the Millennium Age repeating the pattern of the first reset where Mankind finds itself once again in a place of judgment from God. The redeemed will be saved and transition into life in the New Heavens and New Earth. The animate and inanimate things will be, redeemed, restored, or replaced. Angelic evil within people will be completely absent from the New Heaven and Earth. This judgment differs in that the entire physical realm is reset to a new supernatural realm where fire instead of water dissolves everything that was made. This is as the Apostle Peter states. (2 Peter 3:7-13). In response to the coming judgment of God, the Apostle Peter asks us but also those in the Millennium, *"What manner of persons ought you be in holy conduct and godliness..."* (2 Peter 3:11)

God is also a God of community. It is as a community that we find much of our holy conduct and godliness for the Kingdom of God. We see that God encourages communities, equips them, commands them, holds them accountable, and has made covenants with them. He has given them examples to follow, and He has provided priests, prophets, and apostles as leaders to guide people in His ways so that we can align our lives to His will and be participants in His plan, living as His community.

When we think of our work with God in a community, there are two groups of people that come to mind: the Kingdom of Israel (mostly Jews) and the Church (mostly Gentiles). God accomplished uniquely important things through individuals such as Abel, Noah, Abraham, Moses, Peter, and Paul who inspired change. However, it is through these two groups that God has revealed Himself to fallen humanity in ways that the world could not ignore, because as everyone knows, groups generally possess greater power for change than individuals do, especially groups led by the Holy Spirit.

Christians understand the mission of the Church. Jesus made it quite clear He would be with us when we go out and make disciples for the Kingdom of God and draw them into community together as His manifested body on the Earth. The mission of Israel, in the Millennium Kingdom, will be to become priests once again. To become the restored

Kingdom of God on Earth and serve as faithful subjects to its King. God tells Moses that Israel is to be a Kingdom of Priests and a holy people group. (Exodus 19:6) What is their mission, what do priests do? At its core, priests bring God to the people, and the people to God. They are to serve God in this way as a nation of priests and cause Israel to live a life of worship to the Lord. Israel is to be Messiah's light in the world and bring the Everlasting Covenant to the rest of the world. They are to be living testimonies of God's holiness and power. Israel's presence in the world will be to bring all people who "fear the Lord God," which is always the beginning of knowledge, to experience God with them because God desires that all people everywhere come to the knowledge of Him.

In the Millennium, many of the Gentile nations of the world responded much like Rahab did for example, she was a Gentile who came to fear the judgments of God, then she subjected herself in faith to Him and His people and lived among them. Rahab married a Jew, and she is traced back into the genealogy of Jesus. In those days Israel's orders from God was to execute His judgments upon all the Gentile nations and kingdoms under the man of God, Joshua. In the Millennial Kingdom God will call upon Israel once again, this time to execute the message of the Gospel among the Gentile nations for their salvation, under the authority of their High Priest, Jesus Messiah.

With the Holy Spirit to empower them; they will complete their mission unhindered by Satan and world religions that at one time ruled over the kingdoms and hearts of people everywhere. Israel's success will be worldwide, reaching all nations with the Gospel. People groups from every tribe, language, and kingdom will enter into the Spiritual Kingdom of God, in fulfillment of the Abrahamic and Davidic covenant promises of God.

No one individual could accomplish what these two groups do collectively as a community. No one individual would have the impact to bring glory to God on the magnitude of scale that the Church has done during its age and what Israel will do during the Millennial Age. In every way that God touches our lives we see that He not only desires to restore us but to make us better than we originally were, resulting in a more intimate relationship with God. This is true individually, but it is also true collectively, as members together in relationships, we are better together. This is true of the Church, and this is true of Israel as well. It is true for Gentiles, and it was true for the Jews as well.

These two groups, the Jews and Gentiles, are very different from one another in their histories, cultures, beliefs, and experiences. Throughout all Jewish history, hostility separates them from one another. These differences are not by accident; they are in the Master Plan of God. Only the Messiah has the power and authority to bring these two very different groups of His people into one collective unity. He will reconcile both Jews and Gentiles, in relationship with one another in the household of God. This is what the Apostle Paul shares in Ephesians 2:11-21. The end result of this unity of all His people is a type of supernatural holy temple of the Lord. It seems that this is what the Apostle John is attempting to describe in the New Heaven and New Earth. (Revelation 21) This unity into one people is not possible among people today, but will be in the Millennium when Jesus the Messiah executes this plan of God and brings all things to their completion.

As humans, we have no other relationship, no other union more intimate than that of a husband and wife. By design of God, marriage between a man and a woman is when the two become one. That is the level of relationship that is found in the Master Plan of God for all the redeemed to experience when "God will be all in all" to us. This is evident in the revelation given to the Apostle John in Revelation, chapter 21. In this chapter, an angel tells John that He will show him, *"the bride, the Lamb's wife."* In John's culture Jewish marriage in his day consists of three steps that have to occur before the marriage is final. Briefly said, there is the betrothal period, followed by a bride and groom celebration with a ceremony, and the last part is for the groom to take his bride to her new home with him for the marriage consummation and life as one. The angel talking to John points out that this wife of the Lamb is still a "bride," which John would understand to mean that the third and last part of the marriage has not been fulfilled between the Lamb and His bride.

From the context of the entire book of Revelation, we easily understand that the Lamb is referring to Jesus Messiah, but who is the "Bride," that is not as easy to understand? In several places in the Scriptures, we see that cities are often a personification of the people who live in them. Ezekiel 16:46-48; Revelation 17:18; 11:8 examples of this. In Revelation chapter 21, the angel who is speaking to John shows him a city, the holy Jerusalem. It has ascended out of Heaven onto the New Earth. This is not a person but an inanimate object, which leads us to understand that the city personifies the Lamb's bride; that the bride is not an inanimate object but is collectively its resident of this city, and its residents are both Israel and the Church. In Revelation, chapter 21 we see that the way into the city is through twelve gates, each one named after a tribe of Israel, and that all of Israel as a whole is represented by these gates. The angel goes on to show John that the walls that support these gates consist of twelve foundations, with each foundation bearing the name of an Apostle upon it. It is clear to us that these twelve disciples represent the universal Church. These two images, the foundation walls, and gates, separate the outside world from those inside who collectively represent the "Bride." We understand that this new holy city is constructed within these walls and gates to identify who this supernatural city is intended to be for by accessing the city and bringing together all the Jews and Gentiles as the Bride of the Lamb.

Only those whose names are written in the Lamb's Book of Life enter this City of God, the place where all redeemed Gentiles and Jews live together as children of the Lord God Almighty and the Lamb. (Revelation 21:22-27) Those whose names are written in the Book of Life are God's children; they are not individual wives of the Lamb. It should be understood that the titles of, "bride" and "wife," are reserved for the collective union of the entire "assembly." There are not two wives but only one, the union of Gentiles and Jews, which Jesus Messiah demonstrates for us during the Millennium Kingdom. With all His people in their final state in the New Heaven and New Earth, we can say with confidence that the universal Church is the Bride of the Lamb. (Ephesians 5:32) However, God Almighty has also referred to Israel as His wife in numerous places in the Scriptures, such as in Isaiah 54:5, and elsewhere in the Psalms, also by way of depictions given through His prophets, such as with Hosea who called Israel, the Lord's betrothed for forever. (Hosea 2:19)

Israel is depicted in the Scriptures more often than not as His unfaithful wife who plays the harlot with other gods. But the Lord is always willing to take her back as His wife. (Jeremiah 3:1) It would be mistaken to think that God has permanently divorced Himself from Israel. We know how God feels about human divorce; how much more would He reject any notion of a Godly divorce? In the Millennium Kingdom, Jesus the Messiah reconciles Israel to God, restoring her and making her better than she originally was, pure, a holy people through Jesus, making her into a glorious and faithful wife. We can best understand that the restored "whole of Israel," will also be what is called the "Bride of the Lamb." Both the "universal Church and the "Whole of Israel" together in unity, are one wife in the household of God.

John's descriptions of the city spoken of in Revelation 21:10-21 personifies the Lamb's bride in her beauty and splendor. The imagery of the holy Jerusalem as a bride and eventual wife to the Lamb of God, who is Jesus, is difficult to grasp and even harder to explain. The Apostle Paul uses similar imagery to what John has said in Revelation 21:9-23. Paul brings some clarity to this supernatural bride when he writes to the Gentile church in Ephesus about how Jesus has broken down the spiritual wall of separation between Jews and Gentiles. He concludes by saying, *"Now you are no longer strangers and foreigners, but fellow citizens with the saints and members of the household of God, having been built on the foundation of the apostles and prophets, Jesus Christ Himself being the cornerstone, in whom the whole building, being fitted together, grows into a holy temple in the Lord, in whom you also are being built together for a dwelling place of God in the Spirit."* (Ephesians 2:19-22). It can be said with confidence that this temple in the Lord is bound together by the Spirit of God and it forms the household of God in the New Heaven and New Earth, and is that city, the New Jerusalem.

It is very reasonable to say that the Lord Jesus Messiah will have eliminated all the obstacles to collective unity that have always separated Jews and Gentiles and will make them one people of God. We saw this pattern in the work of the Holy Spirit in the early church, and we will see it proliferate in the Millennium Kingdom. As the apostle Paul said, *"that in the fulness of the times, He might gather together in one all things in Christ, both which are in heaven and on earth-in Him."* (Ephesians1:10). In the hands of the Messiah, both the Jew and the Gentile will come together as one body, with all those who are in the new holy Jerusalem.

The vision of the new Jerusalem itself and its supernatural environment leaves us with much mystery, but not without enough understanding to see that this new relationship with God will be more than a restored relationship with our creator; it will be the apex of the entire human experience, both individually and collectively. One redeemed people of God called from every tribe, tongue, and nation. We can add to this picture the understanding that both Israel and the Church are portrayed in the Scriptures as having never fulfilled that third step in the Lamb's marriage according to the tradition of a Jewish wedding but it will happen. This bride is seen in glorious splendor and taken to be with the Lamb her husband. It is reasonable to believe that this supernatural marriage is consummated when the Wife and the Lamb are face to face before the Father, in the House of God in the New Heaven on the New Earth, standing before the multitude of the angelic hosts of Heaven in a consummated collective unity of all the redeemed.

This collective unity that will occur between Jews and Gentiles, between Israel and the Church is something that is in the Master Plan of God. It is neither Israel nor the Church that does this work, but it is Messiah who will see to it that all people, both Jewish and Gentile and those preceding both, who are in the Kingdom of God will one day be gathered together with Him as His bride, as the whole family of God. (Ephesians 3:14)

In this chapter, we have come to better understand the God of the Master Plan and how it prepares us not only for the Millennial story to come but also what occurs after the Millennium. We see that God does not change, nor does His plan; He is righteous in all that He does. God demonstrates He is in a triune relationship that has an intimacy we cannot understand and there is intimacy in our relationship with God both individually as His children and collectively as His "Bride." God's call to faith, is to trust in his righteousness alone, which redeems us through His atonement made on the cross of Jesus. We understand that God reveals Himself to people progressively over time, and with that, He reveals His plans for us. The God of the Master Plan has made outrageous promises and will keep every one of them. He will continue to add people, not remove them from His promises. He does not include everyone in all of them, yet God is Righteous and Just in all things.

God also uses patterns over time in order to reveal and reinforce the intent behind His plans. We see that God desires to be in a personal relationship with His people, choosing average people to use as examples that show we qualify for a relationship with Him. We understand that God prefers to restore things rather than replace them. In doing so, He makes them better than they were originally, and He makes them in preparation for eternity. This would be true for not only people but could be said for all four parts of His creation.

With a better understanding of the God of the Master Plan, we can produce a satisfactory summary such as this one:

The Master Plan of God is His divine work in the re-creation of a new eternal realm in which both the physical and spiritual creations are brought together into one supernatural union redeemed into a willful submission to God. This planned work of God is completed in spite of any and all possible human or angelic opposition perpetrated in rebellion against God and rejection of the plan of God. The executed plan of God overcomes all enemies who seek to prevent God from fulfilling His purposes for His creation. Those opposed to God's plan do so by seeking to change the set times and key milestone events that God has fixed according to His sovereign will, seeking to cause the plan to fail.

The plan of God reveals that God the Son has been given all power and authority to execute the plan over the pages of history. In the remaining days ahead, that have been determined by God the Father, Jesus Messiah will execute completely all the plans of God, then "all things are to be made new" in the will of God. When the Master Plan is completed so will the Master outcome be achieved, "that God will be all in all," and be experienced by all. Then all people and angels in the supernatural Kingdom of God will experience their ultimate fulfillment with God in the new creation. Where all things, including all people, will be made for eternity. We will have been made in His likeness and will freely love Him intimately when we see Him face to face.

This outcome will cause all things to bring eternal glory to God, and cause His children to respond to this inheritance in all love, praise, honor, and thanksgiving to the Father, Son, and Holy Spirit. The eternal Lord God Almighty, who alone is worthy of eternal worship Amen.

Having a deeper understanding of the Master Plan will help the reader be able to place the Millennial Kingdom story into a proper context of what God is doing with His creation. The Master Plan will also show us what events must occur in the physical and spiritual realms, during and also immediately after the Millennium before all things are made new for the New Heaven and New Earth to come.

CHAPTER 6:
Preparing For The New Heaven And Earth

Many people today, at least many in the United States, seem to be looking for the "End Times," for the Antichrist, and the return of Jesus. There are an abundance of books and videos, TV seminars, radio programs, and Bible studies that present various versions of how it will all go down. Some of these versions are radical departures from traditional beliefs; others offer subtle deviations; there is a flavor for all types. End Times story enthusiasts usually realize that it is not the end at all and that the world continues for another 1000 years after Jesus Messiah returns. Yet so little is understood about that 1000-year period, and even less is said about it. It is often treated much like an epilogue to a main story, when in fact, the execution of God's Master Plan is just getting warmed up. However, we know from the Scriptures that it is not the end at all but only preparations for the next step for humanity in the advancement of God's Master Plan. It is a movement towards the New Heaven and New Earth and that ultimate outcome in which" God will be all in all."

The world that Jesus Messiah will return to is a devastated world at the end of the Tribulation, and there is nothing in the Scriptures to indicate that God pushes a reset button. God will not send something like a supernatural power surge that covers the Earth and everything on it. Then as the surge lifts, the world has become a new supernatural home for the glorified and a much better place to be, a place of glory and majesty, a place fit for a king, especially the King of kings. In a simple review of what happens during the judgments of the seven-year Tribulation period, we will see that there will be much work to be done to this fallen sinful world when Jesus arrives. He will build a kingdom that will bring God glory from the ashes of despair, death, and destruction and His people will help Him. A kingdom unlike any other, one that progresses a thousand years before it reaches its climax. Why is there so much work to be done? Because God chooses to restore rather than replace His creation. And when He does restore, He removes from the bad, and adds to the good, making all that He restores better than what they were originally created to be. In the process of restoring and making better, He continues to pursue new relationships with all people who do not know the Savior King and strengthen the relationships He has with those who do.

Unfortunately for us, sometimes when we complete a long-term plan of ours; a huge project or undertaking that requires multiple tasks, we find that our solution to the problem that we fixed created new problems for us, or did not permanently put an end to the problem but only kicked the can down the street so to speak. When we consider that people and angels retain their free will and the ability to discern what is good and evil, we have to ask, will there be the potential for future or reoccurring problems? Another way to ask the question is, "What kinds of permanent results are needed in order for the Master Plan to be considered a complete success and the outcome God will obtain by the execution of His Plan?

God has revealed to us the following permanent results that will come from the execution of His Master Plan. All that He will bring to pass before the ultimate outcome "He is all in all."

All things newly created by God, and all things re-created by God will, to a greater extent, bring everlasting glory to God.

The physical Heavens and the Earth were summed up by God as being" very good" (Genesis 1:31), even though it was in His Plan for it to be a temporary creation. (Genesis 8:22; 1 Corinthians 7:31; 2 Corinthians 4:18; 2 Peter 3:7) What can we expect God to proclaim about a new supernatural Heaven and Earth that is meant to last forever? If God also calls mankind "good," a living being made out of the dirt of the Earth and formed in the image of God, what will He say about re-created supernatural people, made not of flesh and blood but made in the likeness of the risen Lord Jesus? (1 Corinthians 15:47, 49) The Psalmist states that the Heavens declare His righteousness, and all the people see His glory. How much more for the people and the New Heavens? Will it not be an everlasting greater glory?

Never again will God's words and His truth be doubted or challenged by mankind or any angelic being.

Never again after God creates a New Heaven and a New Earth will man or angel doubt God's word, put into question His truth, or attempt to distort it. Since the early days of humanity and in every generation up through the Millennium Age, people have willfully attempted to discredit God by putting into doubt His words given to the Prophets, Apostles, and the Son. People intentionally poison the pure word of the Scriptures and cast doubt on what He actually said, and to a greater extent, distort what He means by His words. Every generation, starting from the first one in the Garden of Eden until now and on through the Millennium age, will have people who disregard God's words as the truth and exchange them for a lie of their own making. (Romans 1:25) For humanity, this began in the garden, when Eve agreed with the serpent that what God said no longer mattered. For Satan, he was likely rejecting God's words before there was ever a human to walk in that garden.

Before God will be all in all, He will validate that His word cannot fail or be changed by either people or angels. Rebellious humanity and the fallen angels alike that will not submit to God's truth and His words will be given every opportunity to prove God wrong. God has and will allow Human religions of every imaginable kind to form and be spiritually empowered, by a demonic world. God will let humanity discover for themselves worldly religions that displace God's truth in the hearts and minds of people. They will pass on their lies from generation to generation and claim heavenly titles of truth and be representatives of God, all in vain. In the Master Plan of God, it will be made obvious to all people in the days of the Great Tribulation to come that worldly religions are to be judged to be powerless and false. The humanistic systems of the world today that reject divine truth, the God of all creation, and believe that man is the supreme being, will not escape their judgment. God will validate himself as the sole giver of truth. (Revelation 13:1-8; 2 Thessalonians 2:4) Jesus tells us the end result of knowing God's truth. *"Then you will know the truth and the truth shall make you free."* (John 8:32) Free from ever questioning it again.

The God-established offices of Prophecy, Kingship, and Priesthood will be united in one person, Jesus Messiah forever.

In the Master Plan of God, we see that there are three offices to the Kingdom of God. That of Prophet, King, and High Priest. These offices become unified in the person of Jesus Christ. This will be evidently clear to all people before the New Heaven and a New Earth come into being. Under the authority of sinful men, these three distinctly separate offices of God were more often than not, found to be antagonistic towards one another, rather than acting as agents of God who work together in carrying out His will among the people. This was prevalent in Israel and contributed greatly to the destruction of both Judah and Israel. The Scriptures reveal conflict, deceit, and abuse within each of these offices and in their interactions with one another. Yet there were times where various prophets, priests, and kings acted appropriately in their assigned roles from God, but their human frailties and sin limited their effectiveness. When all three offices worked together with one another, they made valuable contributions in service to God's plan.

In the Millennial Kingdom, these three offices will demonstrate to all, a perfect harmony with one another, performing the will of God in the execution of their specific roles. When these three offices come together in Jesus Messiah, they will function perfectly here on the Earth for 1000 years. By the appointment of these three offices given to the Lord Jesus Christ, we recognize that He alone is worthy of all submission, by all people under His dominion and authority. And He alone will subject all things to the Father so "that God may be all in all."

All power and authority over all created things are God's alone, and they will never again be challenged by man or angel.

At the end of the age, before the New Heaven and New Earth are created, all power and authority will be placed under the feet of Jesus Messiah. All challenges to God's authority made by Satan and the demonic realm of angels, both in Heaven and on Earth, will have failed. Every power-grab opportunity that Mankind and Satan had seized upon and will seize upon in the times ahead, will ultimately fail to accomplish their purposes. A war in Heaven that is to come among those in the spiritual realm will result in Satan's defeat and set up the remaining three and a half years of the Great Tribulation. At that time, the devil, that serpent of old, attempts to alter God's Master Plan but fails in his attempts to destroy the Jewish people and those who come to faith in Jesus Christ. (Revelation 12:7-17).

Additionally, While Satan rules over the kingdoms of mankind, he has an enemy on Earth that he has not been able to overcome for over two thousand years. It is the Church of Jesus Christ. It is commissioned and empowered by the Holy Spirit, to set free those who are under Satan's dark domain to become citizens of Heaven. The Church brings the message of Jesus to free those in oppression and set at liberty those who are chained by their own sins and rebellion against God.

A united mankind under the Antichrist, will prove to themselves that they have no power to oppose God except by their own will alone. As the Scripture says, the nations, their kings, and kingdoms are a drop in a bucket to the Lord. (Isaiah 40:15) They will submit to the rightful rule of the King of kings and Lord of lords, or face destruction for resisting Him. (Revelation 20:7-10) At the end of the time allocated in the Master Plan, Satan, the demonic angels, and all unredeemed humanity who have turned away from God will not see the New Heavens and the New Earth. They will be separated for eternity from those who turned to God for their redemption. (Revelation 20:11-15) Those whose will it is to serve God and love their Savior will come into perfect subjection to the Son of God and become sinless and incorruptible. They will become unwilling to dispute or reject God's power and authority, they will claim His righteousness alone. All of redeemed humanity, having served God's purposes in life, having participated in the success of the Master Plan of God, will desire to serve Him faithfully in the New Heaven and New Earth.

Heavenly witnesses will validate that God is righteous in all His acts of judgment towards mankind and the angels

We all have heard the saying, "Absolute power corrupts absolutely." The thought is that as a person's power increases, their moral sense will diminish. We have all seen men and women throughout the ages rise to power and influence only to succumb to moral failures. Even the man after God's own heart, King David, was caught up in that Bathsheba incident of lust, adultery, deceit, and murder. David reigned for only 40 years, and he struggled with kingly power in his sinful hands and failed more than once in that time. In the Scriptures, we are told that Jesus Messiah will reign for 1,000 years and that His Kingdom will be worldwide. Will Jesus be vulnerable to that proverbial saying? No, of course not, Jesus is God the Son, and we identified that God does not change, which includes His moral standards. God's position on morality is never impacted negatively by His power. He is already the God of all things. The Scriptures tell us that, *" Jesus Christ is the same yesterday, today, and forever"* (Hebrews 18:8). If Jesus is righteous, just, and true as the only King over all the kingdoms of the Earth in His first year in power, then it is a given that He will be exactly that same Godly king 1000 years later and every year in-between and beyond into eternity.

There are people who live on this side of life who say God cannot be Just if He chooses to act with vengeance, wrath, jealousy, or destruction. Such behavior from God, they assert, would not be compatible with His claim to be a God of love, grace, and mercy; they have doubts about a God who judges, condemns, and sentences those to whom He has given free will. Not believing what God has said but rather believing a lie is always encouraged by the demonic hosts, especially those things that sound good to people but not to God.

For the free-will-thinking creatures of creation- to accept as truth that, "God to be all in all," such doubts and accusations must be overcome with the validation that God is just and all His actions are righteous. We can recognize the doubter's opinions on the matter, but we cannot ignore the witnesses who are in Heaven and what they are saying. These people hold to a different perspective, such as the one found in Revelation 19:1- 5. *"After these things, I heard a loud voice of a great multitude in Heaven saying, Alleluia! Salvation, glory, and honor, and power belong to Lord, our God! For true and righteous are His judgments, because He has judged the great harlot...* In the context of these verses, God has just passed judgment and destruction on the world's system of religions, values, and institutions (that would be the "Great Harlot") for her sins and to avenge the blood of His servants who were victims of this Scarlet clothed Harlot. These people in Heaven are thrilled to see her destruction.

This great multitude in Heaven in one loud voice, praises God for His righteous judgments. This praise would likely come from all of the redeemed of human history up to that time and would likely include all of the Heavenly hosts of angels. Heaven's witnesses will validate that God is righteous in all of His acts of judgment, just as it is recorded in the Scriptures. In response to God's righteous judgment, the Apostle

John observes the twenty-four elders and the four living creatures who are in the throne room of God. They have observed all that God has been doing in His acts of judgment and react by falling down in praise and worship of God. (Revelation 19:4)

God validates that He is Just and Righteous in all of His judgments, and He does so in the presence of an innumerable Heavenly host of witnesses. True and righteous judgments of God have continued throughout the ages of human history for angels and people to observe, and at specific times participate in their execution. It is in the Master Plan of God to have all angels and all people come to the realization that God has always been righteous in all of His judgments, and He always will be. God the Son, Jesus Messiah, will execute perfect righteousness and judgment in His reign as King in the 1000-year Millennial Kingdom and under the worst of conditions in a world of sinners. When the final rebellion of humanity occurs, God will act justly when He ends this physical realm and creates the New Heavens and New Earth revealed to us in Revelation 20:7-10.

God, the promise maker, is also the promise keeper of every promise that He has ever made.

Before there can be a New Heaven and New Earth, God will have fulfilled every single promise that He has ever made throughout world history and kept every promise given to every person. If God said it, so it is that His will be done. Nothing will be overlooked and no promise will be ignored. The Lord Jesus has taken on a personal role in the fulfillment of every promise and covenant God ever made, and He will see to it that it is sovereignly performed to perfection according to His Father's will.

God will execute final judgments on Demons, Satan, the Scarlet Harlot (worldly religions), and Man.

It is in the Master Plan of God to put an end to these forms of evil and prevent them from ever influencing humanity again. After the destruction of the world's religions, (Jeremiah 10:10,11; Revelation 19) God strips Satan of all authority and power, having taken away his rule over the world's kingdoms and incarcerating him in the abyss for 1000 years. After that, he is released and he will incite a worldwide rebellion. In which he is finally taken away and cast into the lake of fire, the permanent place of his destiny. Then after the old Heavens and Earth have passed away, God brings all unredeemed humanity from all of the world's history to the White Throne of Judgment, where final justice is served in the righteousness and truth of God (Revelation 20:11-15).

God will put an end to all sin and bring an end to death, all sadness, tears, and pain. With that, all the bi-products from the effects of sin will be gone as well.

It is in God's Master Plan to end death and prepare us for life with Him in the New Heaven and the New Earth. When the redeemed are raised up in a resurrection of the dead and others raptured, we will be raised up incorruptible; we will be raised up immortal. *"Flesh and blood cannot enter the kingdom of God, nor does corruption inherit incorruption (I Corinthians 15:50). "So, when the corruptible has put on incorruption and this mortal has put on immortality, then shall be brought to pass the saying that is written: "Death is swallowed up in victory." O' Death, where is your sting?" O' Hades, where is your victory?"* (1Corinthians 15:54,55) We are told that *"the wages of sin is death, but the gift of God is eternal life in Jesus Christ our Lord."* (Romans 6:23) this faithful promise will pass into a glorious reality.

God will give everlasting life to all the redeemed. They will be both spiritual and physical beings in Christ's likeness; in the image of the Heavenly man.

It is in the Master Plan of God that humanity's redemption includes a resurrected body. We are told that flesh and blood (which are corrupted by sin) cannot enter into the Kingdom of God. Requiring that our new physical forms be supernatural, both physical and spiritual, in the likeness of the Lord's body, with which the apostles had supernatural experiences with after His resurrection. (Romans 6:5) The Scriptures tell us that Jesus could be touched, eat food, and yet simply appear and disappear whenever He chooses to do so. To what extent we will have such a body is unknown for now. Our redemption and glorious being will be the result of Christ's righteousness imputed to each redeemed person.

God will have created a New Heaven and a New Earth, and a new holy city, Jerusalem. He will dwell with us there. He will be our God, and we, His children.

In God's Master Plan, there will be a supernatural Heaven and Earth. A new spiritual and physical realm for all His people and angels to dwell in. A realm where God declares that He makes all things new! However, it will not just be a place where the redeemed live as God's children, they will in fact be with their Heavenly Father. This entry into the New Heaven and New Earth is likely when Jesus Christ subjects Himself to the Father.

The Scriptures tell us that the plan is for the physical realm to end and that a New Heaven and New Earth will emerge. (Revelation 20:1, Psalm 102:25, 26) At that time, God declares from His throne," *Behold I make all things new!"* (Revelation 20:5) Then He proceeds to show the Apostle John a gigantic three-dimensional cubed city that John can barely describe. It is a city about 1500 miles long in three dimensions. The angel shows John the New Jerusalem, (Revelation 21:6-22) this new city is a supernatural and it descends out of the Heavenly realm of God onto the New Earth. The city has a river and trees; it needs no sun or moon for light because God is its light and there is no nighttime.

Being that John is describing for us something never seen before, we cannot know with certainty what this jeweled capital city of God is all about, but we do walk away from this knowing that it is supernatural in nature, both physical and spiritual. It is probable to say that this city is what Jesus referred to as His "Father's house," the place where Jesus will take us when He comes to get us. (John 14:2-4) This city will be home to all of the redeemed in the history of mankind and also to the Lamb of God. In this new realm, the Lord God Almighty and the Lamb (Jesus Messiah), are themselves the temple of God in the New Jerusalem (Revelation 21:22). The redeemed enter that temple and will live as inheritors of all that is God's. (Revelation 21:7) The redeemed will live life at a level that we cannot really conceive of now, but one thing that satisfies our souls more than any other is that we will be with God Himself. (Revelation 21:3) The redeemed will come face to face with God, but not before they are prepared to come into His presence (Revelation 22:4).

Maybe the most unexpected thing about this New Heaven and Earth is that people from every walk of life and from every period of time in history, every culture, and every tribe will be able to live together in Godly harmony and love for one another. Does this happen instantly once we become immortal in Christ-likeness, or is it possible that we continue to learn to be the people we should be?

The Master Plan of God shows us that we are not ready for this new Kingdom, that angels are not ready for this Kingdom, and that Heaven and Earth are not ready for this Kingdom. God is showing us in His holy Scriptures that there are some objectives that need to be reached and that His standards for them are high. Holy high standards, perfect standards. And we also see that there is a reasonable, logical progression of changes that occur to prepare all things for God and the New Heaven and New Earth. These changes that occur as outcomes of His Plans will bring us through our journey with our Lord and with one another.

The Master Plan of God makes it clear that every person who was ever born will be in the New Heaven and Earth or in the Lake of Fire. Every soul who has the capacity to consciously exercise their own free will in life will know that their destiny was determined by their faith. Trusting in God that their sins have been paid for will lead to life, and rejecting God's will leads to death. Free will has a lot to say about people's destiny and their responses to the objectives that God will fulfill. The fact that before our birth, God knows our destiny, does not require God to explain Himself nor does it affect human free will. God is a mysterious God for sure in matters of predestination and free will. This truth is something we cannot understand at this time. Motivated by His love for you and me individually, we subject ourselves to His Lordship and become Christ's own possession, and our God calls us to join Him in everlasting life.

The new supernatural realm is where mankind and the angels of Heaven will be prepared to live together with God in the new reality. In the New Jerusalem, and wherever we go in this new world, we will go in the presence of the Father, Son, and Holy Spirit. God will not restore us to be only like that first man, Adam, but will recreate us in a glorified likeness of the Son of His love, Jesus Christ, the man from Heaven. (1 Corinthians 15:46-49) To that end His, love, mercy, grace, and cause for thanksgiving to God, glorifies Him.

Love for one another will be the commandment to abide by, temptations and sin will be no more. He will be our God, and we will be

His people. Our life's work on Earth that was invested in unredeemed things will not survive the judgment seat of Christ. However, it is reasonable to think that our memories will be retained, including both the good and bad experiences that helped to form who we are. They will survive the trip into the new realm in new ways that bring God glory. We who are redeemed will be prepared to do whatever God calls on us to do in that age and in the ages to come, ages to be revealed in the Master Plan of God. We will live in the majesty of reigning as a Kingdom of Priests and as the adopted children of the great "I Am."

It isn't always easy to accept that all unredeemed people who take the pathway to damnation do so willingly, there will be no new kingdom for them. They will have made it known to all that when God reached out to them during their life on Earth, they preferred to exist without Him in their life. Their own words, spoken from their hearts will condemn them. When they stand before God as one of the condemned, He grants them their heart's desire as they enter into the terror of their final destiny. God's justice and God's holiness will come upon them, and they will be sentenced to a hellish existence without God, stripped of His image, and all His goodness. There in the Lake of Fire, all the condemned will join the Antichrist, the False Prophet, the demon angels, and Satan himself for eternity. (Revelation 20:10-15) With the end of evil and the calls for justice satisfied, God is glorified. Gone will be a temporary imperfect creation with its gaps. Replaced with a new creation of Holy perfection bearing in it the fullness of God's Glory for eternity, A creation where God will be all in all.

PART TWO:
THE MILLENNIAL AGE STORY

CHAPTER 7:
The Millennial Age Link To The Master Plan

The Millennial Age is arguably the least understood period of time in the Bible. The fact that it is a future time yet to be played out leaves it open to the misunderstanding of prophecies and subjective thinking that can easily conflict with God's words about it. The Millennial Age is identified in the Scriptures as a 1000-year period of time that exists after the Great Tribulation ends and before the final rebellion that is led by Satan begins. We can begin to understand this "Age" by looking at how Jesus reveals it to His church in the Book of Revelation, chapter, 20, verses 4-6, as follows:

And I saw thrones, and they sat upon them, and judgment was committed to them. Then I saw the souls of those who had been beheaded for their witness to Jesus and for the Word of God, who had not worshipped the Beast or his image and had not received his mark on their foreheads or on their hands. And they lived and reigned with Christ for a thousand years. But the rest of the dead did not live again until the thousand years were finished. This is the first resurrection. Blessed and holy is he who has part in the first resurrection. Over such, the second death has no power, but they shall be priests of God and of Christ and shall reign with Him a thousand years.

The Apostle John introduces us to the Millennial Age. In the text that John gives us, we can understand the following: Christ (the Messiah) will reign as King of kings and Lord of lords over the Earth for 1000 years, which is why He came back to Earth. (Revelation 19:15-16) Also, there are multiple thrones; these are seats of authority to make judgments, sentences, and awards. These thrones are for the co-rulers who serve Jesus Messiah. We do not know who they are or where they come from. However, we are told that they were killed as martyrs, and beheaded for their witness to Jesus and the word of God. They are to be resurrected and reign with Jesus for those 1000 years. It is certain that there will be twelve of these thrones in Israel and that the twelve resurrected Apostles are its judges, as Jesus said. *"So, Jesus said to them, assuredly I say to you, that in the regeneration (renewal), when the Son of Man sits on the throne of His glory, you who have followed me will also sit on twelve thrones, judging the twelve tribes of Israel,"* (Matthew 19:28) that would be one per tribe. This judiciary office is not one in the New Heaven and New Earth but in the renewal of the Kingdom of God on Earth.

These co-rulers, are people who became believers in Jesus after the rapture had occurred, so they are not a part of the Church. There are two additional things to know about these martyr witnesses; First, we can be confident that there will be many, possibly thousands. Since the twelve Apostles have already been assigned to rule over the Jews in Israel, we can say that it is highly probable that these witnesses will be assigned to rule over the Gentile nations worldwide. Second, these witnesses are resurrected martyrs from the Tribulation and are included as being in the first type of resurrection. Verses 5 and 6 make a distinction between the types of resurrections there are to be, not their quantity. There are two types of resurrections, those of the "Just" and those of the "Unjust." Of which all of the "just" will resurrect before the "unjust" will. The Apostle Paul says, *"I have hope in God, which they themselves also accept, that there will be a resurrection of the dead, both of the just and the unjust."* (Acts 24:15; see also Revelation 22:11)

There is nothing here in Revelation 20: 4-6 that would compel us to believe that these witnesses who are martyred during the Great Tribulation are included in the resurrection event of 1 Thessalonians, 4:13-16 which is when the Church is raptured and the dead in Christ (Messiah) are raised up. It would be in error to think that the "First Resurrection" was to mean a one-time-only event, one that included the Church and its rapture. To hold to such a position would place the resurrection near or at the end of the Tribulation in order to include these resurrected martyrs found in Revelation 19:5. This would also require the Church to suffer through the Tribulation events, which presents its own unique set of difficulties that are reasonably dismissed.

Any thought of a one-time only resurrection cannot be reasonably accepted knowing that there have been other people who have already been resurrected prior to that event. In Matthew 27:52, 53, after Jesus was resurrected, these dead in Christ were raised up in one of their own resurrections, and they came out of their graves and "appeared" to many. Note that these resurrected people do not live again physically, they were not raised up from the dead as Lazarus of Bethany was, only to face death a second time. These resurrected people in the Matthew account only "appeared" to others in their glorified state as Jesus did and then were raptured away. Additionally, an untold number of other people will be resurrected to life after the Millennium Age has passed, having their bodies resurrected before the Earth is dissolved. To expand on this thought logically, anyone who dies a believer in Jesus Messiah after the resurrection event of 1 Thessalonians 4:13-16 will also take part in that first type of resurrection, that of the "Just." Also, all who take part in the first resurrection type will be raised up before the "Unjust" are raised up. Otherwise, we would have to conclude that all people who live beyond the resurrection event of 1 Thessalonians 4:13-16 are a part of the resurrection of the "Unjust" which isn't worthy of consideration.

Also, there is nothing here in the Revelation, chapter 20 text, to indicate that all of the resurrected dead of the 1 Thessalonians 4:13-16 event will be living and ruling on the Earth with Christ for 1000 years; that would not be plausible. Rather, the point being made here in Revelation, chapter 20:5-6 is that it is this specific group of resurrected martyrs who were beheaded during the Tribulation because they refused to take the mark of the Beast, they will rule with Jesus Messiah in the Millennium. There will be more discussion on these saints as we develop the Millennial Kingdom events.

That's it; that is all that Jesus has shared in His letter to the seven churches about the Millennial Kingdom. The Apostle John delivers to the churches fifteen inspired chapters about a seven-year period of time and then just three verses about the following 1000 years! In fact, there is so little given in the whole of the New Testament about this 1000-year period, that maybe the Millennial Kingdom is not to be of much importance to the Church. To think that would be a mistake, rather, we are taught by Jesus to pray to our Father in Heaven, asking that "Thy Kingdom come on Earth as it is in Heaven." Christians are to want the Kingdom to come to the Earth. So, then we ask ourselves questions like, "What is the nature of this Kingdom on the Earth, what will it be like? We may ask, "Is this Kingdom a spiritual Kingdom, maybe a Church Kingdom?" As said previously, the Kingdom of God that Jesus will reign over, will be uniquely physical and spiritual, unlike any kingdom that will ever exist on Earth. There will be much more on this as we go forward.

Why are the New Testament letters largely silent about this time on Earth? This is most likely because the Church will have been raptured to Heaven by Jesus and also because this time is not for the Church, but a time for the renewal of the Kingdom of God on Earth. The Old Testament writers have much to say about this Kingdom form, its King, and Israel's relationship with God, during the Millennium Age. For the Jews, it will be a time of renewal, the restoration of Israel that Jesus taught His disciples about, and it was something that His disciples were expecting to happen. They asked Him after His resurrection, *"Lord, will you at this time restore the kingdom to Israel?"* (Acts 1:6,7) The Promised Land and the Children of Israel are directly connected to the events of the Millennial Kingdom and central to a renewed, ongoing relationship with God. This is also in the Master Plan of God.

The nation of Israel is last seen in the Holy Scriptures as being cursed in their iniquities and unreconciled with God. They proved to be unfaithful to the Lord, and they came to reject the very Messiah that they had hoped would return to be their king. They went so far as to have the God who became flesh and dwelled among them, killed and they became enemies of His Gospel. (Romans 11:28; Acts 3:14, 15) Their Old Covenant priesthood died along with the destruction of their temple, along with the failed hope of a renewed Kingdom of God. Is that the end of their story? Is it time for Christians to put that Jewish Bible on a shelf to be used only for principles for living and object lessons? The Scriptures tell us that God does not change and that His promises will be kept, that will include His promises to Israel. It is in the Master Plan of God to restore and renew, to make better those things that will bring Him glory. Israel is going to be one of those things and He is going to do it through Jesus Messiah.

The redemption of the Jewish people, and their impact on the Gentile nations of this world through the Kingdom of God, are solidly embedded in the prophetic Scriptures. There is not now and never could be a Plan B, or some kind of reset in God's plans. The incarnation of Jesus Christ in Bethlehem did not put an end to one story and start another. It was a time for the first physical visitation of God to His chosen people. A time for Him to step into their world physically and make the final sacrifice for the redemption of all the ages. Opening the door to the spiritual Kingdom of God to Israel. Not through the Old Covenant laws and the physical Kingdom of God but through His Gospel, His Church, and the body of Christ where His grace extends to the Gentiles.

Jesus Messiah is the only one who will execute God's Plan through the Millennium, and into the New Heaven and New Earth. During the Millennium He will bring all things under His authority and rule. And when all things are fully executed, He will deliver all things to the Father including Israel. (1 Corinthians 15:24-28)

Before we get any further into a narrative on the Millennium Age, we must address potential objections. In doing so, we will endeavor to take God at His word and not attempt to make what is said mean something else. One possible objection put into a question is: Do the verses in Revelation 20:4-6 mean a literal 1000 years, or could it be an allegory, a metaphor? The idea that the 1000 years is symbolic of something else is a notion that is not supported in its context within the Book of Revelation, nor was it revealed by an angel to John as being symbolic as with other symbolism. When symbolism is used in Scripture, its meaning is validated independently in another part of the Scripture, or by an angel, or by simple common knowledge. For example: Daniel's vision of a lion, a bear, and a leopard-like creature in Daniel 7:4-6 are confirmed later in the chapter by an angel to be kingdoms. Without that validation, you are left with the choice to either accept the explanation given to you by an interpreter or reject it for another, maybe even one of your own interpretations. At times when we do not understand a particular passage of Scripture, we are tempted to resort to using symbolism as a way of getting around the passage or use it to further advance a particular line of thinking. This is a common occurrence in the study of future events in the Scriptures and should be avoided as much as possible.

Visions given in the Scriptures do contain symbolism, such as the one John is given in Revelation 12:1-3; which will serve as a needed Tribulation example. We know that the "sun" and "moon" in the text are symbolic of Jacob and Rachel and that the "twelve stars" are the twelve sons of Jacob, collectively they are symbols for the House of Jacob, that is Israel, because the Scriptures validate that this is so in Genesis 37:9-11. Therefore, in Revelation 12:1, the woman who bore the Child is known to be the nation of Israel. There is no scriptural validation that states any other meaning symbolically for the sun, moon, and stars when they are used together. So, the use of the word "woman" is not to be connected to Mary, the mother of Jesus, or to something unrelated to the story, but to the people who brought forth Jesus. This becomes obvious when looking further into chapter 12, when Satan makes war with the rest of this woman's offspring when there is no one around to save the Jews who are coming to faith in Jesus. (Revelation 12:17)

An underlying desire to see the 1000 years as symbolic may be found in the heart of the objector. Thoughts of unnecessary redundancy and having a worn-out world endure more of the same in life, leave them feeling something like an airline passenger only wanting to go home, but is stuck in an airplane, having to continually circle around the airport in a holding pattern unable to land. All we want to do is to land in that New Heaven and New Earth, hoping that God will speed things up and get everyone to the gate. Such a perspective of the Millennium Age could not be further from the glory that emerges out of the Kingdom of God and the revelation of its great King!

Another common belief is that the 1000-year Millennial Kingdom is representative in some way of the Church and the 1000 years as part of a Church Age. This line of thought remains suspect for the reason already mentioned, it is purely subjective and is not supported at all in the Scriptures. We are not in the Millennial Kingdom, we are however living in and among kingdoms under the authority of Satan, according to the Scriptures. (Luke 4:5-7)

But what about a popular idea going around today that this 1000-year kingdom is a time to come when this Earth will be occupied by the glorified saints of the past and or, Christ's Church? The Scriptures do not tell the Church this is the case, also, this line of thinking does not fit into the pathway that has been developed in God's Master Plan. The logic of it all isn't there either. It posits that Jesus takes us to the Father's home for a time and them empties His house of multiple hundreds of millions of the redeemed to take them to a temporary Earth, to do things that Messiah can do without them, with a Kingdom of people who are already on Earth. Before we can settle on a specific understanding of events to come, we need to examine how such an understanding would align with what else the Scriptures do say about that event. A wrong understanding will often conflict with who God is and His character. Obviously, any understanding that would position God to no longer keep the promises He made to Israel would also open up the door to the possibility that one day He may not keep the promises He has made to Christians as well. Furthermore, the idea of a Church-led and occupied Millennial Kingdom lacks many logical reasons for doing so. However, what the Scriptures do tell us through the messages of several prophets and in much detail is who will be occupying the Earth during Messiah's Kingdom, and it will be the surviving Jews and Gentiles of the Tribulation judgments and their generations that follow.

Another line of wrong thinking is to believe that when the prophetic Old Testament writers speak of Israel and God's people, we should understand that this is in reference to the Church, seen as God's replacement for Israel, and His replacement in the Millennial Kingdom. We need to understand that such a theology exercise turns simple-to-understand verses of Scripture into confusing or patently misleading statements that have nothing to do with the Church. One such example offered is found in Luke 1:32-33, which in its context is about an angel speaking to Mary at the time before Christ's birth, saying, *"He will be called the Son of the Highest; And the Lord will give Him the throne of His father David. And He will reign over the house of Jacob forever, and of His kingdom there will be no end."* What level of blind understanding is needed in order to actually believe that this angel is talking about Jesus and the Church rather than about Jesus and Israel, who the last time we checked, is the House of Jacob! Is the Church now supposed to be Jacob in this verse and in this role? Confusing for us yes, but especially for poor Mary, she would go through life thinking that the angel meant exactly what was said and so should we. Besides, what would it matter to anyone anywhere, that Jesus is going to be reigning on a throne that was at one time occupied by King David, but now the Kingdom that Jesus will be reigning over is really the Church and not the Jews? We must take God at His word!

Those who struggle with the whole plan of God for a Millennial Kingdom ask questions such as, "Why have a Millennial Kingdom at all, it all appears to be so redundant and brings little value to the Plan of God?" "Why wouldn't God put an end to Satan when He had him at Armageddon?" "Why keep Satan incarcerated for a time, only to let him out again?" "Why let humanity be deceived once again, and why let humanity rebel one last time?" "What is the point of it all?" The answers to these questions can be found in the Millennial Kingdom story itself. In the story, God will be glorified in amazing ways that otherwise would be lost in any other scenario given for those 1000 years.

Revelation 20:7-10 is an easy-to-read, simple-to-understand text in that Messiah reigns for 1000 years, and afterward, Satan roams free again. Satan leads humanity in a rebellion that leads to their end, where God delivers a crushing blow to their evil intentions and they all go up in flames. In reply, it would be simple to say, "It will happen this way because it is God's will to do so." Although that statement is true, it is not very satisfying. However, when understood in the context of God's Master Plan, the Millennium Age and the final judgment that follows it will advance God's Plan and prepare humanity and the angelic realm for the New Heaven and Earth.

During the Millennium Age and shortly afterward, before the world and the entire physical realm are no more, there will be several things that will occur that have never happened before in Human history, situational changes in the world we live in that will bring God great glory!

#1 GOD WILL PHYSICALLY REIGN OVER A PHYSICAL KINGDOM.

When Jesus Messiah returns to set up His Kingdom on Earth, (Daniel 2:44) it will be the first kingdom in history to ever have a Holy King. One who is incorruptible, the perfect judge and administrator of truth, and a giver of wisdom. A King above all kings and a Lord above all Lords. One who demands that justice be served and who will dispense grace, mercy, and love for all people with equity. One who will know when to bear the rod of iron and when by grace to pardon for sins. And this King will do so for 1,000 years without sin impacting His thoughts or actions. Jesus Messiah will descend out of Heaven from the very throne room of God with the name "King of kings and Lord of lords" written on His thigh. He will return to the Earth as its rightful ruler. (Revelation 19)

#2 THE KING WILL RULE OVER A JUST, ONE-WORLD CENTRAL GOVERNMENT

There will be a level of control and authority as determined by Jesus Messiah over a world of sinful people. The world will experience a one-world central government that ministers to all nations with equity, functioning for the good of all people everywhere. With the Messiah in control of it all, the world will change from its despair and corruption and experience prosperity, the fruits of righteousness, and goodness, in spite of our flawed humanity.

#3 SATAN WILL NO LONGER HAVE ANY POWER OVER PEOPLE AND THEIR KINGDOMS

With the dominion of Satan broken and his removal from the Earth, all the kingdoms of mankind will be free. Free from the spiritual oppression and darkness that incites people and drives them to destroy one another out of the lust for power, greed, security, and the desire for superiority.

#4 THE DEMONIC INFLUENCE UPON THE WORLD'S RELIGIONS WILL BE REMOVED.

As a result of the demonic removal from the Earth, world religions will become impotent and meaningless. In reaction to the judgments of God throughout the Tribulation, faiths of every kind will lose all hope and see no evidence of power at work in their deities. The Kingdom of God will experience no spiritual opposition forces, but only the sinful natures of people and their free will.

#5 THE MESSIAH WILL CAUSE ISRAEL TO BE A KINGDOM OF PRIESTS THAT LEADS PEOPLE INTO THE SPIRITUAL KINGDOM OF GOD

Israel is to become the Kingdom of Priests that God had always planned for them to be, and Messiah will lead them as High Priest. The covenant promises made to Abraham and to David will be executed under the authority of the High Priest of the Kingdom of God, both in Heaven and on the Earth and God will be glorified.

#6 THE PHYSICAL KINGDOM OF GOD WILL SPREAD THE GOSPEL WORLDWIDE

With the expansion of the Physical Kingdom of God, its spiritual form will reach out to a sinful and lost world again, through the ministries of the redeemed Jews, equipped with the good news. Leading people who are in the physical Kingdom to a transformation into the Spiritual Kingdom of God, much like the Church did as the body of Christ. Salvation and redemption by faith will move across the nations in the name of Jesus Messiah, who died for their sins.

#7 AFTER 1000 YEARS, SATAN WILL INSTIGATE A UNITED WORLDWIDE REBELLION AGAINST GOD.

Revelation 20:1-3 states that Satan is released and deceives the nations once again. A rebellion at the end of world history occurs, as shown in Revelation 20:7-9. This will bring to light the fact, that aside from God's grace and mercy none of humanity is righteous in the sight of God; all people deserve God's judgment. Salvation and redemption from sin come only through the One who died for the sins of the world. All people everywhere bear the sinful nature and deserve the judgment they receive from a Holy God. And only those who are saved by faith in the redeeming blood of the Lamb, Jesus Messiah.

We can better understand the plan and purposes of God for the Millennium Age when we see that it is in His Plan to change many things about life on Earth after the Tribulation judgments. The link between this present age and the Millennial Age to come is not going to be some supernatural reset of life on Earth complete with supernatural citizens. But rather a continuation of God's dealings with sinful humanity, under a whole host of new conditions that will eventually lead to a necessary end to all things. In the Millennial Age to come, we will see Messiah executing the Master Plan and bringing all things into subjection, under His authority, and power, and then bring about a climactic end to the physical realm.

CHAPTER 8:
Finding The Millennial Story

This Millennial story is an account of the Millennial Age and beyond, where the kingdoms of this world have become the kingdoms of our Lord and His Christ, who shall reign forever and ever. (Revelation 11:15, 16) This story has its start at the end of the Tribulation judgments found in Revelation chapters 6-19 and extends beyond the Millennium Age to include the final rebellion and end to this world. Also, the story will include the following Judgment Day event and concludes with the revealing of the New Heaven and the New Earth.

Extending the story beyond the Millennium Age is necessary in order to show the readers the continuing saga of humanity's journey towards its destiny with God, and how the Millennium story is a critical component in the continuation of God's Master Plan. At the story's end, we will be able to see the outcome of God's Master Plan. That it is just as stated by the Apostle Paul, "that God will be all in all." (1 Corinthians 15:28)

The Millennial Story has to be drawn out of the pages of the Scriptures and be put together much like we would put together a jigsaw puzzle. We shouldn't be alarmed by that thought, many people put together jigsaw puzzles successfully every day! The story this puzzle tells comes to us much like a bag of a 500-piece puzzle that is dumped out on a kitchen table. Each piece tells only a fragment of the story, and each piece requires that it be properly linked to its adjoining pieces in order to make sense of the images that will form as a result. By looking at any common puzzle box cover we can generally tell which area of the puzzle many of the pieces will go. We easily determine for example, that the blue puzzle pieces are the sky, rather than water and the colorful pieces are birds and butterflies, rather than fall leaves, and so on; we understand how puzzles work. The puzzle at hand is the Millennium Age that is spread across the pages of the writings of the Prophets and the Gospels, and it requires assembly if we wish to see the whole story.

There will be some readers who may oppose the story outright or in portions, this is understandable. In response to such objections an "Afterword" written by the Author, "Framework of the Millennial

Kingdom" has been prepared. That narrative explains how this puzzle went together the way it did. It will be said now that there is an overwhelming amount of Scripture that supports the positions taken in the story presented and done so without any abuses taken with scriptural context. Also, these positions take into consideration the fact that God has a Master Plan and that He is executing His Plan; this story gives many probable and very many plausible descriptions of how that Master Plan will be completed before there can ever be a New Heaven and a New Earth.

As stated previously, God has revealed Himself to us progressively, and with that, He has also revealed progressively, aspects of His Master Plan to us, and that Plan tells us that it will bring God great honor and glory. The story presented brings to fulfillment all of the objectives we have looked at in the Master Plan, and it successfully arrives at its ultimate conclusion when it can be said, "That God may be all in all."

We can take note of these things that have been previously reviewed by the reader: The gaps found in the four parts of God's creation must be satisfied before "God may be all in all." That the character of God in the execution of His Master Plan will be revealed and validated, and that God is Righteous and Just and worthy of all honor and glory and praise! Lastly for consideration: There are expectations to come as a result of an executed Master Plan. All of these factors, that is, pieces of the puzzle must be successfully included in any Millennial Kingdom puzzle in order to tell its story well.

As with most puzzles, we like to start with the border. The border gives us the extent of a puzzle's size and determines what it will take to fill it all in. The extent determines the overall shape the puzzle will take, and it determines which images in the puzzle reach the boundaries and which ones do not. When we read Revelation chapter 20 verses 1-10, we have found the border to the Millennium puzzle. With its pieces already put in their place and connected together to make the four sides to our puzzle. Everything that happens in regards to the Millennium Age will need to fit within the context of these four truths of Scripture. 1. Jesus Messiah, who we know to be the rightful King of the Earth, returns to reign over a judged Earth for 1000 years. 2. The Kingdom of God that Jesus rules over in the spiritual realm of Heaven is now manifesting itself physically once again on the Earth and is to be a Kingdom of Priests of

God. 3. The previously reigning ruler over the Earth, who is Satan, is removed from power and dominion and incarcerated for those same 1000 years, and then released to deceive people once again for a "little while." 4. After the 1000 years of the Kingdom have expired and after Satan's release, humanity rebels against God's will and gathers together for the battle to destroy the saints at Jerusalem, but God destroys the rebels and Satan. In these ten verses, Jesus gives the Church the most critical pieces of the Millennial Age puzzle. Without these border pieces, there could be no understandable story of great glory or an understanding of why the world ends in the way that is revealed in the Scriptures.

Unlike a common puzzle with a picture of the puzzle's images on the box cover, we find that our puzzle has no Millennial Kingdom picture on the box cover. Rather, our box cover offers imagery only with text, rather than by shapes and colors. With the four sides of the puzzle border intact, we will look for evidence among the many pieces and begin the process of connecting those pieces that show commonality or relationship and eventually drop the images we assemble within the puzzle border until the entire picture is completed and the story told.

More often than not, when we are reading the Scriptures and we come across a clearly prophetic text from an Old Testament book where the prophet appears to be speaking about the Messianic Kingdom of God, we often will give it a moment's thought, nod our heads with acknowledgement and move on to something else. We will rarely go through other prophetic texts seeking commonality or relationship and then connect the prophecies to form a bigger picture in the Millennium Kingdom. We know the text in hand has to fit in somewhere, and we understand that when we do make the right connection then the text tells us more about the story. But often, we don't seek to make these connections because the task seems daunting, it's a puzzle.

Now we have to ask, "Why would God give us a spiritual puzzle to put together? What we can say about such a thing?" In God's wisdom, He has decided which truths will be easy to understand and which will not. Generally, we see that truths about the present are easier to assemble for one another than truths about the future. We must also accept the fact that God doesn't always hand us spiritual truths in easy-to-read chapters and verses.

The Jews also had their spiritual puzzles, especially about their future. For them, "Was the Messiah going to be a humble, suffering servant, or was He a conquering king?" "Was there one Messiah or two?" The Scriptures pointed to both roles, and the spiritual puzzle remains a puzzle until it was played out on the pages of history. We will need to accept the spiritual puzzles by faith, but not with blind faith. There are no guarantees that we have it all exactly right.

With the extent of the Millennial Kingdom border pieced together with four sides of the puzzle, we then need to begin forming the specific images within it; this is the bulk of the work. To study the Millennium Kingdom is really to study the Old Testament and the words of the King Himself. Once we get beyond Revelation 20:1-10 we will find some, but precious little information about the Millennial Kingdom for the New Testament Church. That is because the Church is not going to be in the physical Kingdom of God. But also, because the Church is already in the spiritual Kingdom and will reside in the Father's house. Should this be disputed, examine the Scriptures and see if the Church is ever called into a physical Kingdom scenario. What we will find is an abundant amount of Scripture written by the Prophets of Israel in a physical Kingdom of God to come and their various descriptions of the Messiah.

The prophet's writings are not orderly accounts of future events as they unfold. They wrote to warn the people of their day and to tell them what to expect when judgment comes upon them. But they also wrote words of encouragement to those who were faithful to God. The people understood that they would be caught up in the wrath of God, which was to come upon the whole House of Israel. To them, God made promises of a new and better day that would come to the people of God. And He gave them glimpses into what the land and the people of Israel would experience under a new covenant, with Messiah as their king. They would see that the Gentile nations who hate them now, will one day look upon them with reverence and seek them out so they may come to know God as well.

He also gives understanding to all of us who read the words of the Prophets to see that His words are true as they are spoken and that the promises of judgment came upon the condemned just as He said it would. But also, the promises of hope and deliverance by the acts of God would come just as He said, in those "latter days."

If we are to find the story of the Millennial Kingdom in the writings of the prophets, then we need to understand the context for the prophet and the people he is speaking to. We need to examine what the prophet has said and clarify who he is speaking of. We also need to make sure we understand what is being said, how it is written, and what God wants them to hear. We also need to understand in sufficient detail the history of the Jews and their Kingdom of God. All these understandings are useful in order to know who the prophet is speaking to and for what time he is speaking. These understandings help us be able to determine if the prophet's message is intended to be for their generations or is it for a future generation and time? An example of this is the text in Jeremiah 33:14-17. We can be confident that this prophecy is a millennial event because historically this event has never occurred to date. In Jeremiah's day, Judah existed but the House of Israel was mostly scattered. But the text says that one day these two will be reunited and grow up to David a Branch of righteousness. There is nothing in history that even comes close to a fulfillment. However, this prophecy connects well with the Millennial Kingdom story. Connecting the prophecy to the correct event in time takes diligence, but it is essential to getting the right puzzle pieces to form an accurate image in the story.

We have to accept that many prophetic messages speak not only about people who are contemporaries of that prophet but also about people and events in a distant future. This acceptance is logical for two reasons. First, if God were only speaking to those generations in and around the times of that prophet, then their messages from God have no further accomplishments to make in the Master Plan. We could say those prophecies were fulfilled, and a greater portion of the Old Testament would become ancient history to us and the messages from the prophets will have little to no relevance to Christians except to serve as a source of examples and exhortations for Christian living, and how God revealed Himself to His people in the past. This statement is true for some prophecies, but not all. We cannot write off all prophecies because some have been fulfilled. Rather, this should cause us to examine the remaining prophecies and look for their time for fulfillment.

There is no rule from God that says that a prophecy can only be relevant to the prophet's present time or a future time, but not to both.

There is a reason for accepting that a single prophecy can speak to people who live in two different times. If God were only speaking through the prophets about future events beyond the generations of that prophet, then that prophet would be telling people who desperately needed to hear from God that this prophecy would have had no immediate value or application for you, your situation, or your time. This would solicit a kind of "that's nice to know, but what about me?" response from the faithful in Israel. The prophets speak messages that are for their contemporaries and also for people in future days ahead, often for both with the same prophecy. Both the people in the past and in the future, as well as the people of our day, need to hear the messages of the prophets for hope, edification, and consolation. Prophecy is a call to His people of all times to take to heart what God has told us and is telling us still. We are to observe the mysteries unfold over time into fulfilled promises that cause us to be in wonder of Him and give Him glory; this is in the Master Plan of God. In other words, we should pay attention to the unfolding of the prophetic word, seek to understand it, and observe its pathway to fulfillment and glorify God in doing so.

Common to the prophetic books and their messages is that the Creator God, who covenants with mankind, will keep His promises that He has made with us. Promises that He will remain good even though we are not. He will prove to be faithful in His relationship with us even when we prove to be unfaithful to Him. That He will be known by His people and by those who are not. That He is the Lord God, and they are His people, regardless of the situation at hand. The Prophets also make it known in much of their writings that there is something desperately wrong with mankind. People's hearts are corrupted beyond repair, not physically but as spiritual beings. Our minds and consciences bear this out to be true daily. Israel, whom God had given His "Law" to, proved for us all, that just because you have God's laws and just because you desire to keep them doesn't mean that you will. Rather, we found out that by having these laws, they serve to stimulate our sinful nature into breaking them. (Romans 7:5-11) The messages that come from the prophets bring God's solution, but we don't always accept it.

In order to find the Millennial Kingdom of God story, we must have an understanding of the historical Kingdom of God story. Without a well-grounded knowledge of what God has already done about His

Kingdom when it was on Earth for the first time, we will experience some difficulty in understanding what God is doing with the Kingdom when it is restored, that is only common sense. We must not think of these two Kingdoms as two separate Kingdoms because of the centuries that have passed. We must remember that God prefers to restore rather than replace the things of His creation and that all things He creates are good. So then, the Kingdom of God, that is Israel, was a good thing. And in the Millennial Age, God will restore Israel in many ways as He originally created it, but He will not stop there; He will make it better. He will make it a Kingdom that lasts 1000 years on Earth before He makes "all things" new again in the New Heaven and New Earth. We find this renewal of the Kingdom of God and its impact on the world written in the words of the prophets and given to the people of Israel in the form of many promises from God.

The Prophets specifically spoke of times of hope and a time when their Messiah would come. He would be their High Priest, King, and Prophet of God, who would give the people new hearts in place of their hearts of stone, and fill them with a new spirit. He would gather them from around the world and bring them to Himself. They would be made new, reconciled to God by His righteousness, just like Christians are made new. Messiah would be a light to the Gentiles, who can find their hope in Him. The Messiah, this Son of David, will usher in glory to the Kingdom of Israel that will surpass that of his father David's kingdom and achieve worldwide recognition and glory.

Tragically for the Jews, when "Immanuel," God is with us, came into the world and Jesus presented Himself to the Jews as their savior from sin, offering them life in the spiritual Kingdom of God, He was rejected. They would not accept God's Messiah on His terms and in God's way but rather, insisted on the fulfillment of the physical Kingdom from the prophecies of their choice or nothing at all. Promises and prophecies that God had chosen for another time and in other circumstances, but the Jews would not hear of it. When Jesus demonstrated that He was their Lord and Messiah, the King of the Jews, the Jews became enraged and had Him killed on a cross. And as in one voice, the crowd who witnessed Jesus' crucifixion spoke prophetically saying, "His blood be on us and on our children." And so, their own curse has been upon them from that time on and continues to the Millennial Age.

Soon after that event, the Jewish people lost their temple and their city, they lost the priesthood and the practices of temple worship. They became a lost nation, scattered around the face of the world. They lost their Promised Land and became unreconciled with the God who gave it all to them. Little has changed for the Jews since the death of their King. They remain scattered sheep without a shepherd. A people who are cursed and whose name is derision among the nations of the world because God said it was to be so. And these things will remain this way until that day when all Israel knows, "I am the Lord their God." This is also a part of the glorious Master Plan of God, as we will see in the Millennial Kingdom story.

There are thirteen Prophets plus some of the Psalmists who prophesied about events during the Millennial Age. In these prophecies, there are several themes that run in common between prophets, all of these are directly related to the time of the Millennium. The most common themes and their numbers are as follows: 1. The Lord, who scattered Israel all over the world will gather them together to Himself in the land of Israel and to Jerusalem. (17 times) 2. The nation of Israel will be a blessing to the Gentile nations; the nations world-wide, will bless Israel in return. (18 times) 3. Israel's iniquities will one day be pardoned when they repent and humble themselves before the Lord. (5 times) The Lord will give Israel and all the peoples of the nations an "Everlasting Covenant" to live by. (7 times) In the prophecies of Ezekiel, the prophet repeatedly states in those days of the Millennium that "Israel shall know I am the Lord their God." (4 times) and in several other places that the nations shall know, "I am the Lord" and "that there is a God over Israel."

Even with a thorough understanding of what the Scriptures say about the Millennium Kingdom to come, there remains much mystery about the execution of God's Master Plan as it moves into and through those millennial years. These prophecies from God were given to a variety of men at various times and locations, during the earthly Kingdom and even after its fall. Yet they tell a story of a King and a Kingdom to come and that Israel will be there to experience them. These prophecies were for all of Israel, but would Israel's people trust in these prophecies from God in the centuries to follow?

Often the words from God about the "latter days" came to the people like a gift shop postcard with a picture. These prophecies, created by God through the prophets, were given to the people in the prophet's day, some, over twenty-four hundred years ago. This leads us to one more mystery about God and these millennial postcards. Those prophecies that are for the "latter days," present a picture of an event or scene without a context, just a title called "latter days" or something similar. They clearly speak of a time in the future, even in our future, in a time of modernity but the pictures that are featured on the postcards are shown for those people in the prophet's day to see and understand. Fortunately for us, we who are living closest to those "latter days" have the better vantage point to see with the most accuracy and least deviation, of what God is telling us about the future and the intent behind the prophecy.

For example, what appeared to be miraculous or supernatural to a person twenty-four hundred years ago could be commonplace in today's world of technology and human achievement. Consider what ancient people would say if they were to see the results of one day's work by one person who harvested grain using a huge combine machine rather than by hand with a scythe. The prophets, when explaining future events, would have to see these events in terms of what is normal for them in their time period and be able to describe them in understandable ways to their people. With few exceptions, God would not show them a vision of the future that could not be understood at all or something futuristic that they could not reasonably describe. There would have to be elements to what the prophets were seeing or describing that gave them enough of what is recognizable to be able to make some sensible explanation or statement about it. For example, a prophet could easily recognize many weapons of warfare, horticultural practices, transportation, the environment, and cities. But how would a prophet ever explain mass communications, electricity, chemicals, or technologies? God would not likely have put them in such a predicament.

We can see how the Apostle John may have struggled to understand what He was seeing about the future supernatural Heaven and Earth to come and the description of the New Jerusalem in Revelation, Chapter 21. Yet under the Spirit's inspiration, he was able to pull together enough understanding to convey a description for us to understand. Although not a perfectly clear picture of what was happening in the vision, the message given to us is in sufficient detail; the rest is hidden from us as a mystery. As to the Millennial times being described by the prophets, we need to keep an open mind that the words being used to describe such things as modern vehicles, weapons, explosions, equipment, military forces, cities, agricultural practices, governments, and so on will be done in ways familiar to the prophet in his time and understandable to the people who hear that prophet speaking to them.

Lastly, when considering the millennial story, there are critical positions that could be taken opposing the story in whole or in part. A person may propose that the Prophets wrote only of the times that have already passed and that we are simply not aware of those times. Or that the prophecies were a kind of "overblown" account of events that occurred in history, accounts that were never recorded in history or elsewhere in God's word. Another position is that the claims being made in the prophecy were intended to inflate the effects of a fulfilled prophecy event recorded in the Scriptures. Something kind of like making mountains out of molehills, pumping up what God has done with inflated effects that are intended to give encouragement or bring significance to the insignificant. Another maybe, is that the prophet is making an effort to lift up people with new hope for a brighter tomorrow. Possibly as a distraction from the unpleasant life they are living or will face in the near future.

Such claims were they to be true, cannot be true without damaging God's integrity. Such claims minimize the impact of God on the people of the Earth and would be an act of intentional deception by both God Himself and His Prophets. Rather, we should expect that God will act in mighty and amazing ways that only "the God who may be all in all" would reveal about Himself and His Master Plan. God has given us the means to find and understand enough about the Millennial Kingdom to react to it in positive ways. This Millennial Story is but a humble attempt to capture what will truly be an amazingly powerful chain of events that will take humanity into a New Heaven and New Earth through the Master Plan of God.

CHAPTER 9:
The Story Begins

9.0 FIRST THINGS: ABOUT THIS STORY

About this Story:

The following story is not a fictional account of one person's perceived future of the world, like some post-apocalyptic adventure novel. This writing is a non-fictional accounting of what the future is likely to look like when derived from Scriptural texts. Prophetic statements that connect with one another and support images of the future that fit within that defined four-sided border of Revelation 20:1-10. Scriptures, when understood in relation to one another bring a conclusion to the revealed Master Plan of God.

The statements found in the story are gathered together by chapters, put into an orderly account that works chronologically together. Many statements made in the story will have been formed not only from the Scriptures and their context but also with consideration of historical facts, the chronology of historical events, simple logic, and rational thought that all contribute to the story. The writing will also make use of reasonable speculations where the word of God does not speak directly. "Reasonable speculation," of course, is open to subjectivity and therefore will need to be carefully monitored in its use. The reasonable speculations in the story are formed on the basis of what the Scriptures have told us about God's character and the past actions of God, people's emotions and their human nature, sin, relationships, prophecy, etc.

Reasonable speculation, when handled correctly is a positive contribution to a story. We are aware of the reasonable speculations that are found in a Nativity story for example. These speculations can be used to help us to consider truths that we have never experienced before; examples of this would be, "What daily life in this world will be like when there is no longer any satanic influence?" And another: "How will the economy work during the Millennium?"

Let us explore an example of a "reasonable speculation" on the impact miracles will have in the Millennial Kingdom? Miracles are very likely to occur, but it is reasonable to think that they will be limited in their use, likely for the purposes of advancing of the Kingdom. When it comes to people, God has proven that He prefers to work with people and through people and not apart from people to accomplish His plans. Miracles are plentiful in the Scriptures, but they are never the cause of a person obtaining a redeeming faith. Faith is not the product of a miracle, but rather as Romans 10:17 states, *"So then faith comes by hearing, and hearing by the word of God."* This prerequisite will not change in the Millennium Age to come. Miracles can cause fear, confusion, and supernatural awareness but these are conditioners for faith to enter in. Miracles will cause people who believe Messiah, to grow in their faith. Those who do not believe in the words of God, are not going to believe in the Messiah by the work of a miracle in any proportion just as Jesus said. (Luke 16:27-31)

Yet speculation about miracles occurring in the Millennium Age appears to be reasonable based on what we know about God and His word.

9.1 Survivors Of The Tribulation

The Tribulation period ends with the last of the triune judgments from God, which includes the Armageddon event, when the "Beast" (Antichrist) and his armies are destroyed by Jesus Messiah and Satan is bound and incarcerated in the abyss for 1000 years. This begins a new age for humanity, the Millennial Age. A brief assessment of who remains alive on Earth at the time of the Messiah's return, and at the start of the Millennial Age, is as good a place as any to begin looking at humanity's living conditions after those catastrophic events of the last seven years described in Revelation, chapters 6-19. The Tribulation event is when God judges unrighteous humanity for their rebellion against God's authority and His right to rule over the nations of the Earth. The Tribulation is also an act of God's judgment against all the dark forces of evil, and their dominion of darkness. God's judgment will have put to an end all the demonic supernatural power that fed upon humanities weaknesses and brought spiritual power into the religions of the world. God's third judgment put an end to Satan's control over all the kingdoms of this world. That is, all governmental leadership, power, and authority were stripped from Satan when He was taken by force and bound.

When you factor in all the Tribulation judgments found in the Book of Revelation, and look at the death counts that mount up as a result of the fourth seal, the sixth seal, the trumpet judgments including the sixth trumpet, and that of the seventh bowl, the death count is staggering. Add to those numbers the Jews and Gentile believers of The Way, who are hunted down and executed by the reign of the "Beast" (Antichrist). Add in factors for collateral deaths such as suicides, murders, and human reactions to all the general and supernatural mayhem, and it would not be surprising to see that out of the eight billion people alive on the Earth (using today's number), only three billion would live to see post-Tribulation days and the start of the Millennial Kingdom. It is possible that the number of survivors could be lower yet. A reasonable estimate would be between 2.5 billion and 3.0 billion survivors, with that number continuing to decline downward, given that the death rate would not drop to normal levels just because God stopped His judgments. These survivors will be both Jews and Gentiles living among the surviving nations around the world. With more details to follow, we will place the survivors into four groups. The Remnant Wilderness Jews, the Remnant Scattered Jews, Believers of the Way, and the Surviving Gentile Nations.

Who isn't living on the Earth is also a factor to consider: Satan, Demons, The Antichrist, and the False Prophet and, the Armies and Kings who were at Armageddon. With the exception being Satan, these are all in the Lake of Fire. Satan has been removed from the world and is incarcerated. The Church had been previously raptured, and the resurrected have been taken up from the Earth and taken by Jesus to His Father's house in the Heavenly realm of the Kingdom of God.

Who has returned to the Earth with Jesus when He comes to begin His reign on Earth? As previously reviewed, there will be individuals who are to co-reign with Messiah. (Revelation 20:4) These are likely to include the twelve Apostles. (Matthew 19:28; Luke 22:24-29) Also, returning with Jesus to fill out His governmental cabinet are those resurrected souls who were beheaded for their witness to Jesus and the word of God. *"Those souls who would not worship the beast or image…. They live and will reign with Christ for one thousand years."* (Revelation

20:4) We don't know how many of these saints there will be, but it is very probable that they will be in great enough numbers to be appointed to official positions throughout the world, and possibly serve in the very communities in which they were martyred. These martyrs will probably include those martyrs that the angel shows to the Apostle John during the fifth seal. Those souls are not in the Father's house but under the very altar of God. They have been set apart for a very special purpose, which at this time of the fifth seal had not yet come. John is told that a certain total number of martyrs had not been completed. (Revelation 6:9-11) We are not told what their being singled out will mean but certainly the total number that God has in mind will be achieved before the return of Christ.

It is very probable that those martyrs identified with the fifth seal will see their numbers swell during the reign of the Antichrist. Each killed for their testimony and for the word of God. Each having been beheaded, likely singled out for public execution, not just killed or die randomly from the result of one of God's judgments but rather, by order of the False Prophet. (Revelation 13:15, 16) These martyrs are publicly murdered during the Tribulation, but now in the Millennium Age, they will be living testimonies of the resurrected life of the believer in the Messiah, who chose to die for their faith in Jesus rather than deny Him.

These glorified martyrs will very likely be reigning as the King's official representatives in every region of the world, directing Kingdom affairs. They may even serve in the presence of people who personally witnessed their public execution during the Antichrist's reign. These martyred rulers are what will be referred to in the story going forward as "Immortals," because that is what they are. They will be given the authority to execute power, assign local governments, and establish their leadership. They will re-establish civil law and order, which will be needed after the mayhem caused in the Tribulation years. These Immortals have proven their commitment to Jesus Messiah, and know what it takes to face up to those who rejected Him as the rightful king. Many people in the lands where these Immortals set up their formal offices will treat their new rulers much like any other occupational force. Some will seek to gain favor, while others look for opportunities to drive them away or cause them to be ineffective authorities.

The Immortals will seek to do the Messiah's will and advance His Kingdom in all righteousness, justice, mercy, and truth. They will execute authority according to the Lord's will. These rulers are no longer fallible human beings with a sin nature and vulnerable to corruption. These rulers will enact all that the King decrees without hesitation and with total trust from the King. They will determine and correct activity that does not meet the requirements of the Kingdom's criminal and civil laws. These rulers will have the support of believers who have come to faith in Jesus as their savior and has lived through the Tribulation, as well as those who will come to faith in the generations that follow. As resurrected leaders, the Immortals are spiritually powerful people who will provide needed services and bring governmental support for the work of ministry. Their limits of glorified power and ability are not known, but they will be in the likeness of their Lord, bearing His image. (1 Corinthians 15:42-49) The Promised Land of Israel will likely be ruled in a very similar fashion by the twelve apostles, just as Jesus said.

It is likely that some people who saw these Immortals be killed would become early believers in Jesus and be moved by the Holy Spirit to become followers of "The Way" (John 12:9-11), and inherit the spiritual Kingdom of God. There will not be any forced phony confessions of faith foisted upon unbelievers, they will be left to their own free will to believe. Jesus tells us in His parable about a rich man and the beggar who both died. The rich man begged Abraham to send the beggar back to His living brothers in order to convince them that there was an accounting and resurrection to come. Jesus said, *"If they do not hear Moses and the Prophets, neither will they be persuaded, though one rises from the dead."* (Luke 16:22-31) Like the rich man's brother's, many, many people will not come to a saving faith when they come into the presence of these Immortals.

The Apostles will likely teach Jews how to become "sent ones" like they themselves were, serving Messiah and living inside and outside of the Promised Land. All people will hear the Gospel message about the saving faith in Jesus's sacrifice on the cross, redemption from sin, and the call to seek the spiritual Kingdom of God and its King. They will likely teach the lesson that the Jews of the past did not learn, that being in the physical Kingdom of God does not assure you a place in the spiritual Kingdom of God.

9.2 Wilderness Remnant Jews

When we look at the midpoint of the Tribulation, we can identify who these Wilderness Jews are and how they came about to be isolated from all other Jews and end up in the wilderness. As determined previously in Revelation 12:1-6 the "woman," who is described as being clothed with the sun, with the moon under her feet, and on her head is a garland of twelve stars, is a symbolic description for the House of Israel, the Jewish people who brought forth Jesus. The symbolism is confirmed in Genesis 37: 9-10.

Speaking of this woman, Israel, Revelation, Chapter 12, verse 6, says that *"the woman fled into the wilderness, where she has a place prepared by God, that they should feed her there one thousand two hundred and sixty days."* In that verse, several points are to be noted. That certain Jews, not all Jews everywhere in the world (12:16-17), coming from somewhere, fled into the wilderness to escape Satan. God had planned for this escape and provided both a place and provisions for these Jews to last them for 1,260 days. Also note that the wilderness is a specific place, also confirmed in the chapter in verses 13-17. It has been suggested that a place called Petra may be the location, this is possible. These verses are as follows: *"Now when the dragon saw that he had been cast to the earth, he persecuted the woman who gave birth to the male Child. But the woman was given two wings of a great eagle, that she might fly into the wilderness to her place, where she is nourished for a time, and times and half a time from the presence of the serpent. So, the serpent spewed water out of his mouth like a flood after the woman, that he might cause her to be carried away by the flood. But the earth helped the woman, and the earth opened its mouth and swallowed up the flood which the dragon had spewed out of his mouth. And the dragon was enraged with the woman, and he went to make war with the rest of her offspring, who keep the commandments of God and have the testimony of Jesus Christ."* (Revelation 12:13-17)

There is much symbolism in this sign. The fact that the dragon is Satan is clear, as is the fact that he is annihilating the Jews because of Jesus the Messiah. The identity of the dragon is validated in verse 12:9. The flood of water called out by Satan is symbolic for his calling out for an army, a satanic army. The word "flood," is a symbolic description of an army that is used to catastrophically destroy non-military people. The words "an army" is meant by the words, "a flood," the use is proper in that the prophet Daniel used the word "flood" symbolically when it clearly meant an army. This symbolism is validated in the 70-week prophecy in the Book of Daniel. The prophet is describing the military destruction of the city of Jerusalem and its temple when he says, *"The end of it shall be with a flood."* (Daniel 9:26) An army, not water destroyed the city. There are similar references elsewhere in the Scriptures.

The two wings of a great eagle are a symbolic picture of God's providence to pick up and move people at His will to do so, for their own good. Just as He did with Israel in Egypt, saying to Moses and Israel *"You have seen what I did to the Egyptians, and how I bore you up on eagle wings and brought you to Myself."* (Exodus 19:4) Although Israel walked during their time in the wilderness, it was God who raised them up by His power and providence and brought them into a deeper relationship with Him. Now, many centuries later God will provide for wilderness Jews once again.

It is very probable that these Jews, who are in the wilderness were led by God to escape out of the City of Jerusalem and travel beyond the border of Israel, at the time when the Antichrist was intent upon destroying their sovereign nation, its people, and desecrate their temple. Prior to this wilderness event, there is to be a peace treaty that the nations have honored, and Israel was to have been assured of their right to peacefully exist in their own land, and have the opportunity to build a temple to God, complete with a Levitical priesthood. It is very probable that because of the newly built temple in Jerusalem, Jewish pilgrimage's coming from around the world to the Holy Land and to the temple would be in abundance. This is a temple that God will greatly disapprove of, a temple without its High Priest, Jesus Messiah, a temple led by lost shepherds, built without the Son's authorization and without His presence. The flight to the wilderness by Jews is likely in reaction to the nations under the Antichrist breaking the treaty and viciously attacking Jews everywhere, over running Jerusalem and killing both residents and its pilgrims. This attack comes not only upon Jerusalem but all of Israel and is highlighted by what is called the "abomination of desolation" referred to in Daniel 12:11. Jesus, appears to be speaking of this event in

Matthew 24:15-20, where He warns Jews to flee from where they are in Judea and head for the hills. Telling them not to stop to for anything or you're at risk of getting caught up in the coming tribulation, and that this will be especially difficult for those who are pregnant or have babies to carry to make their escape.

It is fitting then that God provides a miraculous escape from the city into the wilderness hills. As the Prophet Zechariah writes that the Lord will provide for Israel *"In that day His feet will stand on the Mount of Olives, which faces Jerusalem on the east. And the Mount of Olives shall be split in two, from east to west, making a very large valley; Half of the mountain shall move toward the north and half of it to the south. Then you will flee through My mountain valley, For the mountain valley shall reach Azal. Yes, you shall flee from the earthquake as in the days of Uzziah king of Judah."* (Zechariah 14:4,5) It is likely that this is the event that allows Jews to escape the city and flee to the wilderness to live for a time and times and a half time, which is three and a half years, for the remaining duration of the Great Tribulation. The same amount of time (1260 days) that is identified in the vision John had in (Revelation 12:6) These Jews flee through a newly created valley that opens up when a major earthquake splits Mount Olivet in half providing a way of escape from Jerusalem and direct then in a way out of Israel. Those who escape are but a small remnant of the entire population of Jews worldwide. Those who do not escape Israel are either killed or taken to be modern-day slaves by the international regime of the Antichrist. (Zechariah 14:1-5)

It should be noted that geographically, a major fault line runs through that entire region from north to south and that the "Jordan Rift" fans out in every direction from this primary fault line with numerous secondary fractures that crisscross most of Israel, making the entire area vulnerable to earthquakes. Large quake events are in the historical record of Israel, and quakes in the area have been recorded to have had multiple epicenters. Seismographs have recorded between 200 and 300 tremors on a daily basis in Israel. An earthquake event in Jerusalem directed by God is very probable.

Once in "their place" in the wilderness (Revelation 12:14) God provides for His chosen people with both provisions of food and water, and also protection for them from the army (the flood) that Satan (the serpent) sends out to destroy these Jews. In response to it, God opens up the earth and swallows the attacking army. What happens here is very reminiscent of what God did to Pharoah's army at the Red Sea when the Lord opened up the waters, letting the Jews pass through and then closing them up on the Egyptians. Resulting in God getting the glory so that "the Egyptians shall know that "I am the Lord." Exactly what transpires here is not perfectly clear, but it is plausible to say that this Satanic army, this flood, that was sent to utterly destroy these Jews was a vast number of earthbound demonic angels. These demons likely took bodily possession of people and were intent on eradicating God's covenanted people. When the earth opens up and swallows up the demonic army in its entirety, it becomes plausible to believe that God has judged the demonic realm by sending every demon to their fate, and into the lake of fire. (Matthew 8:28, 29)

During the short time that he has left on Earth and now without his demonic army, Satan will with great urgency focus on eradicating all people who become believers in Jesus and every Jew as well through the acts of the Antichrist, (Beast) his primary resource. This makes sense logically because if there are no Jews, then there is no Israel; there would never be the execution of God's promises to fulfill the Davidic Covenant, and there can be no throne over the House of Jacob for the Messiah to reign from. Satan's goal is obvious to us, he plans to prevent the physical Kingdom of God from coming to Earth, so that he can maintain his rule over mankind and hold his dominion over all the Earth. After being driven out of the Heavenly realm, the Earth is all he has left and Satan is quite aware of the time he has left to hold it. (Revelation 12:7-17) By destroying all of Israel and converts of "The Way," he would effectively disrupt the Master Plan of God and cause changes to be made by God. (Daniel 7:25)

When these Wilderness Jews escape Jerusalem, they come to realize that it was not good fortune that brought them to a place of refuge. They realize that it is the Lord God who has brought them to a desolate place to be with Him. In Petra, or wherever else this place is, they find themselves completely dependent upon God for their circumstances. Any thoughts of returning to the city or going for provisions to feed and clothe themselves would put them at high risk of death should they leave their safe haven. All communication with the rest of the world will likely be cut off, isolated from the world; However, leaving this place proves to be unnecessary. It is certain that these modern-day Jews, who had just experienced a supernatural deliverance from death, will begin to live new experiences with the Lord God by living the next 42 months just as their ancient ancestors did in the days of Moses, live as Israel in the wilderness once again.

This place is where God will bind these modern-day Jews to the ancient faith that their ancestral fathers held when Israel became the Kingdom of God. There in the wilderness, these Jews will be protected from the plagues of God's Tribulation judgments just as their ancient fathers were protected from the plagues that came upon ancient Egypt. God will provide for their needs. Although not stated, He will likely once again send them manna from Heaven to eat and cause water to flow from the rock to drink and to bathe. They will have fled for their lives, unable to bring even the basics of supplies. The clothes they wore when they fled will last them the next three and a half years, as did the clothes of their ancestors which lasted for 40 years. (Deuteronomy 29:4-6) God will no doubt send the people leaders and teachers, maybe a risen prophet, possibly even Moses, even Elijah, possibly even the angels of Heaven. Teachers who are led by the Holy Spirit to teach these people the meaning behind the experiences that their ancestors had with God Almighty. We cannot say for sure who the "they" will be in Revelation, 12:6 that feeds the remnant both food and the Word of God, but for those 1,260 days, God will be preparing the Wilderness Jews for that day when they return to Jerusalem and meet Jesus, their Messiah.

Added note: The following verses are pieces to the Millennial story puzzle and contribute to the narrative message above: Jeremiah 31:1-7, Hosea 2:23,

9.3 The Scattered Remnant Jews

The "Wilderness Jews" will be kept by God in the wilderness hills beyond the border of Israel for the duration of the Tribulation; they are a relatively small group of people when compared to the "Scattered Remnant Jews." The scattered Jews live all around the world, but in the last half-century, they have been gathering in great numbers in the U.S. and Israel. These scattered remnants will experience the Tribulation judgments in a completely different way from those Jews whom God has placed in the wilderness. These scattered Jews will have a different calling from God, they will not be supernaturally protected from their enemies or provided with a place of safe refuge. God does not provide for their needs during those last three and a half years of the Tribulation. How many Israelites are we considering, and where in the world do they live is useful. Using rough estimates for numbers, there are about 14.8 million Jews living today, depending on the purity of their ancestry. Approximately 50% of these live in the United States, and about 30% live in Israel today. The remainder of the 14.8 million live scattered throughout the rest of the world, as many of the prophetic Scriptures say. A prophecy from Zechariah is a significant "Tribulation" times message from the Scriptures, Zechariah 13:8, 9 states, *And it will come to pass in all the land that two-thirds in it shall be cut off and die, but one third shall be left in it; I will bring one third through the fire. Will refine them as silver is refined. And test them as gold is tested. They will call upon my name. And I will answer them. I will say, "This is my people"; And each one will say, "The Lord is my God."*

Several points that can be made about this critical prophecy, which is directed at the Jewish people. It speaks of the time of the Great Tribulation to come, but only one point is needed to be made that makes the puzzle piece fit. The refining and testing that are to happen to them will result in a strong relationship between God and those who are refined. However, Israel, even today, remains unreconciled with God because they killed their Messiah and King. How can we know this prophecy is a piece to the puzzle? History fails to reveal that this prophecy has been fulfilled to date, the three Jewish Wars with Rome, of which the last war in 135 A.D. was the greater of the three, it had cost an estimated 500,000 Israeli lives. But that does not even come close to the numbers needed to satisfy the prophecy. Even the Holocaust numbers fall short of what we can expect at this time of great trouble. No historical event following the destruction of the temple and Jerusalem can satisfy any of the content of this prophecy. Even the prophecy's reference to the "land" is not specific to Israel but refers to the earth in general, to God's domain. Israel today, remains unreconciled with God because they continue to reject their Messiah and King and continue to exist with the consequences for it. Only after the Tribulation, when Jesus Messiah builds His Kingdom, will this prophecy fully come to pass.

Should this piece fit into the Millennial story as expected, then this prophecy will result in a world-wide judgment upon Israel during the Tribulation rather than any isolated regional judgments. By simply doing the math, nearly 10 million Jews will die, many of whom will no doubt die in the United States. Such an outcome would suggest that both the U.S. and Israel today will likely experience catastrophic violence and destruction. The familiar prophetic words, "Times of Jacob's Trouble" will have come upon Israel, as written by the prophet Jeremiah in chapter 30:7. *"Alas! For that day is great, so that none is like it; And it is the time of Jacob's trouble. But he shall be saved out of it."* Should those numbers prove to be close to being accurate, even the Holocaust will be eclipsed by the devastation to come and only a remnant will be saved. There are several other prophecies that reveal Israel will be reduced to a remnant but will survive to enter into the Millennial Age and turn to the Lord.

What triggers this intensified aggression against the Jews deserves a reasonable explanation. No group of people left in the world will be impacted more by the rapture of the Church than the Jews. When the Church is taken away by Christ from this earthly scene, Satan will be able to place his full attention and demonic resources into his plan to prevent the return of the Kingdom of God, rather than battle the Church in spiritual warfare. It is logical to understand that his plan is to eradicate all the Kingdom people of Israel off the face of the Earth, along with all those who come to faith in Jesus Christ. With great rage, the dragon (Satan) goes on the offensive against all Jews and all new believers in Jesus Christ. (Revelation 12:17) With the loss of his demonic army to pursue the Jews, Satan must rely mostly on human resources and concentrate his power through the use of the Antichrist and False Prophet in order to accomplish his plans to destroy the saints of God and force changes in the times and plans of God.

The Prophet Daniel tells us about the "Little Horn," known to most as the Antichrist. This man is to be under the control of Satan to work His plans. Daniel says this in chapter 7:25. *He shall speak pompous words against the Most-High, and shall persecute the saints of the Most -High, and shall intend to change* (alter, that is, vary away from) *the times* (appointed occasions) *and law*, (a royal decree). the Prophet goes on to say, *"His power shall be mighty, but not by his own power;*(that would be Satan's power) *He shall destroy fearfully and shall prosper and thrive; He shall destroy the mighty, and also the holy people."* (Daniel 8:24) The Antichrist, will make bold declarations against God and certainly against the Lamb, who revealed Himself to the world during the sixth seal event. (Revelation 6:16,17) Satan and his Antichrist will likely use that event to blame the Jewish people for the wrath of the Lamb and the plagues that has come upon the world; thereby adding to the hatred that the nations already have against the Jewish people and placing the whole house of Israel into Satan's crosshairs.

According to what the Apostle John sees in Heaven, there will be a great multitude of the redeemed who lost their lives during the time of the Great Tribulation. It is likely that some of these people will be Jews, who will become saved by faith in the Lamb of God and are killed for refusing to take the mark of the beast. For many others, whether it be in the testimonies of their fellow Jewish brethren, or the Rapture event, or because of what happened during that sixth seal event, a horrifying realization will come to many Jews, that Jesus of Nazareth is who He said He was. He is the King of the Jews, their God-appointed Messiah and the faith that Christians held over all these centuries has proven to be true to God's glory. To these Jews, it will seem that the God who had once called Israel His "chosen," has abandoned them for their rejection of the Messiah and has turned them over to a world that hates them and will wipe them all off the face of the Earth. With millions perishing, the survivors, many more of them being women and children, will fall victim to modern-day slavery and oppression and eventually death when their value as a commodity fails.

By the end of the Tribulation, using the simple math above, the Jewish population worldwide may decrease to as little as 4.5 million, based solely on the prophecy from Zechariah. But God has a plan to restore the Kingdom of God on Earth and make it even better. He will continue to fulfill His Master Plan and these surviving Jews have a lead part in that plan. Thus says the Lord, *"Although I have cast them among the Gentiles and although I have scattered them among the countries, yet I shall be a little sanctuary for them in the countries where they have gone." Therefore say, "Thus says the Lord God; I will gather you from the peoples, assemble you from the countries where you have been scattered, and I will give you the land of Israel." And they will go there, and take away all its detestable things and all its abominations from there. Then I will give them one heart, and I will put a new spirit within them, and take the stony heart out of their flesh, and give them a heart of flesh, that they may walk in My statutes and keep My judgments and do them; and they shall be My people, and I will be their God.* (Ezekiel 11:16-20) When the time comes for the Great Tribulation to come to an end, there will be a monumental turn of events for all who survive in this world. But no group of people will be impacted more by this change than the scattered remnant of the Jewish people.

Added note: The following verses are pieces to the Millennial story puzzle and contribute to the narrative message above: Ezekiel 11:11-20, Ezekiel 34:12-14, Psalm 14:7, Isaiah 51:1-6, Joel 3:1-3, Jeremiah 30:3, 4, Isaiah 30:18, 19).

9.4 Believers Of The Way

During the Tribulation days, God will not be without a witness among the people of this Earth. The gospel message of grace and truth through faith in Jesus Christ as Savior and Lord, will be proclaimed and offered to people during those judgment days. There will be most likely Gentile people who come to be redeemed by the blood of Lamb and gain an inheritance in the Eternal Kingdom of God in the New Heaven and New Earth. These new believers are redeemed after the Church has been removed and now reveal the way to salvation, thus named for the reader, "The Way."

These believers are recipients of the message of salvation that will go out from the 144,000 redeemed followers of the Lamb of God (Revelation 14:1-5) and possibly from the Two Witnesses in Jerusalem (Revelation 11:3-10), and certainly, from the angel who would fly among every nation, tribe, tongue, and people, to proclaim the everlasting gospel. (Revelation 14:6) With the Church now gone, they will with great difficulty be the light and salt of the Earth that Jesus expects of His followers. As a result, there will be a great harvest of God before the bowls of judgment are poured out upon an unrepentant world. During the Tribulation, people will be reaped into the Kingdom of God and in numbers greater than at any time in history, because God desires that none perish.

In Revelation, chapter 14, an angel coming out of the temple in Heaven declares to Jesus in a loud voice, *"Thrust in your sickle and reap, for the time has come for You to reap, for the harvest of the Earth is ripe."* And so, the Tribulation will prove to be not only a time of God's judgments but also a time of great reaping of the redeemed by the Lord, a final harvest that comes before the final judgments from God come upon an unrepentant world. (Revelation 14:14-16) Like any kind of natural reaping of grain, the plant has to be cut down and die in order for the grain is taken, here the same occurs. Many, many saints will die at the hands of the Beast (Antichrist) and their spirits reaped by Jesus. He harvests a great number of the redeemed and brings them into His Father's household just as He said He would (John 14:1-3). The Antichrist will glorify himself in the shed blood of the believers in "The Way." In contrast the great multitude of victims will stand before the throne of God and glorify Him for the blood of the Lamb, shed for them. (Revelation 7:9-14)

Those believers of The Way who survive the Tribulations on the Earth will live to witness the return of Messiah. They will not only be of the spiritual Kingdom of God like those who died before them but will also be called to play a critical part in the physical Kingdom of God, in the early days of the Millennium, when Jesus Messiah returns. These people are sinners like all other people who survived the judgments of God. They will have struggled to stay alive during the worst seven years of world history and yet when they became new creations in the faith, they choose to help others around them who like themselves, are persecuted or in need. They will witness to the unsaved, and do whatever they can for other people, doing so out of love and conviction through the Holy Spirit, often at a cost of their own life, much like those first believers in the "Way," who were willing to die in the place of others at the hands of the Romans during the early days of the Church. (Acts 9:2)

The believers in "The Way," who are not reaped by Jesus in the Tribulation harvest will be called into a special service by their King and become His servants in the renewed physical Kingdom of God. There is much more to be said about the people of "The Way" in the chapter to come.

9.5 The Surviving Gentile Nations

The last group of people to survive the judgments is also the largest by far. The Gentile nations are non-Jewish ethnic groups of people, not to be confused with governmental or political bodies. These Gentile nations include all the people groups that exist throughout the world. These groups consist of men, women, and children who will have survived the worst seven years of world history and enter into the Millennial Kingdom age. It should be noted when talking about judgments that there is nothing in the Scriptures to indicate that God will change who is judged among the Gentiles and Jews. The act of sparing children from a judgment day would be inconsistent with God and foreign to His purposes. God did not spare children in the days of Joshua. God did not spare Israel's and Judah's children in the days before their exile, and He did not spare the children in the days of Noah, or those children living in Sodom or in Gomorrah. Any act to save children from the Tribulation days to come would put into question why God didn't save those other children in the past. The character of God and His actions that we previously reviewed show God to have validated that He is a Just God and Righteous in all His works of judgment. (Revelation 19:11) We can count on God to be just that, with the souls of children during the Tribulation and after the last rebellion as well.

In the days leading to the return of the King, all nations around the world will be in utter chaos. Life will be mostly unbearable, and the suffering physically, mentally and emotionally will likely continue long after the Tribulation ends. Every people group on Earth will have experienced death and destruction of a magnitude that is unimaginable. The population of the world will have declined from 8 billion to maybe 3.0 billion, possibly 3.5 billion people. There is likely no family on Earth who will not have felt the sting of death that takes somebody away from them in some kind of hyper-natural event, a horrible supernatural event; or in war.

The horrors of a world war could be understood and endured; there is a long track record of people everywhere rising up once again above the ashes of war. However, the supernatural attacks from God and the

Lamb will be a uniquely terrifying experience, with humanities reactions replayed all over the world much like the way people reacted to the sixth seal. John records humanities reactions: *"And the kings of the earth, the great men, the rich men, the commanders, and every slave and free man hid themselves in the caves and in the rocks of the mountains and said to the mountains and rocks, "Fall on us and hide us from the face of Him who sits on the throne and from the wrath of the Lamb! For the great day of His wrath has come, and who is able to stand?"* (Revelation 6:15-17) Those verses and the three before them make it clear that all people regardless of who they are will be overcome with fear. The great and small go into hiding expecting that their judgment day has come upon them.

Does the "Sixth Seal" event coincide with the Resurrection of the Dead and Rapture events, we cannot tell? But it is plausible to think so because the events recorded in Revelation 6:12-14 do align very well with what Jesus said about His coming to gather His elect to Himself in Matthew 24:29-31. That God would not only announce His arrival with a trumpet sounding but also make it clear to the world's inhabitants that there is a judgment day yet to come. In the Rapture, Jesus Christ has suddenly returned for His people just like He said He would do. And He has taken them away from wherever they happen to be at the time of His coming, and the world will know it when it happens. For one group of people, there will be the experience a great joy in a rapture. For another, shock and trauma in witnessing the resurrection of the dead, and the taking up of the living to their supernatural Lord followed by the feeling that doom is coming upon them. This act of redemption would bring some sense to what had just happened during the sixth seal. This would seem to be a more plausible scenario than some kind of mysterious disappearance of believers that leaves a world scratching its head wondering what just happened.

Regardless of these things, we can understand from the Scriptures that the result will be this: All the nations who survive the Tribulation and live to see the days of the Millennial Kingdom will have experienced both the removal of the world's Christians, the resurrection of the dead, and they will have gone through those events revealed in Revelation

6:12-17, whether they are experienced in separate events or together as one.

Another experience that the nations will have gone through when they see the days of the Millennial Kingdom is that the world will have had some kind of reaction to the Antichrist (The Beast). To the people of the world the Antichrist will have been a mystery to them. Some would have rejected him outright not trusting in his promises, others will fear that a judgment from God will come upon all who would take sides with the Antichrist. These people may seek to defer from taking the "Mark of the Beast." Still, others will have gladly taken his mark, looking at this man as their savior; the person they hope will bring humanity through all these natural and supernatural calamities. Someone who has shown he has supernatural abilities as well, possibly able to protect them from the wrath of the Lamb, whom everybody fears, everyone except for this world leader and his prophet. In these people's minds, it will be that this man who was once dead is now their Messiah. The one who they witnessed conquer the grave and rise up from the dead to become ruler over all the world. Speaking praises of this great god-like man, *"Who is able to make war with him?"* (Revelation 13:15-17 and 13:16)

However, a few years after the Antichrist's run at being the world's Messiah, the survivors of the Tribulation will have experienced his fall with the return of the true Messiah along with his heavenly army. At that time, the Antichrist with his kings and armies will make war against the heavenly invader who returns to Earth and brings renewed fear to all the nations. Spoken words of destruction that come out of the mouth of Messiah will swiftly and completely slay Antichrist's army and kings. The dead will become food for a great number of flocks. Birds that will be gathered to Armageddon for the purposes of eating upon the fallen warriors. (Revelation 19:17-21) Then at that time, the Antichrist and False Prophet are thrown alive into the lake of fire and the people never hear from their potential savior again.

The people who survive it all to see the Millennial Kingdom will likely see the conquering King of kings and Lord of lords send out His Heavenly army to slay every individual worldwide who had taken the mark of the beast. (Revelation 19:15-21) The nations will experience the conquering King's rod of iron and they will know that there is a God in Heaven to be feared above all things, who has now come upon the Earth to rule over them. Messiah will have slain His enemies after He has plagued the world for the last seven years with great acts of judgment upon all people. It is reasonable to believe that most of the survivors of the Tribulation, both Jew and Gentile alike will dread the days ahead and live in terror of what is to come upon them next. Fearing that they have fallen in the hands of such a vengeful enemy as the Lamb of God. (Revelation 14:9-11)

Much will be said about the surviving Gentile nations in the chapters to come.

CHAPTER 10:
Transition From Tribulation To Tribute

10.1 Situational Awareness

There is one thing that we can be certain about when Jesus Messiah comes back to Earth and restores the Kingdom of God, it will be a time unlike any time in history. As reviewed previously, it is very, very improbable that there will be a supernatural resetting of the Earth for those who survive the Tribulation. A reset is not in the Master Plan of God or what we have seen of His nature. God prefers to restore and to make that which He restores better from what they once were, this is the direction that the world will go in during the Millennial Age. We will look into how the Master Plan develops during the Millennium Age but first, we will be taking a realistic look at how a world in tribulation transitions into a tribute to Messiah.

When Messiah returns to the Earth to begin His Kingdom work, it is to be expected that He will be returning to a world that is in utter ruin. Planet Earth is in critical condition, its oceans have been poisoned, and the beaches and shorelines are filled with the stench of dead sea creatures of every kind. None had survived the plague of the second bowl, the oceans have become watery graveyards. Entire freshwater sources that served major metropolitan areas are now poisoned. Fresh water needed for life to exist is scarce; the lack of water worldwide is a crisis greater than any prolonged drought has ever caused. Water once clean and drinkable has become as blood. The sun and its light will have been supernaturally struck as well, reducing its light and its power reduced by a third. Fears grow, knowing that photosynthesis will fail and with it the survival of all plant life.

But when the fourth bowl of wrath is delivered, people everywhere will become plagued with a sudden reversal of a sun once diminished in its light, now burning so hot as to scorch the Earth and men with massive fires and great heat.

Also, there will have been a world war involving three great armies (identified by their colors) with forces numbering 200,000,000. This war will kill one-third of all the people on the Earth (possibly 2 billion people) that survived the world's trauma up to that point. (Revelation 9:14-19)

At the "Seventh Bowl," when the worldwide earthquake strikes, every city in the world will experience its destructive power, having its infrastructure of power, water, gas and transportation destroyed. Fire storms will breakout in residential areas with no water to fight them. (Revelation 16:18-20) With the global-wide quake, every volcanic island that exists will have sunk into the sea; all the great island nations and cities will perish with them, their mountainous peaks no longer visible from above the water line. All other islands will be swept under water by the shifting tectonic plates moved by God hand so that none survive the judgment. The quake will cause Tsunami's to build and crash into every mainland of every ocean, like something out of a disaster movie, but it is no movie, multiple millions will die and the coastal cities will be obliterated. Animal habitats will be severely threatened, mass extinctions are a possibility. Power plants, manufacturing, and supply chains from the field to market for food will have been crippled. If all that man has built is not destroyed in the worldwide earthquake, then a plague of great hailstones weighing 70 pounds, will have fallen everywhere, crashing down on people, homes, businesses, education facilities, governmental institutions, hospitals, city centers, and industry. The destruction is so exceedingly great that people blasphemed God because of that particular plague of hail. (Revelation 16:20,21)

"Behold, the Lord makes the earth empty and makes it waste, distorts its surface and scatters its inhabitants. ...The land shall be entirely emptied and utterly plundered. For the Lord has spoken His word. The earth mourns and fades away, the world languishes and fades away; The haughty people of the earth languish. The earth is also defiled under its inhabitants, because they have transgressed the laws, changed the ordinance, broken the everlasting covenant. Therefore, the curse has devoured the earth, and those who dwell in it are desolate. Therefore, the inhabitants of the earth are burned, and few men are left." (Isaiah 24:1-6) The world-wide population will be relatively sparse compared to what it was. This everlasting covenant that God enacted is the Noahic Covenant. (Genesis 9:5-12) It was broken throughout all of human history and now humanity is being held accountable for the shedding of

man's blood, the image of God, over the centuries of time. The judgment for this may be why there is vast amounts of blood used in the judgments found in Revelation, 8:8-9, 16:3-4 representing the shed blood of humanity over all time.

It is certain that when Messiah arrives in the land of Israel there will be social and economic collapse. Governments will cease to function; banks emptied and police departments that no longer serve the greater good. Burying the dead will become a major task everywhere, wherever, there is people. Diseases will spread among the people and winter and summer will bring their seasonal hardships. The Earth for a time, will be a great graveyard for mankind, a world of poisoned water, filthy air, and land that has been scorched by fires, littered with dead people and creatures of every kind, in every country in the world. The oceans are dead and the natural balance of nature will likely be unbalanced. The majority of the nations who survive will fear God and the Lamb. People everywhere, will hate the Lamb of God for what had been done to their world and to their lives; many will prefer death rather than bow down to the one who has come to rule over them. Only one thing that will not change by God's judgments, that all survivors of the Tribulation remain sinners.

This is the situation the world finds itself in when He whose name is called "The Word of God," comes and takes the kingdoms of mankind out of Satan's control and ends his domain. This is He who arrives to Earth with the name written on His thigh and on His robe, KING OF KINGS AND LORD OF LORDS. (Revelation 19:13; 16)

10.2 Return To The King

Before Jesus left this world in the days of Pontius Pilate, the man asked Jesus if he was a king, Christ responded by saying, *"My kingdom is not of this world. If my kingdom were of this world my servants would fight so that I should not be delivered to the Jews; but now my kingdom is not from here."* (John 18:36) Jesus makes it clear in that verse that He is a king and that His Kingdom is not on the Earth. Yet, He then inserts the thought that this is a temporary situation as things stand for the time being, suggesting that His Kingdom's absence in this world will change. We understand His words to mean that Jesus, is the king of the spiritual realm, which is the Heavenly Kingdom of God. It is that Kingdom the

Apostle Paul believed he is a part of while yet living on Earth, and that Jesus will keep him for that Kingdom, (2 Timothy 4:18) and so does the Church. We understand that when we leave this world, we will experience a Kingdom life in Heaven under the kingship of our Lord and Savior Jesus Christ. And that as things stand for us today, we are citizens of that Kingdom.

When Pilate asked Jesus directly and to the point, "Are you the King of the Jews?" Jesus' response is a clear yes, *"It is as you say."* (Luke 23:3) Born the King of the Jews, Jesus never ruled a day in His life over the Jews. And from the reactions of the Jewish leaders towards Him, they would never allow it; they would see to it that He was dead first. When Pilate, looked for reasons to let Jesus live, the Scriptures tell us, *"All the people answered and said, "His blood be on us and on our children."* (Matthew 27:25) So God granted them what they asked for. Jesus the Messiah, did not rule over them or their children. From that time forward they bear the weight of that decision. But it has been this way for Israel from its beginning as a kingdom. It was in the days of the prophet Samuel, that people of Israel first rejected God as their king, wanting a man to rule over them like the other kingdoms. So, when God became a man and lived among them preaching a spiritual Kingdom of God, they rejected Jesus and His Kingdom, wanting rather, a physical Kingdom on their terms.

The people of Israel, no matter how hard they would try, always defaulted back into rejecting God's king on His terms. During the Tribulation, God begins to execute His plan for Israel's redemption and restore the physical Kingdom of God to the Earth once again. We are told in the Scriptures that after the Lord reveals Himself during the sixth seal, God, handpicks 144,000 people, 12,000 from each of the twelve tribes of Israel to be sealed and to be His servants (Revelation 7:3-8) This is remarkable in that God appoints a full representation of the nation of Israel to be put into service during the Tribulation, after they have witnessed the Lamb's return for His Church and the resurrected dead. The events of the 144,000 are picked up again in Revelation 14:1-5.

It is here that the Apostle John tells us He sees the Lamb, now standing on Mount Zion in Jerusalem and with Him are the 144,000 sealed Jews, having His Father's name written on their foreheads. The

144,000 follow the Lamb (that is Jesus Messiah) wherever He leads them on mission as their Lord and King. We should understand this event to mean that these 144,000 Jews are redeemed by the sacrificial death and imputed righteousness that comes by faith in Jesus Messiah. We can also understand that they follow the Messiah and live as first-fruits to God and the Lamb. These 144,000 are the first fruits among all of the Jewish believers who come into the restored Kingdom of God, for the duration of the Millennium. (Revelation 14:1-5) Reconciled to God, these Israelites have returned to the King and when they do, Heaven erupts in praise to celebrate the long-awaited occasion with a song that no one on Earth knew to sing, but only the 144,000 could sing it. It is very probable that this gathering of Jews to the Lamb is an actual supernatural event. Jesus sets his foot in Jerusalem, on the very spot where He will build the temple and rule His Kingdom from. But the world around them does not witness this. Like the song that is sung, only the 144,000 participate in this supernatural event. However, after that event, when the 144,000 go on mission, it is likely a Spirit-led following, because Messiah's physical return for the world to witness is identified in the Scripture to occur later, at the end of the Tribulation, found in Revelation, chapter 19.

Continuing with John's account of the Lamb and these 144,000 Israelites in Chapter 7, we are given a glimpse of the results of their ministry. John is shown a great multitude of people who worship God in Heaven in the throne room of God. They are seen blessing and glorifying God, who sits on the throne, and the Lamb for their salvation. When John asks the angel where all these people come from, the angel tells him that these are those who came out of the Great Tribulation and made to be white in the blood of the Lamb. (Revelation 7:9-14) This great multitude of people from around the world die during the Great Tribulation, as believers in "The Way." Some people may see in this vast loss of life, a great tragedy, but the Son of Man sees as a harvest, from an Earth ripe for the reaping of souls to be saved. (Revelation 14:14-16)

Having laid the circumstances that will begin Israel's redemption during the times of Jacob's Trouble, we return to the early days of the Millennial Kingdom of the previous chapter. The Great Tribulation ends with the incarceration of Satan and the destruction of the Antichrist, False Prophet and all people who will have taken the mark of the beast. Also, the 1,260 days will have ended for those Wilderness Jews whom

God had supernaturally saved from the Dragon's (Satan) army. Now is the time for their return to the city that they fled from.

At some point following the end of the Tribulation, God will lead the remnant into the Promised Land once again and back to Jerusalem. They are returning for the last time, into the land that was promised by God Himself to be theirs always. They likely hear from the Lord, words from their Torah: *"You shall be my people and I will be your God."* They will likely be told that when they return to Jerusalem, God has restored the Kingdom of God, with Messiah sitting upon the throne of David as promised in the Covenant. They will be told of a new covenant that brings peace, an Everlasting Covenant. They will hear that the Kingdom of Israel will once again flourish before God and its people will increase to great numbers as He had promised to Father Abraham. They will be told that Messiah will build His sanctuary and tabernacle and will never forsake them again. *"I will set my sanctuary in their midst forevermore. My tabernacle also shall be with them; indeed, I will be their God and they shall be My people."* (Ezekiel 37:36,37) *"But I am the Lord your God, who divided the sea, who's waves roared, the Lord of Hosts is His name. And I have put my words into your mouth. I have covered you with the shadow of my hand, that I may plant the heavens, lay the foundations of the earth and say to Zion, 'You are My people."* (Isaiah 51:15,16) Encouragement and confidence in God's promises such as this will likely be given from the Scriptures, *"Behold the days are coming that I will do the good thing which I have promised to the household of Judah: In those days and at that time I will cause to grow up to David a Branch of righteousness; He shall execute judgment and righteousness in the earth."* (Jeremiah 33:14-15)

How this remnant returns to Jerusalem is not known and how God leads them back from the wilderness is not known. When they return to Jerusalem, they will find the city horribly disfigured, in ruins from a great earthquake that split the city into thirds. (Revelation 16:19) The quake also caused the ground which will become known as Mount Zion, to dramatically rise in elevation like a mountain, while others including Mount Olivet will drop in elevation causing Mt. Zion to be the high point of the city. They will likely enter the city where Mt. Olivet had split in the quake and walk the route they took when they escaped the city three and a half years earlier. It is possible that when they approach Mount Zion that it is there where these Wilderness Jews will come face to face with Jesus Christ, their Messiah. Their spirits will quake within them at the at the sight of seeing His face once again, this time up close where they will see the nail marks upon His hands.

On that day, they will come into the presence of He whom their ancestors have always denied, despite the witness of His Church. They will realize in an instant, that the One whom they have always rejected, has been the One that their forefathers had put to death on a cross. He was now their king, Israel's King, the Son of David. Shock and fear will eventually be overcome with a desire for repentance for their iniquities, shame and disgrace will come upon each person who is before the Lord. No doubt, many of the Jews will fear to even venture near to Him for fear of retribution. They stand exposed, spiritually bankrupt in the presence of the Messiah that they have rejected for over 2000 years. There will be nothing they can say to Him in their defense. What could they say, that they were "good Jews" and "children of Father Abraham, they dare not.

The Jews of the Tribulation were the first Jews in 2000 years to have a temple built in Jerusalem before all of this happened to them. They worshipped in that temple with zeal and in their reformed religious ways, but God rejected their temple and their worship outright, for they had not reconciled with God Almighty and with His Messiah. They had not given recognition to Messiah their High Priest and His everlasting covenant that comes from God and not from man. God called for an end to that temple, *"He shall bring an end to sacrifices and offerings."* (Daniel 9:27) The end of worship in that new temple is a judgment from God. The prophet Daniel records for us, *"Because of transgression, an army was given over to the horn to oppose the daily sacrifices: and he cast truth down to the ground. He did all this and prospered. Then I heard a holy one speaking: and another holy one said to that certain one who was speaking, "How long will the vision be, concerning the daily sacrifices and the transgression of desolation, the giving of both the sanctuary and the host to be trampled underfoot?" And he said to me. For two thousand three hundred days and then the sanctuary shall be cleansed."* (Daniel 8:12-14)

The Tribulation temple is destroyed along with much of the city with a massive earthquake. Eventually, a Messianic temple is built, but not on the Temple Mount of days past but on Mt. Zion. And temple worship will once again be made right, vindicated as morally righteous. (Isaiah 2:2,3) This occurs 2300 days after the temple grounds and likely the entire city is purged of all of the unholy abominations found within the city.

What these Wilderness Jews will be able to attest to is that none of these things happened to their worship in the temple until after the Antichrist, (the Little Horn) broke the very covenant he made with the Jews when they built the temple and resume a sacrificial system. (Daniel 9:27) And then in an act of blasphemy that was revealed to the prophet Daniel. The Antichrist makes known that he is the "Little Horn." This man that Daniel prophecies of, and Jesus speaks to His disciples about, brings the "abomination of desolation" into the Jewish temple, standing in the very Holy Place of the temple. (Matthew 24:15) There, the Antichrist speaks blasphemy against God, His name, His tabernacle, and those who dwell in Heaven, (Revelation 13:5,6) *And it was granted to him to make war with the saints and to overcome them." (Revelation 13:7)*

That was to be the beginning of the end for Israel and all Jews. That will be the start of "Jacob's Trouble when two-thirds of Israel will perish before Messiah comes for them. *"Alas! For that day is great, So, that none is like it; And it is the time of Jacob's trouble. But he shall be saved out of it. For it shall come to pass in that day, Says the Lord of hosts, That I will break his yoke from your neck, and will burst your bonds; Foreigners shall no more, enslave them. But they shall serve the Lord their God and David their King, Whom I will raise up for them.* (Jeremiah 30:7-9) But God stops short of allowing their destruction by telling the prophet, *"Yet I will not make a complete end to you. But I will correct you in justice, And I will not let you go altogether unpunished."* (Jeremiah 30:11b)

When these Wilderness Jews return to Jerusalem and realize who their Messiah is, they will remember that the people of their heritage have been blinded for centuries. Having lived as enemies of the gospel and unreconciled to the God they claimed to worship. (Romans 11:25-

36) They know for certainty that this Holy God should judge them without mercy, for rejecting God's Son and sentence them to that place out of His presence.

In a moment's time, standing there in the ruins of Jerusalem, they come to terms with the reality of Messiah, that "God is with them." Every person there will know that they do not need saving from the world, the Antichrist, or hell itself, but that they need saving from themselves. And there standing before them is their Redeemer and Lord. When Messiah comes face to face with them, they will see Him reach out to them with His nail-pierced hands. Jesus Messiah will fulfill the promise, the words of the prophet that will come to pass, *"I will pour on the house of David and all the inhabitants of Jerusalem the Spirit of grace and supplication; then they will look upon Me whom they pierced. Yes, they will mourn for Him as one mourns for his only son, and grieve for Him as one grieves for a firstborn. In that day there will be great grieving in Jerusalem, like the morning at Hadad Rimmon in the plain of Meggido. And the land shall mourn, every family by itself: the family of the house of David by itself, and their wives by themselves; the family of Nathan by itself, and their wives by themselves; the house of Levi by itself, and their wives by themselves; the family of Shimei by itself, and their wives by themselves, all the families that remain, every family by itself, and their wives by themselves.* (Zechariah 12:10-14)

These Israelites do not mourn the destruction of their city, and temple, and the massive loss of life that occurred, they mourn for their sinful hearts and their rebellion against the one who died for their sins. Repentance and reconciliation will be the order of the days ahead.

The city is in ruins, but their lives are in ruin more. The remnant Jews will hear words from their Lord and Savior that will bring healing to their souls and also, a new spirit that reveals a heart in them that was never there before. Messiah speaks to them with the voice of God, with assurances that they will never be treated as they have been in the past, by either God or man. They will prosper and the nations of people that cursed them in the past, will become blessed by your redemption. Jesus Messiah, tells them that He will bring reconciliation and salvation to the Gentile nations as well. As King, Jesus Messiah will tell them that He has taken away the Gentile nation's right in the judgment of Israel and that He has cast out their enemies, Satan and the Beast, (Antichrist) along with his False Prophet and all those who would be the death of Israel. Messiah will likely tell them that they will see no more disasters, not to ever fear ever again, but to be strong. (Zechariah 8:4-15)

He will tell them that never again will Israel trust their security to a man like the one who had just deceived them, who defeated them. (Antichrist) that they will be faithful and depend upon the Lord the Holy One of Israel. They will be told that the destruction they see now, which was decreed by God, will overflow with righteousness, as promised through the prophet's word. (Isaiah 10:20-23)

He will likely tell Israel once again what He told the Church, that He is their God, *"I am He", "I am the First and the Last."* That it is He who laid the foundation of the Earth, and He who created the Heavens with a wave of His hand. And now the Lord God your redeemer, the Holy One of Israel has returned to you. I am the Lord your God who will teach you to prosper, who leads you in the way to go. (Isaiah 48:12-17)

The Lord Messiah begins to shepherd His people and to be their provider. *"In that day the Branch of the Lord shall be beautiful and glorious; And the fruit of the earth shall be excellent and appealing for those of Israel who have escaped. And it shall come to pass that he who is left in Zion and remains in Jerusalem will be called holy- everyone who is recorded among the living in Jerusalem. When the Lord has washed away the filth of the daughters of Zion, and purged the blood of Jerusalem from her midst, by the spirit of judgment and the spirit of burning. Then the Lord will create above every dwelling place of Mount Zion, and above her assemblies, a cloud and smoke by day and the shining of a flame by night. For over all the glory there will be a covering. And there will be a tabernacle for shade in the daytime from the heat, for a place of refuge and for a shelter from the storm and rain."* (Isaiah 4:2-6)

After the arrival into a devastated city without an operating infrastructure and without safe structures to dwell in. It is very likely that those who lived in the city during the tribulations of the last three and a-half years, would have already scavenged through the houses and commercial buildings that stand empty, looking for all manner of shelter, clean water, and provisions. Not so when Messiah arrives. It is likely that the Lord will provide supernatural shelter and supernaturally cause the produce of the land to flourish for His chosen people.

Cleansed in His righteousness, they have come to know that they have been saved by grace alone by the One who died for their sins, who lives again over 2000 years later, and now He stands before them in His resurrected glory. Spared from the horrors of the Tribulation, the Wilderness Jews will praise the God of Glory and draw near to the Lamb, to worship the One who has returned to them for no other reason they can see other than that He loves them.

Those people both Jews and Gentiles alike, would either come to believe in Messiah for their salvation and worship Him or they could be driven from the city, leave at their own will, or possibly be judged for crimes or rebellion. The remnant Jews spend one thousand two hundred and sixty days in the wilderness under the protective care and revelation from the Lord God of their ancestors. (Revelation 12:6) They will come to know their Messiah face to face when they spend those early days of the Kingdom in Jerusalem with Jesus. Called to ministry by Messiah himself, these chosen Jews will likely be the "sent ones," and to walk among their people and nations of the world just as He called the Apostles, their Jewish brothers, many centuries before them. Called to labor for the Kingdom of God and do their part in the Master Plan of God.

"Thus says the Lord of Hosts: "In those days ten men from every language of the nations shall grasp the sleeve of a Jewish man, saying, "Let us go with you, for we have heard that God is with you." (Zechariah 8:23)

Added note: The following verses are pieces to the Millennial story puzzle and contribute to the narrative message above: Ezekiel 18:31,32, Ezekiel 18:31,32, Ezekiel 36:2,23-28, Jeremiah 30:1-11, Ezekiel 39:21-29, Hosea 1:10,11, Micah 2:2,13, Isaiah 4:1-6, Isaiah 10:20-23, Isaiah 27:12,13, Isaiah 48:12-17, Zephaniah 3:4, 15-17, Zechariah 8:11-13, Zechariah 12:7-9, Malachi 3:2,3, Isaiah 49:20,23, Micah 7:15-18, Micah 5:4-7, Isaiah 35:8-10, Isaiah 1:27-31, Ezekiel 36:1-9, Joel 2:28-32, Micah 7:18-20, Isaiah 54:3-15, Isaiah 28:16, Isaiah 30:18,19, Isaiah 43:1-7, Jeremiah 31:31-34, Zechariah 13:1,2, Isaiah 51:12-16, Psalm

72:1-5, Isaiah 49:3-6, Isaiah 59:6-21, Ezekiel 21:25,27, Isaiah 56:7,8, Isaiah 42:6-9, Isaiah 52:

10.3 Gathered For Glory

In the days of Hoshea King of Israel, the Assyrian Empire invaded the land of Israel, conquered it and proceeded to exile people from their land. Many captives from the Northern Kingdom were scattered throughout the empire, never to return to their Promised Land. Scattered so much and so far, that they are often referred to as the ten lost tribes of Israel, being that we have very few ideas as to where they are today. Some people doubt that their descendants could ever exist anymore.

The Southern Kingdom of Israel, Judah (including the House of David) and Benjamin took a different path in history. They too, went seeking their own way without God and were eventually conquered by the Babylonian Empire. Many Jews were taken out of the Promised Land into exile. When God's manifested presence left Solomon's temple His glory departed from its threshold. (Ezekiel 10:18,19) After which the temple was destroyed and the House of David ceased to rule over the people of Israel.

God had told the Southern Kingdom Jews, through the prophet Jeremiah, that they would be exiled for seventy years and then allowed to return to their land to live under the sovereignty of their Gentile kings. God kept that promise. When they came back to the Promised Land, they built another temple, rebuilt Jerusalem and rededicated themselves to God. However, that essence of glory, that manifested presence of God that departed from Solomon's temple did not return and the city and nation never returned to their former glory as a sovereign country. History tells us that their land was overrun several times by the latest super-power from the north, or from Egypt, coming from the south. At times, they were overrun by one of the smaller powers that rose to dominate their region and for a short time through violence. became a sovereign Israel once again only to lose it once again.

The Jew's turbulent existence nationally, their city, and their temple were ended by the Romans in 70 A.D. They crushed the city and slaughtered Jews by the ten-thousands. This judgment occurs approximately 37 years after the Jews had the Messiah killed, when they proclaimed, 'they have no king but the Caesar in Rome.' So now, for over two millennia, Israel disappeared as a sovereign country and its people remain scattered all over the world, yet He preserved them, according to the Master Plan of God. *"Thus says the Lord God:" Although I have cast them far off among the Gentiles, and although I have scattered them among the countries, yet I shall be a little sanctuary for them in the countries where they have gone."* (Ezekiel 11:16)

For the last 2000 years, God has not forgotten about the Jews or abandoned them. He has a plan for them. Only recently, in the mid-twentieth century, by working through Gentile rulers, God once again caused the sovereign country of Israel to re-appear in the Promised Land. From its start the people and their sovereignty struggle to survive in a world where many nations are bent on its destruction. Without going into details, this secularized Israel will be overtaken and destroyed before the Great Tribulation ends. The small nation has become a centerpiece in world affairs and will remain so into the Millennial Age.

At the time of the Tribulation, after the Church will have departed from Earth, Satan will turn his full attention upon all who are Israel, in his effort to stop what has been decreed by God and attempt to force changes in His Master Plan. One such assault upon the Jews is the failed attempt to destroy the Wilderness Jews. (Revelation 12:13-17) Satan's great rage and power over the Antichrist and False Prophet, will result in the days of "Jacob's Trouble" that will come upon the people of Israel. They will be overrun, many will be taken prisoner, and taken as captives among the nations once again. But God steps in to prevent their certain annihilation, (Daniel 12:1) and Israel will be scattered around the world for the last time.

When Messiah returns to Jerusalem and is among the remnant of Wilderness Jews, He will likely tell them what has happened to this world and to the people of Israel. The Scriptures will speak of what God has done and will do going forward.

"I will set My glory among the nations; all the nations shall see My judgment which I have executed, and My hand which I have laid on them. So, the house of Israel shall know that I am the Lord their God from that day forward. The Gentiles will know that the house of Israel went into

captivity for their iniquity because they were unfaithful to Me. Therefore, I hid my face from them. I gave them into the hands of their enemies and they fell by the sword. According to their uncleanliness and according to their transgressions I have dealt with them, and hidden my face from them." Therefore, thus says the Lord God: "Now I will bring back the captives of Jacob, and have mercy on the whole house of Israel; and I will be jealous for My holy name." (Ezekiel 39:21-25)

The call of God upon the scattered of Israel is not just directed to Messianic Jews who expect Messiah's return and to those Jews who have come to faith in Jesus during the Tribulation. But also, the call will go out to all secularized Israelites everywhere, who have abandoned the redeeming faith of their ancient fathers. Although many of them hold to a worship with traditions that bond them with one another in community and includes readings of the Torah, they remain in an unreconciled relationship with God.

Blinded to the truth, they do not know God as the Father, and they want nothing to do with God the Son. Jesus makes it known that you cannot have one without the other, saying, *"No one comes to the Father except through me,"* also, *"And this is eternal life that they may know the only true God and Jesus Christ whom You have sent."* (John 17:3 and John 14:6) These truths will never be more clearly evident than in these days immediately after the Tribulation when Jesus Messiah gathers the lost sheep of Israel like a shepherd who seeks to bring His scattered flock together. They will hear His voice once again and be within the reach of His rod and staff. Just how Messiah brings the whole of Israel back to the Promised Land, we are not told in detail. It is very plausible that Messiah acts with supernatural power, by transferring 2.0-2.5M. people from where they are now, spread out around the world, by sending out a great multitude of angels to gather them and bring them bodily to Him in Israel.

An example of this type of harvest is given in the Scriptures, that of Jews, who happen to be in Egypt and Assyria. The prophetic language suggests a supernatural relocation of God's people will occur. Since it has not ever occurred in the past it is another piece to the puzzle. *"And it shall come to pass in that day That the Lord will thresh from the channel of the river* (that is the Euphrates River, added) *to the brook of*

Egypt; And you will be gathered one by one, O' you children of Israel. So it will be in that day: The great trumpet will be blown; They will come who are about to perish in the land of Assyria, and they who are outcasts in the land of Egypt, and shall worship the Lord in the holy mount at Jerusalem. " (Isaiah 27:12,13)

In these foreign lands, it is the Lord doing the threshing and gathering of His people. One at a time, that is individually and at a moment when a trumpet is blown. Most assuredly this would have to be done by legions of angels. The gathering of Israel will be worldwide and will likely happen soon after the Wilderness Jews have returned to Him and become willing witnesses to this ancient promise that will have come true right before their very eyes. That the Lord will gather His people to Himself, from Egypt, Assyria and from all over the world. Those taken to Him will no doubt be shocked into submission, how shocked may depend upon what they had come to know beforehand.

There is a second possible scenario for gathering His people, Israel. It is by conventional means of modern-day travel which will still be possible, but will be very limited for a time; It is likely that all types of travel will be difficult and dangerous immediately after the Tribulation, causing people to slowly arrive in Israel. While on their call to return to Israel, experience hardships and supernatural deliverance on the way. In either scenario, we do not know the duration of time that it will take to complete the new exodus to the Promised Land. It could be a very short period of time should Messiah send out the angels to gather all of them up to Him, or it could be a lengthy duration of time, as Jews from around the world find their own way individually and or in groups. The word of this call to return will likely get out to the Jews, God is going to gather His people to Himself in Israel and they will come into His presence whether they want to or not, they will return to God's Anointed One, Jesus Messiah.

He will likely call them by strong promptings of the Holy Spirit and also in response to the word that He is spreading out across the globe; that Messiah has destroyed the Beast, (Antichrist) and his government, and has put the nations of the world on notice, that the Lamb of God is Jesus Messiah, He will be their king and they will be His subjects. For secular Jews, it may seem prudent to go to Him and seek favor with the new king, rather than be seen as a Jew who still rejects this Christian

Savior. For religious Jews, they may reluctantly go to Him in fear, understanding the ramifications of their rejection of God's Anointed.

The first order of business as King over the Gentile nations will likely be the demand to end all Jewish persecutions, their release from slavery, and the end to all oppression. He will likely demand that the nations assist all Jews that are among them with their call to return to Israel and to the King; out of fear, many will likely do so. With promptings from the Holy Spirit, those who had oppressed the Jews will likely respond out of fear that their conqueror will inflict additional judgments upon them should they disobey His decrees.

Gentiles may feel an incentive to provide the means for Jews to leave their presence and their lands, by giving them the provisions needed to travel to Israel. Something reminiscent to what the Egyptians experienced in the days just before that first exodus, when Israel suddenly found favor with the Egyptian people who gave them their valuables as plunder. Another incentive for assisting the Jews will likely be an increased belief in the covenant promise made to Abraham and his children; that "God will bless those who bless you and curse those who curse you." A message shared with them by the new believers in The Way.

Regardless of how they arrive, Messiah will require all who are Israel to return to Him and to the land of promise. We should expect that many will not go willingly. They have been afflicted by the plagues of judgment from God and the Lamb and now they hate Him. Others fear it may be a trap of His, intended to exact vengeance upon them. Some will rebel against the command to obey Jesus their Messiah and want nothing to do with Him. Many, will go if only to escape the oppression they have been living under, seeing no better option. Still others will want to return to the homes and families that they were taken from during the Tribulation, this will be an opportunity to do that.

Still others will join those who remain of the 144,000; they will be led by the Spirit as new believers and eager to be with their Lord. Many will want peace and security, and they see this as a chance for a new start in life. Regardless of the many reasons, Messiah will bring them to Himself for His glory and for His purposes. Come they will, willingly or unwillingly, but the whole of Israel will be gathered to Him in the Promised Land for the last time.

The Messiah King is likely to announce exactly what He will do with all of His gathered people, saying something such as what we see in the prophetic Scriptures, *'Thus says the Lord God: "I do not do this for your sake, O house of Israel, but for My holy name's sake, which you have profaned among the nations wherever you went. And I will sanctify My great name, which you have profaned in their midst; and the nations shall know I am the Lord, says the Lord God," says the Lord God, "when I am hallowed in you before their eyes. For I will take you from among the nations, gather you out of all countries, and bring you into your own land. Then I will sprinkle clean water on you and you shall be clean; I will give you a new heart and put a new spirit within you; I will take the heart of stone out of your flesh and give you a heart of flesh. I will pour out My Spirit within you and cause you to walk in My statutes, and you will keep My judgments and do them. Then you will dwell in the land that I gave your fathers; you shall be My people, and I will be your God... Be ashamed and confounded for your own ways, O house of Israel!"* (Ezekiel 36:22-28, with verse 32 added)

Jesus Messiah will make it clear that He is intent upon bringing changes to the people of Israel and see to it they respond in subjection to Him as their Lord God. The people of Israel will no longer be allowed to profane the name which is above every other name, among the nations of people, throughout the world. They are to be ashamed of their rejection of Messiah and for the profaning of His holy name and will face the consequences if they do. But like all the redeemed of the Church before them; if they come by their own free will with repentance, He will cleanse them of their unrighteousness and give them a new heart and the Holy Spirit will indwell each person who becomes a new creation in Messiah, born again with the desire to walk in His ways in obedience. He will take them from the countries of the world and cause them to dwell in the land that God has promised to their fathers. There they will be His people and He, their God.

It is the time in the Master Plan of God to set the record straight as to who He is and who the people of Israel are. Messiah will bring all things in subjection to His will. It is time to manifest the Kingdom of God on this Earth once again and complete the mission of glory among all nations. (Psalms 67:1-7) A renewed Kingdom of God on the Earth, with the King of Glory to shepherd over His people and to rule over all the nations.

Many of the people who return to Israel will be women and children who were bought and sold like a commodity during the Tribulation, and used as slaves. These will be in greater numbers than the men who will not have been spared. (Joel 3:1-3) There will also be a large population of the lame, crippled and blind due to the judgments of the last seven years and the harsh treatment they experienced at the hands of their oppressors. *"In that day, "says the Lord, I will assemble the lame, I will gather the outcast, And those whom I afflicted; I will make the lame a remnant, and the outcast a strong nation; So, the Lord will reign over them in Mount Zion. From now on even forever."* (Micah 4:6-7)

The scattered remnant of Jews who survived the Tribulation have witnessed massive annihilation of their people worldwide at a scale greater than any previous Holocaust. They have also experienced the terror brought on to them by the Lamb and His supernatural presence during the sixth seal event and those that followed. They witnessed the rapture of Christians, while they were left to the lies of the False Prophet. Struck with the fear of God by these events, they will likely be haunted by the thought that Yahweh, God Almighty, is real, just as their ancient fathers experienced Him in the Torah, just as they had described Him to be! What the Lord did to His stiff-necked people was right because of their unfaithfulness to Him in their day. And now, He has afflicted them for their unfaithfulness until they submit to Him, their Lord and King.

They will clearly see that Messiah is alive and powerful to save, but that they were not the ones chosen to be saved from the worst of God's tribulations and the wrath of the Antichrist. Shouldn't they have been saved, they were the children of Abraham, they were the descendants of Jacob and the children of promise. Yet, they were left behind and the Christians taken. Their people were rejected by the Nazarene Messiah, the Son of God. He came for the Christians just as they always believed that He would.

These Jewish survivors will remember that it was the Jews who have been rejecting Jesus of Nazareth, since those days of the Roman occupation of Jerusalem. And now, they will experience what that carpenter's son said to the Jews in His day, *"I say to you hear after, you will see the Son of Man sitting at the right hand of the Power and coming on the clouds of Heaven."* (Matthew 26:64).

These Tribulation Jews all around the world along with everyone else will have witnessed the bizarre sight of people ascend bodily, being changed in an instant, and then taken up to the Lamb of God by angels into the clouds above, then taken away with Him. (1 Thessalonians 4:15-17)

Yet, possibly only moments earlier, this supernatural chaos is preceded by an even greater nightmare. One that happens when all the Earth shakes in an earthquake, and the unmistakable terrifying sound of a trumpet horn blaring everywhere all at once and a great supernatural voice calling out from Heaven. Then an event occurs that results in what can only be described by those witnessing it, human life rising out of the earth like an angel. Not like in some horror movie imagery, but rather human forms bathed in a glorious light of energy, that was so holy it was a fearful thing to behold or to be anywhere near these people. Each person appearing in glorious bodily forms, the dead came to life as they rose out of their graves by an unseen power. Rising out of the ground itself then ascending up into the sky above them, up to where He was. (1 Corinthians 15:51-53, John 5:28, 29) and Romans 8:11)

It all happens so quickly yet the terrifying experience is always fixed in their minds. Although many people have seemingly vanished and many opened graves are now empty. Those who remain ask, "Was this the act of God or was it something else entirely?" When it is all over and many people begin to rationalize away the events they just witnessed, they will confirm that experiencing the miraculous does not translate into believing.

During those Tribulation Days, many Jews will experience an awakening and their spiritual blindness removed like a veil from their eyes. Many will come to faith in Jesus as their Messiah, their Savior and Lord and they will be killed for it. These are spoken about by the angel in Revelation chapter 7:9-17. But also, some will turn their backs on others to save themselves, even at the cost of the lives of their fellow Jews. Others still will not submit themselves over to any power or authority but only do what they think it will take to survive, even denying that they themselves are Jews.

For the Jews that live past the Tribulation's last days, they will likely begin to abandon their reformed religious practices, and its leaders, and struggle to come to know Yahweh, the God of their ancient fathers. For some Jews, they could never submit to this Messiah who destroyed their lives and killed so many of their brethren and family with plagues. It would take a new spirit in them, and a new heart, to even consider worshipping Him as Lord, and accept Jesus as their High Priest and King, and to become willing subjects in His Kingdom. Nothing short of that would do and that is precisely what Messiah can offer them.

Some of the Jews will search the Torah, and read from Law and the Prophets and have to come to terms with what this prophet and others tell them about Jesus Messiah. *"But you, Bethlehem Ephrathah, though you are little among the thousands of Judah, Yet, out of you shall come forth to Me. The One to be ruler in Israel, whose goings forth are from of old, From everlasting. Therefore, He shall give them up until the time that she who is in labor has given birth; Then the remnant of His brethren shall return to the children of Israel."* (Micah 5:2-4) This prophecy is precisely what is happening. Messiah will have given up Israel to those days of "Jacobs Trouble" until that tribulation time when the birth pangs of Israel give way to the expected One when Messiah comes into the world. Then the "Scattered Remnant" will return to the Promised Land and join the "Wilderness Jews" in Israel who will have their own stories to tell.

In time, the Jews will come to understand that Messiah will be the good shepherd to His flock, *"For thus says the Lord God: "Indeed I Myself will search for My sheep and seek them out. As a shepherd seeks out his flock on the day he is among his scattered sheep, so will I seek out My sheep and deliver them from all the places where they were scattered on a cloudy and dark day. And I will bring them out from the peoples and gather them from the countries, and will bring them to their own land; I will feed them on the mountains of Israel, in the valleys and in all the inhabited places of the country."* (Ezekiel 34:11-13)

The King of kings and Lord of lords, states in these verses, that He will seek out those who are His wherever they are on the Earth, and that He will be their deliverer, freeing them from the places and people they were scattered to. He will gather them up from the countries and bring them up to their homeland; there He will feed them, and give them safe haven with His presence. In their land, He will bring healing to the broken and to the sick. Instead of vengeance, they receive mercy, instead of punishment, grace, instead of rejection they receive acceptance but not wholesale acceptance, not at the cost of truth and justice.

When they flock to the Good Shepherd, they will come to know that He was the One who laid down His life for His sheep. With this flock gathering in the land of Israel, we can understand the beginnings of a manifested Kingdom of God on Earth, but also, see the execution of the Master Plan; to gather all things under the subjection of Christ (1 Corinthians 15:27) where there will be one flock and one shepherd. But before the flock is called into service there will be a time of judgment within the flock. The Messiah acts in the power and authority as one in the Trinity of God, all that He does is in perfect submission to the will of His Father. (Matthew 28:18) The Messiah will act in the land of Israel and judge His people when they have returned to Him, for not all Israel is in fact Israel.

"As for you my flock, thus says the Lord God: "Behold, I shall judge between sheep and sheep, between rams and goats. Is it too little for you to eaten up the good pasture, that you must tread down with your feet the residue of your pasture- and have drunk of the clear waters, that you must foul the residue with your feet? And as for my flock, they will eat what you have trampled on with your feet, and drink what you have fouled with your feet. Therefore, I will judge between the fat sheep and the lean sheep." (Ezekiel 34:17-20)

When all the people of Israel are gathered into the land of Israel there will be a time of judgment to come upon Israel. Messiah will make a separation within the people of Israel and reveal that it is not those who say they are Israel that are Israel, not all of Israel are children of Abraham spiritually. Before the King begins to execute justice among the Gentile nations. He will first execute justice upon His flock which He has brought into the land. There Messiah will separate the sheep from the goats so to speak. These people will be separated from one another according to the injustices they caused to fall upon their brethren.

He will *"seek what was lost and bring back what was driven away, bind up the broken and strengthen what was sick; but will destroy the fat and the strong, and feed them in judgment. As for you my flock, thus says the Lord God: "Behold, I shall judge between sheep and sheep, between rams and goats."* (Ezekiel 34:16,17) This time of judgment will be swift, necessary and righteous in the eyes of God, for the King does not bear the rod of iron in vain.

It is likely that there will be among the Jews those persons who willfully caused fellow Jews and believers of The Way to become exposed to the persecution that came upon them during the Tribulation years. Spineless people who will have benefited from their acts of cruelty and rejection of others and their traitorous treatment of their fellow Jews that likely, ended in their death or victims of slavery, or imprisonment.

Those unjust Jews will be judged according to their wickedness in God's sight and justice will be served. No injustice will be overlooked by the King. He will not only judge between the goats and sheep and separate them but He will judge between sheep and sheep, (Ezekiel 3:22) meaning that justice will be served among those whom He allows to remain within the flock. Although their offenses were punishable, they did not require a death sentence to be given to them.

With Godly justice executed among His flock, Messiah is demonstrating to Israel that He will not tolerate wickedness among His people. Jesus spoke about the Kingdom of God to come and the separating out of His servants, the execution of the wicked and unprofitable, as well as the severe punishment for the lazy and careless. And in doing so, making no distinction between His Jewish or Gentile servants, showing no preferential treatment. (Matthew 24:45-5), (Luke 12:42-48)

The Lord has promised to make a covenant of peace with His sheep, spare them from the threat of those who would prey upon them, He will be their safety. The Lord promised to make them to be a blessing and the places they live a blessing, causing them and their land to prosper in safety. There will never again be hunger in their land and they will no longer bear the shame of the Gentiles. They will know that, I the Lord their God is with them, and they the house of Israel, are His people. *"You are my flock, the flock of my pasture; you are men, and I am your God,"* *says the Lord God."* (Ezekiel 34:31)

The remnant gathered back to Israel before the Lord are still sinful people with a sin nature. The fact of their redemption does not change that. They will be called to obedience to their shepherd King and learn the ways of this Savior and Lord. They will come to see that He is all things to all people, a righteous king who bears the rod of iron for judgment and power; they will submit in all humility and look to Him for their redemption.

"In that day the deaf shall hear the words of the book, and the eyes of the blind shall see out of obscurity and out of darkness. The humble also shall increase their joy in the Lord, And the poor among men shall rejoice in the Holy One of Israel. For the terrible one is brought to nothing. The scornful one is consumed. And all who watch for iniquity are cut off." (Ezekiel 29:18-20)

The prophecy of Isaiah speaks of this time in the Millennium when Jesus returns to Jerusalem to rule and gather all Israel to Him, and eventually all the nations of the Earth. *"Of the increase of His government and peace there will be no end. Upon the throne of David and over His kingdom, from that time forward, even forever. The zeal of the Lord of hosts will perform this."* (Isaiah 9:7)

God will at some point pour out the promised Holy Spirit upon the redeemed of Israel. They will have borne their shame and repented of their iniquities and unfaithfulness to Jesus their Messiah. They will by faith place their trust in the Heavenly reality of the Lamb of God who takes away the sins of the world. The Lamb of God that died for their sins on a cross on the outskirts of Jerusalem at the hands of their forefathers.

Each person who repents and confesses that Jesus is their Lord and Savior will receive the Holy Spirit. When this happens is not clear, will it happen all at once as it did on the day of Pentecost or in similar ways as recorded in Acts chapter 2:1-4? It will likely occur after the Jewish people publicly forsake all that remains as a public offense to God and their King in an act of reconciliation with God. Speaking of the remnant

Jews who return to Israel the prophet says, *"And they will go there and they will take away all its detestable things and all its abominations from there. Then I will give them one heart and I will put a new spirit within them..."* (Ezekiel 11:18,19a) The generations of Israel that follow will see a continued growth of those who enter into the spiritual Kingdom of God and walk in the faith. *"I will pour out my Spirit on your descendants, And my blessing on your offspring; They will spring up among the grass like willows by the watercourses. One will say, 'I am the Lord's'; Another will call himself Jacob; Another will write with his hand, 'The Lord's' And name himself by the name of Israel,"* (Isaiah 44:3-5)

Centuries of Jewish teachings, Jewish schools and education centers, will be forsaken. Religious doctrines and displays will be to be purged from the public institutions and culture. What remained of the Tribulation temple will likely be taken away as well. But it will not be Jewish abominations only that are removed from the culture, all public displays of all worldly religions as well. They too will be required to be purged from the Promised Land.

In time, the Jewish people will learn new doctrines and come to understand the role they are to fulfill in the Kingdom. Over time and through the sanctifying work of the Holy Spirit Israel will humble themselves individually and collectively as a nation in the presence of their Messiah. A spirit of submission and truth eventually replaces their anger, pride and devotion to their Jewish legacy and begin to look back into their ancestry to re-establish what it means to be the Kingdom of God on the Earth and a holy priesthood of God among the Gentile nations.

"Therefore, thus says the Lord, who redeemed Abraham, concerning the house of Jacob: Jacob shall not now be ashamed, nor shall his face grow pale; But when he sees his children, The work of My hands, in his midst. They will allow the Holy One of Jacob, and fear the God of Israel. These who erred in spirit will come to understanding, and those who complained will learn doctrine." (Isaiah 29:22-24)

When the spirit comes upon the people of Israel, restoration rather than replacement will bring glory to God starting in the early days of the Millennial Kingdom, according to the Master Plan of God. How long this will take before this restoration is completed is not known. Sin remains in the lives of the redeemed but the deceptions of Satan will be absent and the seductions of the world's religious systems will have been rendered powerless to deceive. It is possible that the work of the Spirit will make the transformation of the whole nation of Israel complete during the lifetime of those generations who survived the Tribulation.

Much work will be accomplished in these first generations in the "renewal" that Christ's disciples spoke of in Acts chapter 1:6. A restoration of the physical Kingdom of God is a transition from alienation and rejection of God's appointed King, to citizenship in Messiah's Kingdom, but not just the physical Kingdom on the Earth but also a transference from a dominion of darkness into the eternal spiritual Kingdom of God.

Added note: The following verses are pieces to the Millennial story puzzle and contribute to the narrative message above: Ezekiel 34:12-25, Ezekiel 37:21-28, Ezekiel 39:22-29, Psalm 14:7, Isaiah 59:21, Zephaniah 3:8-20, Isaiah 11:12,13, Jeremiah 30:3,4, Jeremiah 31:8-14, Zechariah 8:1-8, Micah 4:4-7, Ezekiel 11:16-20, Joel 2:30-32, Isaiah 59:16-21, Isaiah 4:1-6, Isaiah 40:10-14, Isaiah27:12,13, Isaiah 48:12-17, Zechariah 8:11-13, Malachi 3:2,3, Ezekiel 36:22-38, Zechariah 9:1,12-17, Isaiah 41:21-29, Ezekiel 11:16-20, Ezekiel 11:18-20, Amos 9:13-15, Zechariah 10:9-12, Psalm 47:3-9, Psalm 94:14,15, Psalm 98:1-3, Hosea 14:1-9,

10.4 Thy Kingdom Come

As the people of Israel go through a transformation so does the Promised Land, both physically and geopolitically as a Kingdom. Geologically the land will experience massive changes as a result of the massive earthquakes during the Tribulation, but the greatest of these changes occur in the city of Jerusalem itself. It is clear from the Scriptures that Jerusalem will experience a major earthquake, where one-tenth of the city fell and seven thousand people will be killed. (Revelation 11:13) The supernatural presence of the Kingdom of God will manifest itself physically with changes from plagues and death like this, to blessings and the life-giving changes spoken of by the Prophets.

In this quake, the Mount of Olives will split open and drop in elevation creating the valley that the remnant Jews use to escape into the wilderness. What is called Mount Zion, will rise in elevation during the quake to become the highest point in the city and in all the surrounding area. So high that it is referred to as the "Holy Mountain" in the midst of Jerusalem. (Zechariah 8:3 Micah 4:1, 2) A large area of land south of Jerusalem from Geba to Rimmon which is hilly country today, will become flattened out into an agricultural plain, while the city itself is raised up in elevation. (Zechariah 14:10)

Another significant change to the city and geography is that two rivers will emerge from the effects of the Tribulation earthquake that strikes Jerusalem. Both rivers find their source at the top of Mt. Zion, at the very thresholds of where the new temple is to be built. Water in abundance will come up from the ground and form the two rivers. (Zechariah 14:8, Ezekiel 47:1-12) One river will flow to the west into the Great Sea. The other flows to the east into the Dead Sea. It is likely that they will be fed with tributaries that will experience the supernatural effects of those two rivers.

The water that flows in these rivers are referred to as "living waters," The river that flows west will begin restoring the waters of the oceans and supernaturally bring on an abundance of sea life to it. The river flowing east into the most saline-toxic body of water in the world, the Dead Sea will turn into a living body of water. No longer dead, net fishing will become commonplace along the shores of the Dead Sea from En Gedi to En Eglaim. Yet the Scriptures tell us that the swamps and marshes about the body of water will remain salty. (Ezekiel 47:7-11) One wonders if those marshy areas are the sites of Sodom and Gomorrah. *"There is a river whose streams shall make glad the city of God, The holy place of the tabernacle of the Most-High."* (Ezekiel 48:4)

Animal and plant life will thrive in and around the banks of these rivers in ways that respond to their supernatural properties. There will be great multitudes of fish and a wide variety of trees that will grow fruit for food and leaves that will be used for medicines. The trees along the river will supernaturally bear leaves and their fruit every month of the year because of the water that flows out from God's sanctuary. (Ezekiel 47:12)

With the people of Israel secure in the Messiah's Kingdom He will likely mobilize the people in the work of agriculture and construction immediately. The agricultural landscape in the Promised Land will have the hand of God's blessing upon it in response to the "latter and former rain" that God has promised to give to the children of Israel, that rain is Jesus. Now that the promise of the latter rain has come, Jesus has returned to Israel and the land promises to be this: *"The threshing floors shall be full of wheat, and the vats shall overflow with new wine and oil."*(Joel 2:23-24) *"Behold, the days are coming," says the Lord "when the plowman will overtake the reaper, and the treader of grapes him who sows seed. The mountains shall drip with sweet wine, and the hills shall flow with it, "* (Amos 9:13)

Clearly, the imagery here tells the story of agricultural abundance that exceeds that of a world constrained by the curse of the fall although the curse remains. (Genesis 3:17-19) In the early days of the Millennium, Israel will likely be the first nation to be able to produce food in great abundance to distribute to other nations, including nations such as Egypt, who will experience desolation in response to their on-going hostilities towards Israel, until they submit to the will of their new King who dwells in Zion. (Joel 3:18, 19)

The fields and flocks of Israel will likely abound to Eden-like levels of abundance. This will move Israel to bring in many foreigners to work the fields and tend the livestock for the shortage of people, especially men. (Isaiah 61:5, 6) allowing them to gather food for themselves and others around the world. Israel will willingly become an early food source for many nations, for the very people who oppressed them, and hate them. They will learn to "love their enemies" just as Jesus told us to do. Their enemies will begin to see the advantages to blessing the Children of Abraham, rather than curse them. With the availability of food and many other resources, Messiah, will begin the process of reconciling people to one another, Jew and Gentiles alike, according to the Master Plan of God., Jesus executes the words of the Father that have come through the prophet Isaiah.

"In the acceptable time I have heard You, And in the day of salvation I have helped You; I will preserve You and give you as a covenant to the people, To restore the earth, To cause them to inherit the desolate heritages; That You may say to the prisoners, 'Go forth,' To

those who are in darkness,' Show yourselves. 'They shall feed along the roads, and their pastures shall be on desolate heights. They shall neither hunger or thirst, neither heat nor sun shall strike them; For He who has mercy on them will lead them; Even by the springs of water He will guide them." (Isaiah 49:8-10)

The geopolitical organization of Israel and the boundaries of the Promised Land will see a transformation, it will be the homeland for the Kingdom of God. The Promised Land is roughly 280 miles long and varies in width from 40 to 100 miles. There are four major changes in the transformation of the Promised Land ordered by the Lord. *"Thus says the Lord God: "These are the borders by which you shall divide the land as an inheritance among the twelve tribes of Israel Joseph shall have two portions."* (Ezekiel 47:13)

The first change is that the borders are divided into fourteen areas. One for each of the tribes of Israel including the two half-tribes of Joseph's sons Manasseh and Ephraim, and also an added Holy District. (Ezekiel 48:8)

The second change is that the borders of Israel will have changed. Lebanon and a portion of Syria up to Hamath which is approximately 70 miles north of Damascus, Syria today, will be added into Israel as well. A portion of the original Promised Land east of the Dead Sea will be given over to Ammon that is Jordan today. This is likely so that they may share in the access to the Dead Sea with Israel. (Zechariah 10:10, Ezekiel 47:15-18,)

A third change is that the tribes of Gad and Reuben will be relocated to a new land allocation from where they were located at the close of the first Kingdom. The fourth change is that "strangers" who enter lived among a tribe at the time of the tribal assignments are to receive an inheritance of land just as the natural-born children of Israel do.

Who these strangers are is not clear. It should be said that these "tribes of Israel" will be made up of the descendants of the original twelve sons of Jacob. These strangers are not the occupiers who are removed from the land, possibly even Gentiles, however these strangers remain a mystery. With the exile and scattering of the northern ten tribes over the centuries, most of the genealogy has been lost, so such a determination is likely to be supernaturally made by Messiah or possibly by the twelve Apostles who will rule and sit as judges over the twelve tribes of Israel. (Matthew 19:28, Luke 22:28, 29)

The Apostles will be the King's co-rulers and judges. They will dictate and oversee the civil government, and its' laws, including the execution of punishments for law-breakers, and provide benevolent services at the tribal level in Israel. They will preside over major disputes that arise and direct tribal activities, including reconstruction of the cities within their borders. These twelve will enact all that the King desires, and correct any activities that do not meet with the King's approval. Unlike people with a corrupt nature within them, these twelve will act in true righteousness according to the will of God, holy leaders of God. Each individual, possesses a Godly wisdom greater than that of Solomon. They will also provide the spiritual leadership and instruction needed for righteousness, judgments, mercy, and the grace needed by all mortals. They will likely be the teachers of the teachers, for the Jews (1Corinthians 15:42-49) and they will certainly maintain fellowship with Jesus throughout their time during the Millennium Age. (Luke 22:29-30)

Another Kingdom act to come will be the extensive work of rebuilding the ruined cities and infrastructure throughout Israel and the rest of the world. War, the massive earthquakes, and the damages done in the Tribulation have ruptured humanity's forward progress in modernity and had setback all societies in ways never experienced globally. The closest comparison to this kind of detrimental situation would be that of devastated war zones, but even war zones had surrounding nations beyond them, who could step in to help with recovery efforts, or simply be a resource to rely on for materials and aid. The Lord will be their resource and aid, He will command and the people will respond. *"To proclaim the acceptable year of the Lord, And the day of vengeance of our God; To comfort all who mourn, to console those who mourn in Zion, To give them beauty for ashes, The oil of joy for mourning, The garment of praise for the spirit of heaviness; That they may be called trees of righteousness, The planting of the Lord, that He may be glorified." And they shall rebuild the old ruins, they shall raise up the former desolations, And they shall repair the ruined cities, the desolations of many generations."* (Isaiah 61:2-4) Messiah will provide the means for the people of Israel to rebuild and re-populate even the ancient cities of Israel. *"Thus says the Lord God: "On the day that I cleanse you from all your iniquities, I will also enable you to dwell in the cities, and the ruins shall be rebuilt."* (Ezekiel 36:33) Messiah will not only begin the work of rebuilding the cities but He will also restructure the House of David, whether it be physically or spiritually or both is not clear, but it will occur at some point. *"On that day, I will raise up the tabernacle of David, which has fallen down, and repair its damages; I will raise up its ruins, and rebuild it as in the days of old."* (Amos 9:11)

The will of the people of Israel will change over time, and as communications begin to function again, a watching world will see that Jesus Messiah who has always been rejected by Jews is now among them again and is being accepted as their Messiah. The world will see Jewish hearts go from sorrow to singing and from suffering to rejoicing at the hand of their Lord and King. He will give them reasons to sing again.

"Sing, O' daughter Zion! Shout, O Israel! Be glad and rejoice with all your heart, O' daughter of Jerusalem! The Lord has taken away your judgments, He has cast out your enemy. The King of Israel, the Lord is in your midst; you shall see disaster no more. In that day it shall be said to Jerusalem: Do not fear; Zion, let not your hands be weak. The Lord your God is in your midst, The Mighty One, will save; He will rejoice over you with gladness, He will quiet you with His love, He will rejoice over you with singing." (Zephaniah 3:14-17)

Added note: The following verses are pieces to the Millennial story puzzle and contribute to the narrative message above: Psalm 2:5-12, Isaiah 9:6,7, Ezekiel 37:1-14, Ezekiel 11: 11-20, Joel 2:21-27, Ezekiel 18:30-32, Zechariah 10:1-11, Zechariah 14:6-9, Micah 4:4-7, Amos 9:14,15, Isaiah 59:6,17-21, Isaiah 10:20-23, Zephaniah 3:4,13-17, Zachariah 8:11-13, Zechariah 12:7-9, Amos 9:11,15, Ezekiel 36:4-8, 15-19, 22-38, Isaiah 43:9-12, Micah 4:4-7, Psalm 72:8-13, Psalm 45:6-9,14, Ezekiel 36:33-38, Isaiah 42:6-13, Ezekiel 21:25-27, Isaiah 60:12-14, Isaiah 11:3-5, Ezekiel 34:13-28, Isaiah 54:9-15, Isaiah 29:17-21, Jeremiah 31:31-34, Ezekiel 45:1-8, Ezekiel 48:1-28, Joel 3:18-21, Isaiah 1:24-30, Isaiah 54:3-5, Isaiah 61:4-9, Isaiah 49:8-26, Ezekiel 28:25,26, Isaiah 30:23-26, Isaiah 35:1,2) Zechariah 7:8-10

10.5 A Holy District And Temple

In the days of Moses when the physical Kingdom of God was being formed, the need for a place for Israel to meet God was addressed. Yahweh God, gave Moses precise instructions as to what to build and the people built it. The "Tabernacle," was a portable worship center made of materials readily at hand while the nation was wandering in the wilderness. It was a "Holy Place" dedicated to God. Within the Holy Place was a sectioned-off area which was called the "Most Holy." The Most Holy space was separated by a veil that was to remain closed. The "Ark of the Testimony of God" (Ark of the Covenant) and the "Mercy Seat" built with two cherubim angels that sat above the Ark, was placed within the Most Holy space. Once a year, the High Priest was allowed to enter into the Most Holy place. There God would communicate from the mercy seat to the priest about, *"everything which I give you in commandment to the children of Israel."* (Exodus 25:22) This physical tabernacle is a symbolic copy of the spiritual tabernacle, in the spiritual realm. A tabernacle in which Jesus, now gives to His people complete access to God. *"But Christ came as High Priest of the good things to come, with the greater and more perfect tabernacle not made with hands, that is not of this creation."* (Hebrews 9:11) Christ brings to us a spiritual tabernacle, a tabernacle that will take us into the New Heaven and the New Earth.

This earthly tabernacle which was made for the physical Kingdom of God was a temporary place for God's people to meet with Him.

Not so with the spiritual tabernacle in the spiritual Kingdom. We will live in the Father's house just as Jesus said. We will live with God just as we are told by the Apostle John who writes, *"And I heard a loud voice coming down from Heaven saying, "Behold, the tabernacle of God is with men, and He will dwell with them, and they shall be His people. God Himself will be with them and be their God."* (Revelation 21:3)

It is of note that God will live with us in eternity in a New Heaven and New Earth and be for us the tabernacle, He will not live in or have us live in a supernatural temple. The Apostle John points this out in the revelation given to him of the New Jerusalem, located in the New Heaven and the New Earth. John does not see some Heavenly temple structure but rather remarks that the Lord God Almighty and the Lamb are the Heavenly temple. (Revelation 21:22) The temple that Christ brings us to is that of Himself and His Father. We don't have a place to go to seek out God, we are already with Him. There will be more on this later.

In the days of King Solomon, the portable tabernacle of Moses day was replaced by a Temple building in Jerusalem. In that exchange, God made it clear to all that He does not need a temple and confirmed that with what Solomon says, *"But will God indeed dwell on the earth? Behold Heaven and the Heavens of Heaven cannot contain You. How much less this temple which I have built!"* (1 Kings 8:27) What the Lord, does agree to do, is to have this temple be for the name of the Lord God of Israel. Solomon, again says of God, *'You said, "My name shall be there."* (1 Kings 8:29) By committing to His name's sake, God, promises Israel, that He will bind His presence and thus His character with the Temple.

Solomon, also declares that he has built a place for the Ark of God, and when the Ark was brought into the temple and placed into the Most Holy, *"the cloud filled the house of the Lord, so that the priests could not continue ministering because of the cloud; for the glory of the Lord filled the house of the Lord."*(1 Kings 8:10) The Lord, validates His presence in the temple with the dark cloud, a manifested glory that traveled with Israel for all their years in the wilderness. It fills the temple at once when the Ark is put behind the veil of the Most Holy Place.

Later in their history, this glory was taken from Israel, and taken from the temple permanently and the Ark it seems, has disappeared from Earth. That event occurs after the seventy elders of Israel, bring their abominable worship practices involving other gods, into the temple of God, provoking God to remove the glory of the Lord, out from the threshold of the temple. (Ezekiel 8:5-18; Ezekiel 10:18, 19) Any and all religious syncretism is not acceptable in the sight of God, and will not be tolerated among His people, both in those days and in our days as well. God does not change.

This manifestation of glory from God has never returned to any temple built after it had left the temple of Solomon, that is until the millennial temple of the Messiah is built. (Ezekiel 43:1-7) In the days of the Millennial Kingdom, there will be a temple, a House of God, and it will be filled with the glory of God. In the early days of the Millennium, Messiah, will have a temple built on Mount Zion in Jerusalem. *"Thus says the Lord of hosts, saying: "Behold, the Man whose name is the BRANCH! From His place, He shall branch out, And He shall build the temple of the Lord; Yes, He shall build the temple of the Lord. He shall bear the glory, and shall sit and rule on His throne; So, He shall be a priest on His throne, And the counsel of peace shall be between them both."* (Zechariah 6:12-13)

The prophet Ezekiel speaks about a temple and sacrificial system that is in form much like that of the old covenant. He writes extensively about it in Ezekiel, chapters, 40-48.

It should not be understood to think that what Ezekiel writes about is the temple built in the days of Ezra and the Jews who returned from their exile back to Judah. One very clear reason that this piece fits in the millennial puzzle only is that the Scriptures tell us that "The Branch," Zechariah 6:12, 13, builds the temple in question, and no one in the Ezra writings can be identified as "The Branch."

Another mistaken thought would be that Ezekiel's prophetic instructions are about the temple that existed in Jesus' day. That temple has a "Most Holy Place" and a veiled curtain that separates it from the rest of that temple, which is torn in two. (Matthew 27:51) The temple that Ezekiel describes does not have a separation between the "Most Holy Place" and the rest of the sanctuary area. (Ezekiel 41:4) Again "The Branch" does not build that temple in Jesus' day, King Herod gets the credit.

Another option to be considered, but ruled out is that the temple Ezekiel is describing is that of the Tribulation. But there are serious doubts about that possibility as well. Should that be the temple that "The Branch" builds, why would God reject it? And why would God allow the Antichrist to defile it? In the book of Revelation, the Apostle John is called to use a measuring rod to measure up the temple that is to exist during the Tribulation. Yet, no further mention of that temple is recorded by John in the remainder of the book. (Revelation 11:1, 2) The Book of Daniel gives us additional pieces to the puzzle about God's response to that temple, stating that: *"He shall bring an end to sacrifice and offering,*

and on the wing of abominations shall be one who makes desolate."
(Daniel 9:27b)

The "He" in that verse is not about the "Little Horn" (the Antichrist) who covenants with Israel, and then defiles their temple. Rather, it refers to the Lord God who brings an end to the temple for their abominations. The abomination of building a temple of God, declaring that The Most Holy is present, then worshipping without the High Priest, the Lord Jesus Messiah. Without *"the BRANCH"* it is an insult to God. They will bring into this temple their abominable practices, possibly as an all-inclusive temple for all people to worship as they choose, all the while unrepentant and unreconciled with Messiah, their God and the God of their Fathers. Whoever builds the Tribulation temple has chosen to continue to ignore what the holy prophets of God have declared about who the builder of the temple will be and that only brings further judgment upon Israel. We can understand now why the Apostle John is silent about the temple after he is called to measure it up. Spiritually, in God's sight, that temple will not measure up, it is fit only for destruction, and that is exactly what will happen to it.

Could it be a temple description for the New Heaven and the New Earth? That idea has to be discarded as a possibility simply because there is no temple structure in the New Heaven and New Earth. (Revelation 21:22) A final failed option to consider is that the temple Ezekiel is describing is one that never gets built., That somehow God cancels it out as a possible existence. Such an idea conveniently eliminates many recognized concerns about having temple worship, animal sacrifice, Levites, Priests and Holy days in the Millennial Kingdom. However, the idea that God would reveal such an extensive vision to a prophet and then not bring it to fulfillment is completely foreign to God's character, and the proven ways He reveals Himself and His Master Plan. There is no plausible reason to deny that there will be a temple for the Millennial Kingdom.

The only logical conclusion to make when reading what the prophet Ezekiel wrote in chapters 40-48 is that he is prophesying about the Millennial Kingdom which includes a temple, and a worship system that is built and led by Jesus Messiah for the next 1,000 years. With the world's religions rendered powerless spiritually and the Church having been raptured up into Heaven. A new temple during the Millennial Age will satisfy many of the promises made to both Jews and Gentiles. It will advance the Master Plan of God towards a unification of all things under the subjection of Jesus Messiah, so "that God may be all in all."

In the vision from God, the prophet Ezekiel is shown the millennial temple, a very large structure like a small city, this temple will be over twice the size of Herod's temple. (Ezekiel 40:2-5) and in the vision, he was watching a man whose appearance was like bronze, who went about measuring up the temple just as the prophet records it so that he can describe it to the house of Israel, which he does do. (Ezekiel 40:5-42:20).

After this, God takes up the prophet, and He brings him into the inner court of the temple and brings him to the east gate. And there Ezekiel witnesses the glory of the Lord that comes in and fills the new temple. (Ezekiel 43:1-5) It will not be until this millennial temple is built, that the manifested glory of the Lord returns once again to validate His name's presence in a temple. In that glory, the Lord God will remain with His people and manifest His presence in the temple for the duration of the Millennium.

After Ezekiel observes in detail the temple to come, he is told to describe it to the house of Israel, that they may keep the whole design, but also, all of its ordinances, all of its forms, and, all its laws. *"Write it down in their sight, so they may perform them. This is the law of the temple: The whole area surrounding the mountaintop is most holy. Behold, this is the law of the temple."* (Ezekiel 43:11b, 12) Then the Lord proceeds to show Ezekiel the altar for offerings, the rooms for the grains, and the chambers to prepare the sacrifices and offerings. (Ezekiel 46:20) He shows the prophet, the roles of Levites and the Priests and introduces a new "Prince" of the Holy District. The prophecy describes what the rights and responsibilities are of the prince as the administrator of the Holy District. Ezekiel is shown how temple worship is to occur and which feasts and ordinances are to be observed during the Millennium.

It becomes clear to see, that in the Master Plan of God, the Lord is not only going to bring restoration to the nation of Israel and bring renewal to the physical Kingdom of God but also, resume temple worship under Jesus Messiah, who will serve as both King and High

Priest. And this is the way it will remain until the end of the Millennial Age.

"How will people worship for the next 1,000 years and how will that worship extend out into the Gentile nations of the world?" The Millennial people of Israel will worship in spirit and in truth. The writer of the Book of Hebrews agrees, by quoting the prophet Jeremiah. *"Behold the days are coming, says the Lord when I will make a new covenant with the house of Israel and with the house of Judah- not according to the covenant I made with their fathers in the day when I took them by the hand to lead them out of the land of Egypt; because they did not continue in My covenant, and I disregarded them, says the Lord. For this is the covenant that I will make with the house of Israel after those days, says the Lord: I will put my laws in their mind and write them on their hearts; and I will be their God, and they shall be my people. None of them shall teach their neighbor, and none his brother, saying 'Know the Lord,' for all shall know me from the least of them to the greatest of them. For I will be merciful to the unrighteous, and their sins and their lawless deeds I will remember no more."* (Hebrews 8:8-12)

As Jesus had taught, God is Spirit, and those who worship Him must worship Him in spirit and in truth. Worshipping in spirit and truth crosses the barriers of the Church and Israel. So, the people of the Millennium will worship the Lord, just as the Church before did, but also, they will worship ceremonially, in ways that will reflect their ancestral heritage of the children of Abraham, Isaac, and Jacob, at a new Temple.

The New Covenant that Christ gave to the Church, He will give to the people in the Millennium. Israel's previous Old Covenant, given by God to Moses was temporary, a physical covenant, a fleshly covenant, as explained in Hebrews chapters 7 and 9. However, this New Covenant will become to Israel, a new "Everlasting Covenant," that was ratified with the shed blood and resurrection of Jesus their Messiah, who is now among them and chooses to redeem them. The Everlasting Covenant will be for the redeemed of the Millennium. It is a spiritual covenant and it is a connection to the spiritual Kingdom of God, to a spiritual tabernacle, and to a new spiritual law, with a spiritual High Priest, just as the Church experienced, yet, *"Do we then make void the law through faith? Certainly not! On the contrary, we establish the law."* The Millennial redeemed will understand by faith that Jesus Messiah, had first appeared in the world, to make the payment for the sins of the world which He made complete by His sacrifice. And that He now appears a second time in the Millennium, apart from making the payment for sin, but for the salvation of sinners from the just penalty of the Law that leads people only to death, but now to live life by faith. (Hebrews 9:27, 28)

Concerning temple worship practices. The Scriptures are very clear about the obsolete and temporary nature of the Levitical laws, ordinances and temple worship. These do not have the power to redeem us. It is only in Christ's sacrifice which redeems those who have faith in Him. He cleanses us from all unrighteousness and our sins are removed from God's sight. As the writer of the Book of Hebrews quotes, *"Their sins and their lawless deeds I will remember no more." Now where there is remission of these, there is no longer an offering for sin."* (Hebrews 10:17, 18) Furthermore, the Apostle Paul writes. *"For the law of the Spirit of life in Christ Jesus has made me free from the law of sin and death. For what the law could not do in that it was weak through the flesh, God did by sending His own Son...* (Romans 8:2,3a)

The people of the Millennium will understand that they are free from the Old Covenant laws and have found liberty in their Messiah, who had become flesh, and humbled Himself even onto death. Having delivered them from their sins, redeeming all who put their faith in what He did for them on the cross. They become new creations in Messiah, they walk in the newness of a redeemed life, no longer slaves to sin, but subjects of the Messiah. This freedom will be prevalent throughout all the worship communities of Israel in the Millennial Kingdom; there is no other means to salvation.

Through their High Priest Messiah, the people of Israel will reconnect with their ancient heritage and the ways of worship to the God of their Fathers, by using temple ceremonies. Jesus Messiah, fulfills the Law and the Prophets rather than destroy them. (Matthew 5:17, 18) Temple activities will symbolically reveal the path to healing and reconciliation with the Lord their God. *'Son of man, describe the temple to the house of Israel, that they may be ashamed of their iniquities; and let them measure the pattern. And if they are ashamed of all they have done, make known to them the design and all its ordinances, all its forms and all its laws."* (Ezekiel 43:10, 11a) *"Now to the rebellious house of*

Israel, 'Thus says the Lord God: "O house of Israel, let us have no more of all your abominations. When you brought in foreigners, uncircumcised in heart and uncircumcised in the flesh, to be in my sanctuary to defile it- My house-and when you offered My food, the fat and the blood, then you broke My covenant because of all your abominations." (Ezekiel 44:6, 7)

This charge that the Lord makes against the House of Israel, picks up right where the Kingdom and the temple ended in the days of Ezekiel, under the old covenant. It is plausible to think that the Messiah will make this charge against those who served and worshipped falsely in the short-lived Tribulation temple as well. Messiah appears to make a similar charge against the Tribulation temple Levites, who went astray from the Lord, causing the house of Israel to fall into iniquity again. Messiah also praises those Levites, who kept to their duties in the priesthood, while the people continued in their iniquity and brought about the downfall of that temple. Those who will serve in the Millennial temple; both the Levites and Priests will have their roles assigned to them according to the will and law of the High Priest, the Messiah. Their Levitical genealogy, assignments, positions, and inheritance will be very much in line with that found in the original Levitical laws. (Ezekiel 44:10-31)

Additionally, it is in the plan of God to re-unite the whole House of Israel. The twelve tribes have at times rejected one another in the past, even warring with one another, having done unspeakable acts of violence to one another. Messiah will act to bring reconciliation on all fronts. *"He shall set up a banner for the nations, and will assemble the outcasts of Israel, and gather together the dispersed of Judah from the four corners of the earth. Also, the envy of Ephraim shall depart, and the adversaries of Judah shall be cut off; Ephraim shall not envy Judah, and Judah will not harass Ephraim."* (Isaiah 11:12,13) and *"In those days the house of Judah shall walk with the house of Israel, and they shall come together out of the land of the north to the land that I have given as an inheritance to your fathers."* (Jeremiah 3:18) Under the new law, all the tribes of Israel will provide equal resources and support for the millennial temple. The Millennial temple will be a tool to unify Israel. A spiritual unity between the "Whole of Israel" will be necessary having lived under two separate covenants, the old and new everlasting covenants, and for a very long time, under no covenant at all. Messiah will bring about Israel's unity in preparation for their future in the New Heavens and New Earth. A unity is to exist to form one "Whole" Israel that transcends tribes and all their generations, just as there is one "Universal" Church that transcends denominations and all its generations.

The Millennial Temple will not reinforce the separation between Jews and Gentiles as temples have done so in the past, rather, it will do just the opposite. It will bring oneness among the faithful, both Jews and Gentiles who are redeemed under one faith under one "Everlasting Covenant." that covenant reconciles all people to God through the sacrificial blood of the Lamb of God whom God raised up from the dead. (Hebrews 13:20, 21) It will serve as a place that will bring Jew and Gentile worshippers together in fellowship.

The Millennial temple has a place in the Master Plan of God to unite all things in the person of Messiah. *"Having made known to us the mystery of His will, according to His good pleasure which He purposed in Himself, that in the dispensation of the fullness of the times, He might gather together in one all things in Christ, both which are in Heaven and which are on the earth- in Him."* (Ephesians 1:9, 10)

Beyond the Temple, both Israelites and Gentiles will very likely gather together in various ways to worship the Savior in an environment of fellowship: devoting themselves to the Scriptures, singing hymns and spiritual songs, praying, and serving their Lord and King who is High Priest of the Kingdom of God, both in Heaven and on Earth. They will serve one another out of love for God and one another. They will be devoted to the mission of Messiah, to advance the spiritual Kingdom of God, and to add to its growth. They will be Spirit-led servants of Messiah, on a mission to redeem lost souls, both Jews and Gentiles, who have not come to know Jesus as their Savior, Lord, and King.

As for Temple worshipping, pilgrimages to Jerusalem by both Jews and Gentiles to participate in festivals and worship activities will resume during the Millennium. With only a few exceptions, there do not appear to be any laws that mandate required attendance, but people worldwide will come and the temple will be a house of prayer for all the nations. (Isaiah 56:6, 7, Jeremiah 3:16-17)

In the days of ancient Israel, the city of Jerusalem, the Levitical laws, the Offerings, Sacrifices, Priests and Levites, Feasts, and Assemblies, were elements that contributed to the experience of worshipping God together at His Temple. In its restoration, temple worship and all the same elements of the worship experience will be for all who are included in the Kingdom of God, both Jews and Gentiles.

In the Holy District, in Jerusalem, on Mount Zion, the new temple that Messiah "The Branch," builds, will reconnect remnant Israel to their ancient heritage, the Jews will join their forefathers as God's Kingdom people. As the High Priest, He will have them worship on temple grounds in ways much like their ancient Fathers worshipped. However, worship will have significant changes and a new purpose. When God makes things new once again, He makes them better than they were originally, resulting in greater glory to God. This will be true of the new Temple, and all its laws.

The Scriptures tell us that the first Tabernacle and its sacrificial system are symbolic. When the Levi's and Priests performed their services to God on behalf of themselves and the people, they were concerned only with food and drink offerings, ceremonial washings and fleshly ordinances imposed until the time of the reformation (Hebrews 9:6-10)

They were concerned with physical things that satisfied the law, but could not do anything to make a person complete in God's righteousness. Both the Tabernacle and Temple acts of worship were symbolic and did not manifest through the Holy Spirit, that a person has access to God. Rather, the Most Holy Place where Israel was to meet with God, remained off limits to all people, but once a year and then it was off limits to everyone but the priest. For the people to receive a cleansing atonement from God, they will have to gain access to God beyond all physical actions performed under the Law. King David relates to this very thing in Psalm, 51:1-17 which is about his sinful deeds in the Bathsheba-Uriah incident. David knew that there was no physical or symbolic fix to his condition. Rather, he confesses his sins and submits spiritually to God's will, by trusting in an imputed righteousness that can come only from the grace of God.

The believers find hope in God's offering, the one Lamb of God, a holy and pure sacrifice that will actually, not symbolically, take away their sins and redeem them to God. *"For the law, having a shadow of the good things to come, and not the very image of the things, can never with these same sacrifices which they offer continuously year by year, make those who approach perfect. For then would they not have ceased to be offered? For the worshippers, once purified, would have no more consciousness of sins. But in those sacrifices, there is a reminder of sins every year. For it is not possible that the blood of bulls and goats could take away sins."* (Hebrews 10:1-4) *"So Christ was offered once to bear the sins of many. To those who eagerly wait for Him, He will appear a second time, apart from sin, for salvation."* (Hebrews 9:28)

In the Millennium temple, Jesus Messiah will have the sacrificial ceremonies performed, but according to the new "law of the temple." *"Write down in their sight, so that they may keep its whole design and all its ordinances, and perform them. This is the law of the temple. The whole area surrounding the mountain top is most holy. Behold this is the law of the temple."* (Ezekiel 43:11b, 12) Temple worship practices will go through similar kinds of rituals that their ancient fathers did. Reconnecting them to their ancestor's faith, and the re-establishment of Israel as a Kingdom of Priests, but also, witnessing to all Gentile nations that salvation had come to the world a second time, not as a copy using bulls and sheep but by the precious blood of God's Lamb. (Hebrews 9:28) The old sacrificial system of worship that emphasized sin, death, and separation from God. But now, under the new law, the sacrificial ceremonies become a worship of remembrance of what once was, a need for redemption, and a new life possible only by the blood of God's Lamb, Jesus Messiah just as the Church does today.

From its beginning, the Church with bread and wine, symbolically eats the body and blood of Christ in what is known as the Lord's Supper. In this act of worship, the individual performs a self-examination and acknowledges what they have done to cause Jesus to die in their place. The whole Church is commanded by Jesus to do this in remembrance of Him, *"Proclaiming the Lord's death until He comes."* (1 Corinthians 11:17-26) In the Millennium Age, the Lord Jesus has come, and Israel will celebrate the Lord's return in the fulfillment of the promises made to their ancestors before them. Temple worship and ceremonies will be acts of worship in remembrance of the unpayable debt of sin that leads to death. But when that debt was paid with the sacrifice made by God's Lamb, once and for all time, that sacrifice turns to joy for all whom the debt is paid.

All the rituals and festivals such as the Passover, with its symbolic Seder meal will take on new meanings to Jews and Gentiles alike, in the fulfillment of what Jesus did for them. Under the law of Christ, liberty is guaranteed in their Savior's shed blood. The new temple laws command that the grim realities of their sins and the sacrificial acts of animal and grain offerings will be performed daily and also during all festivals. Symbolic demonstrative acts of sacrifices are performed under the new law as acts done in solemn remembrance of Him who knew no sin, but was offered up to God for the sins of the individual worshipper.

In the Millennial Kingdom, there will be significant differences in worship and service within the temple and beyond its walls, because the Son of God *"having been perfected, He became the author of salvation for all who obey Him, called by God as High Priest."* (Hebrews 5:9) As the Scriptures state, with a new High Priest comes a new priestly order and with that new order, a change in the covenant law. (Hebrews 7:12) But Jesus is not just the last High Priest forever. He is the only High Priest to be *"seated at the right hand of the throne of the Majesty in the Heavens. A minister of the sanctuary and of the true tabernacle which the Lord erected and not man."* (Hebrews 8:1, 2) Jesus is not only the High Priest in the earthly physical Kingdom of God but also in the spiritual Kingdom of God. And Jesus is also the High Priest of the true Tabernacle, not an earthly copy or symbol of it.

With a better covenant in place, changes in the restored physical Kingdom of God will take place just as the prophets have revealed. A significant change in temple worship will occur because of the new High Priest. Jesus will bring changes in the law for the purposes of bringing all things together as one in Christ. *"For on one hand, there is an annulling of the former commandment because of its weakness and unprofitableness, for the law made nothing perfect; on the other hand, there is the bringing in on a better hope, through which we draw near to God."* (Hebrews 7:18, 19)

One change that occurs is that the Law of Moses, which brought knowledge of sin and death according to fleshly commandments, will be replaced with a Law, according to the power of an endless life. For Millennial Jews, when they become redeemed with the righteousness of Messiah, they can claim what the Church has claimed for over 2,000 years. Having died to the Law of Moses, they now live under a new law, the law of the Spirit. *"But now we have been delivered from the law, having died to what we held by, so that we should serve in the newness of the Spirit and not in the oldness of the letter."* (Romans 7:6)

The sacrificial offerings continue but will change. There will remain the daily offering but not an evening offering, ceremonial offerings for Feasts, Sabbaths, New Moons and appointed seasons will take on new meaning under the everlasting covenant.

Another significant change is that the new "Most Holy Place" is no longer separated from the sanctuary by a very large veil. The space remains open at all times and accessible; its purpose is to be in remembrance for all of our separation from God, before Jesus was sacrificed. (Ezekiel 41; Matthew 27:51) *"Then it shall come to pass, when you are multiplied and increased in the land in those days,"* says the Lord, *"that they will say no more, 'The ark of the covenant of the Lord'. It shall not come to mind, nor shall they remember it, nor shall they visit it, nor shall it be made anymore. At that time Jerusalem shall be called the Throne of the Lord, and all the nations shall be gathered to it, to the name of the Lord, to Jerusalem. No more shall they follow the dictates of their evil hearts."* (Jeremiah 3:16-17) In the Most Holy Place, there will no longer be an Ark of the Testimony, or a Mercy Seat; the people of God have access to God and His will be known, through the Holy Spirit within them.

Lastly, in this temple, inside of the inner court, the throne of Messiah will have its place from which He reigns as King. (Ezekiel 43:7-7, Jeremiah 3:17) No King's palace, rather, a unifying of the offices, according to the Master Plan of God. Nothing further is mentioned of this, but it is likely to be in a supernatural form as is the King, rather than a purely a physical one.

In the Millennial Kingdom, there will exist a new dedicated parcel of land identified as the "Holy District;" this district is something that the previous Kingdom did not have, which added to the problems between the twelve tribes occurred because of it. This restored Kingdom eliminates those problems. The Holy District is approximately 20 square miles in area. At its center is the Holy City of Jerusalem. Everything within the Holy District is under the direct authority of the "Prince," whose role is to be the representative for all of Israel, as it pertains to activities that involve this district, Jerusalem, and the temple. (Ezekiel 45) The Levites and Temple Priests are to all live in this district and the Prince is to possess land on either side of the district

The prince is not the King, he is not the Lord Jesus and he is not a resurrected but demoted in rank, King David, he is a man who lives and dies. He is given land which is his possession until death. (Ezekiel 45:6-12) He has children and can give them an inheritance. (Ezekiel 46:16, 17) This prince is unlike princes of the past who ruled in Israel, they cannot take anyone else's land; Everyone's land is their family's inheritance. (Ezekiel 46:18)

How a man becomes the "Prince" is not revealed, but it is very probable that he is to be appointed by the Messiah, from the House of David. It would be mistaken to postulate that this "Prince" is King David himself. The question arises from Ezekiel 37:24, 25 and 34:23, 24 where Ezekiel states, that David will be king over them and shall be their prince forever. We should understand that this reference to David who is their shepherd and King, is the Son of David, Jesus Messiah. The idea of King David, being the "District Prince" is very forced and brings on confusion by the use of the word "Prince." That word has been applied in Scripture to anyone who has a role of responsibility and commitment to Israel. Even the angel Michael, is called "Prince," he is the great Prince that stands watch over the people found in Daniel chapter 10.

The Prince of the District is Israel's representative of all official temple activities, he has a prominent role in the worship ceremonies and the appointed feasts that occur in the Holy District. One such responsibility is to bring the animal, grain, and oil offerings for temple use. (Ezekiel 46:9-11) The prince will have a unique relationship with Messiah. Also, he will lead the people in worship at the temple on the Sabbath and New Moon festivals at the east gate of the inner court that is only open on those days. (Ezekiel 46:8-12) As the administrator, it is his responsibility to collect the animals, grains, and oil offerings from each of the eleven tribes of Israel, keeping them on his land until they are needed for daily sacrifices, feasts, and other assemblies. (Ezekiel 45:16, 17) It is the responsibility of the Prince to deliver the sacrifices to the Levites and Priests for an offering, (Ezekiel 45:21-25) where they are taken to chambers for preparation and then into the kitchens for boiling and baking. They are not prepared for an offering in the presence of the worshippers. (Ezekiel 46:19-20)

Unlike in the ancient days of Israel, in the days of the Millennial Kingdom, no one tribe will have control over Jerusalem and the Temple. And no one tribe will be responsible for providing all the needed offerings for the temple. The functions of the temple of God, its laws, and worship of the Lord God will not only be restored to what it was intended to be, but it will be made better!

The Millennial Temple will be the place where Israel can reconnect with their ancestor's faith in the Lord God and celebrate their liberty from the law through Jesus Messiah, who provides for them access into the spiritual Kingdom of God. At the temple, Jews can demonstrate to the nations, the wonder of who Jesus is and what He brings to all humanity. It is a place worthy to bear the name of God Almighty, a place where the word of God will be spoken in truth and in spirit for all to hear.

The Messianic Temple of God will serve as a beacon to all humanity. A light of hope and truth that will draw people to Holy God and to experience the joy of submission to Jesus their Savior and Lord. A temple where generations of people are called by His name to come from the four corners of the Earth for 1,000 years, to praise God and worship Messiah as Lord and King, all to the glory of God. '... *I will shake all nations, and they shall come to the Desire of All Nations, and I will fill this temple with glory,'* (Haggai 2:6, 7)

Added note: The following verses are pieces to the Millennial story puzzle and contribute to the narrative message above: Zechariah 1:16,17, Haggai 2:6-9, Zechariah 6:13, Ezekiel chapters 40-48, Isaiah 2:2-4, Zechariah 14:8-21, Psalm 24:7-10, Micah 4:2, Isaiah 56:1-7, Isaiah 28:16, Isaiah 29:17-21, Isaiah 51:17-23, Zechariah 8:1-9 Zechariah 2:3-10, Ezekiel 44:3, Psalm 46:4-11, Psalm 86:8-10, Zechariah 4:11-14, Malachi 2:5-9, Isaiah 59:9-21

CHAPTER 11:
The Worldwide Kingdom Of God

11.1 Gentile Reaction To An Unexpected King

Beyond the Promised Land there is another story to tell about the early days of the Millennial Age, it is a story told through the eyes of unredeemed Gentiles. A story lived out by the millions of people who survived the Tribulation and the wrath of God. These Gentiles have survived the war and violence of the "Six Seals," (Revelation 6:3-8) the "Trumpets," (Revelation 8, 9) and the "Bowls." (Revelation 16) They survived the plagues sent by God and they know and fear the Lamb. (Revelation 6:16) God's judgment has reduced the world's human population down to 2-3 billion survivors from the 8+ billion at the start of the Tribulation. There will be so many dead among all the disasters, that the bodies could not all be properly disposed of. *And at that day the slain of the Lord shall be from one end of the earth even to the other end of the earth. They shall not be lamented, or gathered, or buried; they shall become refuse on the ground.* (Jeremiah 25:33)

God has judged mankind and His wrath has fallen upon every people group, it is likely that every family on Earth will have witnessed tragic, even horrifying deaths of their loved ones and friends. *The nations have sunk down into the pit which they made; In the net which they hid, their own foot is caught. The Lord is known by the judgment He executes; The wicked is snared in the work of his own hands. Meditation, The wicked shall be turned into hell, And all the nations that forget God. For the needy will not always be forgotten; The expectation of the poor shall not perish forever. Arise, O Lord, do not let man prevail; Let the nations be judged in your sight. Put them in fear, O Lord, That the nations may know themselves to be but men.* (Psalms 9:15-20)

Terrified by what God has done to the people in their lives, they now look at their future with an expectation of only death. Most people will not know if the wrath of God has ended or if the supernatural killings have stopped. People who are not familiar with a Christian worldview and what the Scriptures teach will be overwhelmed with what has happened to them and their world. Reactions will be unpredictable, what people will do in response to the latest plague, lies and deceptions, or social breakdown, will only excel anarchy and generalized chaos. The only people who appear to have ever had an understanding about all that has happened were the Christians and they are the ones that went away with the Lamb, leaving everyone else, even loved ones, without a clue as to how to wake up from this seven-year long nightmare.

Many people will have heard and will continue to hear the testimonies of those who proclaim that the Lamb of God, who took the Christians away, is now the King of the Jews and their Messiah. This would add to the fear among many of these Gentiles for taking part in the oppression of those Jews, who now seem to have God on their side. They hear stories claiming that this Messiah from God will reign over all the world, he is going to be King of the world and be some kind of High Priest over all people who remain alive.

Although most people will come to humbly accept many things about the Lamb of God, they will not easily come to believe the testimonies that proclaim after all that he has done, that the Lamb is now interested in their salvation. That God is moved by love and has sent them a redeemer. *"Had these days not been shortened, no man would be saved, but for the sake of the elect those days were shortened."* (Matthew 24:21, 22)

Gentiles will not quickly accept that this new King loves them and that at one time many centuries ago, this same person died on a Roman cross for their sins. Nor accept that they may place their trust in Him for their salvation and acceptance by the God who has been trying to kill them. It's a hard sell to be sure. The testimonies of believers and the work of the Holy Spirit has been fruitful for the Kingdom of God during the Tribulation and the Holy Spirit will continue to draw condemned lives into righteousness and into the Kingdom of God. Early in the Millennium, people will come to faith in their Savior and place their trust in their Messiah. Many, many more will hold a strong hatred for Him and reject Him. They fear Him more than anything else; at best they hope He will leave them alone and many will likely desire to see Him destroyed if that were ever possible.

In those early days of the Millennium. Messiah will make additional enemies when Israel returns to the Promised Land. Those inhabitants of the land both the friendly and those sworn enemies of Israel, will either willingly leave, or by force give up the land God promised to Israel. It will all be re-distributed to the children of Abraham, Isaac, and Jacob.

Messiah will also put an end to the ruling governments and all political factions in those regional countries that are openly hostile to Israel, including Assyria. (Isaiah 14:24-27) Edom and Moab will likely be taken by force and brought into submission and the people of Ammon will be brought under subjection as well. (Isaiah 11:14) These countries today are Iran, Iraq, and Jordan. Egypt will be openly hostile to the Messiah and will become desolated, likely during the Tribulation, but not to their end as a nation; they too will come under subjection. (Joel 3:19) The decrees from God will go beyond the troubled Mideast throughout the entire world._ *"I will declare the decree: The Lord has said to Me, You are my Son, Today I have begotten you. Ask of me and I will give you the nations for your inheritance, and the ends of the earth for your possession. You shall break them with a rod of iron; you shall dash them to pieces like a potter's vessel."* (Psalm 2:7-9) It is likely that Messiah will bring all of the regional threats to Israel under subjection as a first order of business. Bring security and peace to Israel first and then move on to the rest of the world.

In the Gospel accounts, there are several prophetic parables that are clearly applicable to the rule of Jesus Messiah during the Millennial Kingdom. These parables reveal God's intentions for dealing with both His enemies and His servants at His return. Generally, those parables about His enemies are clear to point out that justice will be executed quickly and decisively. The rod of iron will be used without reserve on his enemies which will end in judgment. Those parables that are directed to His servants generally fall into one of these two types. One type of prophecy is a warning that Jesus gives to all of His servants that they must be prepared for His return as King. They are to know what His expectations of them are and to have been found doing them faithfully when He returns. All the servants will have their day before the King, and their work is examined, and their heart is exposed. Then the rewards and the punishments are handed out after each servant stands before Him.

The second type of prophetic parable reveals that when Messiah returns and establishes His rule over the nations, He will reveal to all that

He has both faithful and unfaithful servants under His rule. In those parables, the King will separate the two types of servants into groups. Jesus calls the faithful servants righteous and blessed. These servants have a place in the eternal Kingdom, and continue in service on behalf of the King, but have earned greater honor and responsibilities. The unfaithful servants are also examined, they are found out to be false servants who seek their own purposes and disobey their Lord in His absence; all the while living among the faithful and enjoying the benefits of all that their Master had provided for them. These self-serving consumers of God's goodness are punished and some are sentenced just as His enemies are.

In the parable found in Luke 19:11-27, its context appears to be in the early days of the Millennium Kingdom and for the land of Israel. Jesus makes a distinction between the coming king's servants and those citizens in the kingdom who are not the king's servants. In this parable, the citizens hated him and did not want him to reign over them. So, when the master or nobleman has completed his dealings with His servants, He turns his attention to those citizens in his kingdom and says, *"But bring here those enemies of mine, who did not want me to reign over them, and slay them before me."* (Luke 19:27) Justice in the Millennial Kingdom will be swift and to the point and it will be done with all righteousness and in-line with the Master Plan.

Without fuel for the fire, demonic activity that empowered the world's religions and governments will be missing after the experiences of the Tribulation. Much of the faith and the commitment to all worldly gods and their causes, will erode away quickly with the realization that there is but only one Lord God and He is to be feared. Yet the hostility and long-time hatred of many, for their ancient enemy Israel, will likely flare up in opposition to Messiah. The rightful King of kings and Lord of lords will be met with opposition from near and far, but the opposition will be powerless to resist the will of the Messiah. *"Behold, the nations are as a drop in a bucket, and are counted as small dust on the scales; look, He lifts up the isles as a very small thing."* (Isaiah 40:15)

The warnings will go out to the people of the world and their leaders. *"Now be wise, O kings; be instructed you judges of the earth. Serve the Lord with fear. And rejoice with trembling, Kiss the Son lest He be angry, and you perish in the way, when His wrath is kindled but a little, Blessed, are all those who put their trust in Him."* (Psalm 2:10-12) To what extent Messiah will use force, both natural and supernatural is not known. However, it is highly probable that He will supernaturally cause all forms of military weaponry to become useless against Him and against all people who submit to His authority and Kingdom. How this is done is not clear but it only makes sense. The Prophet Isaiah explains, *"Behold, I have made the blacksmith who blows the coals of fire, who brings forth an instrument for his work. And I have created the spoiler to destroy, no weapon formed against you shall prosper, and every tongue which rises against you in judgment you shall condemn. This is the heritage of the servants of the Lord, and their righteousness is from Me., says the Lord."* (Isaiah 54:16, 17)

In those early days of the Millennium, sin is still strong and the former ways to deal with your adversaries remain firm in the hearts of people. It is reasonable to think that the enemies of God and of Israel, will persist upon the Earth and that there will be attempted acts of rebellion and aggression opposed to Messiah and Israel but also upon one another. In a vacuum of social order, power struggles will emerge and violence will not be uncommon in many parts of the world.

But the King of kings who does not bear the rod of iron in vain will intervene and re-establish order, He will not fail in any way. The prophets write of the weapons and warfare of their day but the prophecy's application is for another time, one of modern weaponry and warfare. *"I will cut off the chariot from Ephraim and the horse from Jerusalem; the battle bow shall be cut off. He shall speak peace to the nations; His dominion shall be from sea to sea, And from the River to the ends of the earth."* (Zechariah 9:10) Messiah will disarm the country's militaries and converge upon them with offerings of peace, rather than war. Through His Kingdom, He will advance the Master Plan of God by subduing the nations and bring all things under His authority.

God has been angered over how the world has treated His people, Israel. Anti-Semitism will not be tolerated and it will be eliminated in the Millennial Kingdom. It is a hard lesson for many to learn, that the promises of God found in the Abrahamic Covenant are a reality. Those who bless the children of Abraham will be blessed and those who curse them will be cursed. *"Thus says the Lord, The Lord your God, who pleads the cause of His people: "See I have taken out of your hand the cup of trembling, the dregs of the cup of my fury; you shall no longer drink it. But I will put it in the hand of those who afflict you, who have said to you, 'Lie down, that I may walk all over you.' And you have laid your body like the ground, and as the street, for those who walk over."* (Isaiah 51:22, 23)

In the early days of the Millennium, people of the nations around the world will come to the realization that Jesus Messiah, the Lamb, whom for centuries was hated by the Jews and stood as enemies of His Gospel, are now are the object of His affections. He will have loved those who hate Him and seek to be reconciled with them. People of all nations will see that He offers peace and reconciliation for them as well. That He came not only to rule as the undisputed King over all the Earth but also for their welfare, calling them to come by faith into the Kingdom of God.

In the early days of the formation of the Kingdom, Messiah will summon all of the Earth's kings and rulers of the Gentile countries or regions who have not willingly subjected themselves to Him. They will be called to stand before Him, but many will not come willingly. Messiah will likely have angels bring them to Jerusalem and have them replaced with one of the "Immortals." He will then judge the non-compliant. *"It shall come to pass in that day that the Lord will punish on high the host of exalted ones, and the kings of the earth. They will be gathered together, as prisoners are gathered in the pit, and will be shut up in the prison; after many days they will be punished. The moon will be disgraced and the sun ashamed; for the Lord of hosts will reign on Mount Zion and in Jerusalem and before His elders gloriously."* (Isaiah 24:21-23)

In the early days of the Millennium, Messiah will judge Gentiles just as He did the Jews. He will apprehend and sentence those who stand against Him and His authority. This He will do in complete righteousness and justice, and publicly for all to see. He will validate who He is and reveal His character as the authority, as the Lord their God. Those kings and rulers who remain in power will have likely pledged their allegiance to their new King and will function as vassal states to the King of kings and His dominion.

In all the days of the Millennium Kingdom the "Immortals," will sit as judges in the Kingdom of God. (Revelation 20:4) These people are in their supernatural state of resurrected glory, they are immortal. These people are also incorruptible physically, mentally and morally and they are made to be in the likeness of their resurrected Lord. (1Corinthians 15:42-49) It is highly probable that they need nothing to sustain their supernatural bodies including food or sleep, they will serve without exhaustion or discomfort. They will spend their time here on the Earth doing the will of their Lord and King and co-rule over the Kingdom of God. They will likely be assigned to serve throughout the world, wherever the King directs them to serve and they will be recognized as priests of God and of Christ. (Revelation 20:6)

These Immortals are those who when martyred during the Tribulation, were not taken by Jesus to heaven, to the Father's house, rather they are taken to the very altar of God, *"that they should rest a little while longer, until both the number of their fellow servants and their brethren, who would be killed as they were, was completed."* (Revelation 6:9-11) only to return with Jesus after the God's judgments to co-rule in the Millennial Kingdom.

The Scriptures tell us very little about these co-rulers, but it is logical to think that these immortal people manifest for people everywhere, the resurrection power of Jesus Messiah. He will do so by returning people who were publicly martyred for their testimony for Jesus and the word of God alive, but changed into a new life, apart from sin and the curse of death. Resurrected in glory, each Immortal will be a living testimony far greater than what occurred when Lazarus was raised back to life from the dead, when many who had seen Lazarus believed upon Jesus and His words. (John 12:10-11) However, there is the possibility that they will not be easily recognized physically by other people, just as Jesus was at His resurrection.

These Immortals will most certainly be powerful instruments of God's glory to change the hearts and minds of those who live among them. They will without question stand out among the people and the place in which they are called to serve on their King's behalf. They will likely teach what Kingdom living is to be and bear witness to what the psalmist declares about Messiah, *"He shall judge the world in righteousness, And He shall administer judgment for the people in uprightness. The Lord will be a refuge for the oppressed, A refuge in times of trouble, And those who know your name will put their trust in you. For You, Lord, have not forsaken those who seek you.* " (Psalm 9:8-10)

In addition to the Immortals who will co-reign, over regions and countries with Messiah, the King will also appoint a large group of people that survive the Tribulation to be given governing authority to rule at the local level, over towns, villages, and cities. These are faithful believers in "The Way." Gentile servants who came to faith in Jesus after the Church was raptured away, they are now His Kingdom people and they will do the Kingdom work. Jesus speaks of these servant types in the parable found in Luke 19:15-19. During the Tribulation, these believers had chosen to live as devoted followers of Jesus and no doubt struggled daily to live out their faith, in a world in turmoil and persecution. Many of these believers of "The Way" are killed during the Tribulation, and others imprisoned or impoverished by society. Those servants who survive the Tribulation, understood and invested what they had been given, into a Kingdom that they were sure would come as soon as their King returned. These people will be appointed to positions of authority in that Kingdom, over towns, villages, and cities as Messiah sees fit just as the parable reveals.

Yet, as identified in the parable, the truly faithful who survive the Tribulation will be joined with the company of other people who are not true believers but only appear to be of The Way. They seek to gain from what they think is needed to benefit themselves and for their future, without regard for how they impact the lives of others. These false believers are convinced there is a God, how could they not, with all the supernatural events of the Tribulation? They feared the wrath of God and His Lamb, and they feared the Beast and his False Prophet, who would have killed everyone who turned to the Lamb for salvation. They saw their existence as life upon a balance beam. On one side, their need for survival requires that they get along with the world around them and get the things that benefit their lives in desperate times. On the other side, they understood that when the wrath of God ends, the believers in The Way will be on the winning side of the Tribulation and be a part of an eternal Kingdom and they want to be there to reap the benefits from it.

These unfaithful people will connect with The Way and fit in among the faithful, but never really become one of them. This is similar to the parables of finding tares among the wheat. It is also similar to the exodus event from Egypt, when a mixed multitude of people joined up with Moses and Israel, seeking to take advantage of God's provisions and live in a land of milk and honey along with all of their herds and wealth. (Exodus 12:38) But the unrighteous will not succeed, they will be found out to be faithless and separated from the faithful and judged while standing before Messiah.

When we look at parables that apply to the days of the Millennium Kingdom, we can start to connect the puzzle pieces of each. We begin to see a greater picture of how Jesus Messiah will form the physical Kingdom worldwide and the type of people He will place into positions of authority as His servants. We also picture how He will separate those who are the false and what can be expected to be done with each. In the very last parable found in the Gospel of Matthew, Chapter 25:14-45, Jesus is teaching His disciples about faithful and unfaithful servants that exist at the time of the Kingdom to come, these would be the Gentile people of The Way who survived the Tribulation. It is spoken in the context of a great discourse that starts in Chapter 24:1, which is about the time to come when He, the Son of Man, returns to the Earth to restore the Kingdom of God. After Jesus completes His telling of the parable, He continues with verse 31 to teach the disciples about what will actually occur and what will determine the value He places on them, what it is that makes them a faithful servant, and what makes them a worthless servant, it certainly won't be that they made more money for Him as in the talents of the parable.

Jesus explains that when He has come in glory and sits in the temple upon His throne of glory, He will send out the angels of Heaven to gather up all of these servants of The Way, from all the nations of the world, those who are alive at the time and bring them all to stand before His throne where He will sit in judgment as King. There He separates them as a shepherd would separate sheep from goats. (Matthew 25:31-32) This separation is determined by what they had done for other believers who were under persecution for their faith in Jesus, during the Tribulation.

Jesus takes it all very personally, saying, those people who were hungry, thirsty, naked, sick, and imprisoned are His "brethren." The compassion the righteous servants had shown to them is as if they had done it for Him personally. Jesus tells us that the righteous had done what they could to help other believers in need. They gave food, drink, and clothing, helped the sick, and provided strangers with a place to stay. In the context of living during the Tribulation, they would not allow the fear of persecution or threat of death to their own lives stop them from helping others. They absolutely trusted in the promises of God and should they die in their faith, they believed that they would enter into glory with Jesus. The King tells them that they are blessed for their righteousness and will inherit the eternal Kingdom prepared for them.

The unrighteous that are among "The Way" are separated to the left of the King. When they had an opportunity to help other believers, whom Jesus identifies as His "brethren," they chose to do absolutely nothing for them to help them in their peril. The Tribulation years were a fearful time when many people in all societies were persecuting and killing Jews and believers of The Way. They had done their best to avoid any personal risks associated with those who were being condemned and they were never the salt and light Jesus expected them to be. Concerned only for their own good, they never had the faith to act righteously and help God's people for fear of being seen as a sympathizer, or worse, accused of being one of them. The unrighteous are not going to inherit the eternal Kingdom of God because they were unwilling to count the cost that was required of His servants. In an act of justice, they will not be allowed to live in the Millennial Kingdom. All that they sought to gain at any cost, they ultimately lost in the end, just as Jesus had said in the parable, *"For everyone who has, more will be given, and he will have abundance; but from him who does not have, even what he has will be taken away."* (Matthew 25:29) These people will survive the Tribulation at any cost, yet in the presence of the King they will be exposed for what they are, tares among the wheat, worthless servants who are sent away from His presence and into the Lake of Fire.

At His return, all the cities are in varying degrees of ruin, governmental leadership, security from outside forces, safety within the community, and public services are all in disorder or missing completely. The task of rebuilding societies will be a long and difficult task. It is reasonable to think that the basics for living will be restored to many people and as soon as possible, through the efforts of the King and His Kingdom servants.

Water, food, shelter, and security will become the top priority for these new regional rulers. How much supernatural dispensation will be used to meet basic human needs can only be speculated on. But it would not be unreasonable to expect that the Messiah King will help people with basic needs which would help people to overcome their objections and hostilities towards the Kingdom. The people groups are called to be reconciled with their new King, who came to save them, or if not, then face His rod of iron. It is highly probable that these regional rulers and the Immortals will likely gain the services of those who become disciples of the Messiah. And in various capacities, they will also be joined by the unredeemed who simply want to be at peace with their new king and rebuild their society so that they may prosper in life once again.

It would be wrong thinking on our part as we look at this time in the Kingdom to believe that Messiah would direct His rulers to use basic needs such as food and water, as a weapon for gaining control and submission or, give preferential treatment or favor to those who claim a newfound faith in their King, as Lord. Kingdom-building tactics such as rewards and punishments will not be used in the physical Kingdom of God. This new Kingdom will not be governed by people who desire power and all that can go with it. Nor will they lord it over one another, like all the kingdoms of man before it, rather it will be a model of the servant-leader that Jesus spoke of. (Mark10: 42-44) The messages of grace and truth in the power of the Holy Spirit will be powerful enough to bring people into the Spiritual side of the Kingdom of God.

Life on Earth in the early days of the Millennium will be extremely difficult. Initially, there will easily be shortages of food, water, and shelter. People will become desperate. There will very likely be outbreaks of violence in every country. Chaos and anarchy will compete with the worldwide efforts to recover societies from the destruction caused by war and the Tribulation. Reforms made in the institutions of government and education at every level will be made as directed by the decrees that come from the King. These will be communicated and overseen by His co-rulers, regional rulers, and the local authorities.

Ethnic traditions and cultural ties to the world's religions will be required to be changed or ended. The days of demonic deception and satanic influence are over and any groups or organizations that adhere to them will be replaced or permanently closed. The light of the truth of God and His righteousness will free all people who want it and it is in their free will to choose. Neither, a united Israel nor a worldwide Kingdom of God on Earth will appear in one gigantic burst of glory that overcomes a sin-filled world. That was the kind of mistaken thinking of the Jews at Jesus' return to Jerusalem, this led Jesus to speak the words in Luke 19:11-27, the parable previously discussed.

Acceptance of the King and His decrees will be resisted and will take time to effectively become the norm in societies around the world. Acceptance of Messiah as King will have to be acknowledged, but will not be instantly embraced by the people and the lands that they live in. Over time, all of the world will embrace the Kingdom of God and will eventually adapt socially and culturally to its expectations and laws. The Master Plan of God to bring all things under the subjection of Messiah will continue to move forward toward the ultimate objective and like the child who helps Papa build a deck, the children of God will help their Lord and King build the physical Kingdom of God.

The spiritual Kingdom of God will continue to grow with people from around the world and from every generation that follows. Sin remains among all humanity, in every generation, but over time it is reasonable to see its effects diminish over time rather than grow. Not all people will be called to righteousness, their presence in the physical Kingdom of God does not assure their righteousness. Free will remains. All who have been called into the salvation in Jesus' righteousness have obtained an inheritance in their Heavenly Father's house. As time goes on from the first generation to the last generation of the Millennium Age, Messiah will continue to bring to fulfillment the promises of God, and bring to pass the messages spoken of by the prophets who wrote them. He will accomplish all of His earthly Kingdom plans, including His plans for each person who is ever born in the Millennial Age, just as He did in ages past. The nations of the Gentiles will bless Mt. Zion, and its King, their King. The glory of the Lord will be their light and many will come to worship the King of glory. They will proclaim the praises of the Lord and will ascend to the altar of God in the Temple and glorify Him. Seas of people from everywhere will bring gifts of thanksgiving, and they will bring honor to the Jews among them and enter into the temple for worship with them. And the prophecy of Isaiah, chapter 60:1-18 will come to pass.

Added note: The following verses are pieces to the Millennial story puzzle and contribute to the narrative message above: Ezekiel 39:21-29, Isaiah 2:1-6, Micah 4:1-7, Micah 5:4-7, Amos 9:11,12, Psalm 2:5-9, Ezekiel 36:33-38, Psalm 2:6-12, Psalm 9:7,10, Psalm 22:27-31, Psalm 25:14, Psalm 45:6,9, Psalm 67:1-7, Psalm 72:8-11, Micah 7:15-18, Isaiah 11:10, Isaiah 40:10-14, Isaiah 45:22-25, Isaiah 49:22,26, Ezekiel 28:25,26, Zechariah 8:20-23, Zechariah 9:9,10, Zechariah 14:16-20, Isaiah 2:2-4, Isaiah 43:10-12, Isaiah 60:10,11-14, Zechariah 10:10-12, Isaiah 35:5-10) Isaiah 40: 15-31, Psalm 9:15-20, Isaiah 50:10, Isaiah 45:2,23-25, Isaiah 56:5-7, Isaiah 54:16,17, Zephaniah 3:19,20, Zephaniah 2:3-12, Zechariah 14:6-10, Psalm 72:1-11, Psalm 47:1-9, Psalm 50:16,17), Psalm 86:8-13, Isaiah 16:5,

11.2 Messiah's Earthly Work Of Glory

At the baby Christ's birth the angels proclaimed, "Glory to God in the highest" but the glory of God the Son was diminished when eternity had entered into time and become like one of us. Living as the manifested image of God, He is found in the likeness of humanity, humbled in the flesh, fully man and yet fully God; it is a great mystery that only God could explain. Only the glory that was due to Him was diminished. When Jesus returns to build His Kingdom, He will come to His own once again and will accomplish all of His earthly work in undiminished glory.

The Scriptures reveal that Jesus is the fulfillment of God's prophetic promises, some at Jesus' birth and others at His return for the Millennium Age. In some of the prophetic messages that are quoted in the New Testament, we see that Jesus fulfills a portion of a prophecy the first time He walks among us and the remainder of the prophecy at His second. An example of this would be in Luke 4:18, 19 where Jesus speaks of His mission by quoting Isaiah 61:1-2. He doesn't claim the remainder of that prophecy, verses 3-11. He fulfills the remaining verses of prophecy during the Millennial Age when Jesus Messiah comes, not as a humble, sacrificing servant in the flesh, but as the glorified Lord, the conqueror of death, who has been appointed to reign over all the Earth He comes as Prophet, King and High Priest of God. He comes a second time to complete His Earthly work of glory!

What Jesus will do when He returns as the King is not a mystery, the Prophet Daniel is a witness to this in His visions, *"I was watching in the night visions, And behold, one like the Son of Man, Coming with the clouds of heaven! He came to the Ancient of Days, and they brought Him near before Him. Then to Him was given dominion and glory and a kingdom that all peoples, nations, and languages should serve Him. His dominion is an everlasting dominion. Which shall not pass away, and His kingdom the one, which shall not be destroyed."* (Daniel 7:13, 14) What Daniel witnesses is the Son of Mankind, coming to the Earth in a supernatural way for the purpose of taking everlasting dominion as King over the rest of Mankind whether they like it or not.

Daniel, 2:40-44 offers up another message about how at the end of the Beast's world rule; there will be ten kings in power over the world kingdoms. *"And in the days of these kings the God of heaven will set up a kingdom which will never be destroyed; and the kingdom shall not be left to other people; it shall break in pieces and consume all these, and it shall stand forever."* (Daniel 2:44) Jesus Messiah will return at the end of the Tribulation to destroy those ten kings who have come to Armageddon to make war against Him. (Revelation 19:19-21)

With the two advents of Jesus, the contrasts that bring Him unmatched glory are striking. At Jesus Christ's first coming, God the Son, lay hidden from the world. Born with humble beginnings, He came and saved His people from their sins. Born King of the Jews, His glory as God He willingly set aside, never holding the scepter of rule over them, rather dying at their hands, Yet He broke the power of death in undiminished resurrected glory. But now at His second coming, He comes in His Godly glory before all the world and He is revealed to be the Son of Mankind and manifests that He is still one of us, He will take the scepter, set up His Kingdom and rule as King of kings and Lord of lords, not only over the Jews but every tribe, nation, peoples and tongue. The prophecies of the Old Testament reveal details of both of these advents.

At His return, Messiah will begin His work to subdue all the physical kingdoms of the world and at the same time continue to expand the spiritual Kingdom. His physical Kingdom will have dominion over a sinful humanity for the next one thousand years. The Prophet Isaiah, identifies for us, Messiah's role and nature by which He will rule as King, one assigned to Him at the incarnation of His first coming. *"For born unto us a Child is born, and the government will be upon His shoulder. And His name will be called Wonderful, Counselor, Mighty God, Everlasting Father, and Prince of Peace. Of the increase of His government and peace there will be no end, upon the throne of David and over His kingdom, to order it and establish it with judgment and justice. The zeal of the Lord of hosts will perform this.* (Isaiah 9:6, 7) Jesus will bring upon humanity a predominate government that will bring peace over all the Earth. It will be utterly excellent, a marvelous kingdom. The King will be seen as the mighty God, who is valiant, strong, and unrestrained. An everlasting Father who can discipline anyone who is out of step with His decrees. King Jesus will be a wonderful counselor who will devise, guide, and bring the solutions needed to heal a broken world and to make it the best that it can be. He will reign as the authority of peace, which is freely given to those who align their will in submission to the authorities established from the throne of David.

The mystery of God when He appears again, will not be who Jesus is, or why He came, that will be self-evident. The mystery of God when He returns is; what will people behold when they are with Him in His resurrected glory? What will He be like, and how will He work with His people? A greater mystery to be considered is how this supernatural kingdom form will manifest itself in the physical world, in creation, in societies and institutions at all levels.

It becomes clear that when Jesus returns at the second coming, He immediately begins to establish His rule as King of kings and Lord of lords in the city of Jerusalem. These early days of the Millennium Age are the time for the "restoration" of the Kingdom of Israel. This is what the Apostles had asked Jesus about and were expecting to come, as recorded in Acts 1:6, 7. It is also described as the time of "regeneration" spoken of by Jesus. (Matthew 19:28) The city is in utter ruins from war and a great earthquake; it has been overrun by Gentiles from numerous nations and under Gentile control. Jerusalem is to be the capital city of the Kingdom of God and the home base for fulfilling the promises of God by executing the Abrahamic and Davidic covenants. Messiah will not only change Jerusalem but change the world's opinion of it, from the *"bloody city"* to, *"a praise in the earth"* (Isaiah 62:7) what it is that will make Jerusalem the most praised city on the Earth? It will change because of who it is that is there. *"The name of the city from that day shall be: THE LORD IS THERE."* (Ezekiel 48:35) Messiah will claim the city of God as His city, and rebuild it for His own. Jerusalem never at any time throughout its history, ever achieved the praise and glory so boldly proclaimed by these two prophets, but it will. (Zechariah 14:16-21, Micah 4:1-2) In the hands of Messiah, Jerusalem will rise up to become the greatest city to have ever existed or ever will exist on the face of this Earth. We can only imagine the splendor and majesty that people from all over the world will behold when they come to the city built by the Messiah to the glory of God.

The Scriptures tell us much of what Messiah will accomplish during the Millennium Age and very little about how He will go about accomplishing them. Consider the following: *"Now it shall come to pass in the latter days, that the mountain of the Lord's house shall be established on top of the mountains, and shall be exalted above the hills; and all nations shall flow to it. Many people shall come and say, "Come, and let us go up to the mountain of the Lord, to the house of the God of Jacob; He shall teach us His ways. And we shall walk in His paths." For out of Zion shall go forth the law, and the word of the Lord from Jerusalem. He shall judge between the nations, and rebuke many people; they shall beat their swords into plow shares, and their spears into pruning hooks; Nation shall not lift up sword against nation, neither shall they learn war anymore.* (Isaiah 2:2-4)

In just this one passage it is understood that during the Millennial Kingdom, Messiah, as the High Priest will establish temple worship in the city of Jerusalem and draw people from everywhere in some kind of pilgrimage, causing a continuous flow of Gentiles from all other countries to come to Jerusalem, to the temple, to hear the word of the true God. They will come by air, land, and sea. They will come and learn what it means to be among the spiritual Kingdom of God and many will enter into it. They come to learn from the Messiah, obey His laws, and follow in His ways. After the festivals, when a person leaves the temple grounds, they will depart by another gate from that which they had entered. Thereby, symbolically demonstrating that they are a new creation and now a changed person from when they first arrived, changed by the power of the Holy Spirit, validated by the presence of the "Prince" and all to the glory of God! (Ezekiel 46:9-11)

Messiah is the sovereign world ruler over the physical Kingdom of God for the duration of the Millennium. He will act as judge in all major disputes among people groups, and rebuke all nations that need it for failing to meet Kingdom expectations. For the first time in human history, there will be no wars anywhere. There will be world peace for nearly 1,000 years when the organized rebellions and Kingdom enemies are quickly subdued. Countries around the globe will likely disagree but will no longer need to fear one another; there will be no need to factor into their budget, money for national security. Peace among the nations will come through the end of violence by Messiah, who bears the rod of iron until voluntary submission becomes the norm and a new Kingdom world-view forms.

"And it shall come to pass that everyone who is left of all the nations which came against Jerusalem shall go up from year to year to worship the King, the Lord of hosts, and to keep the Feast of the Tabernacles. And it shall be that whichever of the families of the earth do not come up to Jerusalem to worship the King, the Lord of hosts, on them there shall be no rain. If the family of Egypt will not come up and enter in, they shall have no rain; they shall receive the plague with which the Lord strikes the nations who do not come up to the Feast of Tabernacles. This shall be the punishment of Egypt and the punishment of all the nations that do not come up to keep the Feast of the Tabernacles." (Zechariah 14:16-19)

Early in the Millennial Kingdom, getting the nations to participate in Kingdom-wide festivals in submission to the King, will likely require Messiah to use supernatural means as a consequence for not obeying their King. The Lord will require those nations who were once enemies of Israel, to send a delegation from every ethnic group to go to Jerusalem every year and participate with Israel in the seven-day festival at the temple, the Festival of Tabernacles. It is a harvest festival celebration, a convocation in which all of Israel stops work and comes to the temple for a time, to bring offerings and joyful worship to each participant. They will also live in a small tent or booth for the duration of the feast.

The Feast of Tabernacles will bring new meaning to those who attend it during the Millennial Kingdom. First, it is done as a reminder to every generation of Israel's deliverance from Pharaoh and Egypt as promised to Abraham, that God is a promise keeper. It will be a reminder of what Jesus did at His second coming, bringing Israel out of bondage and oppression back into the Promised Land, once again keeping the promises of God. It will be a reminder that Israel lived in small booths for forty years while in the wilderness, completely dependent upon God Almighty. Humbled submission is expected of everyone who attends the festival, even those nation's delegations. It will be a reminder for all who attend, that a time long ago, Jesus stood in the temple of His day, during the Feast of the Tabernacles and proclaimed to all, *"If anyone thirsts, let him come to me and drink. He who believes in me, as the Scripture has said, out of his heart will Flow Rivers of living water." But this He spoke concerning the Spirit, whom those believing in Him would receive; for the Holy Spirit was not yet given, because Jesus was not yet glorified."* (John 7:37, 39)

The Feast of Tabernacles and all other worship will point to Jesus. The promise of the Holy Spirit is for all who believed at His first coming but also in His second coming. The offer of the Holy Spirit is given to all who come to the temple seeking the truth and redemption from their sins. They find it by faith in Jesus, who died and rose again from the dead over 2000 years ago. He now stands before the nations, reigning as King of kings and Lord of lords, to the glory of God! Many pilgrims who seek to know the truth will find the Way and the Truth and the Life when they come to the temple festivals. Repentance and faith will cause many to leave the festival born into the spiritual Kingdom of God. For the people who meet Jesus and stand face to face with Him, speak with Him, or are touched by Him, they will react in awe of Him. Coming to understand that their King who stands before them is the same man that died on a Roman cross for them over 2000 years ago to save them from God's wrath. They will likely react much like the disciple Thomas did saying, *"my Lord and my God!"*

In lands where there is rebellion, there will be fear of judgment, fear of Messiah who will strike the nations that resist their new King and His sovereignty, Jesus may not come to them in an approachable form of a man, but as the unapproachable God that He is, causing great fear and reverence in those who live to witness to others about the experience. Rebellion and fear will pass away and give into willful submission and trust, even to love. Traditional enemies of the Kingdom, such as Egypt and Assyria, (part of Iran, Syria, Turkey, and Iraq) will eventually become closely associated with Israel and the Kingdom of Messiah. *"In that day Israel will be one of the three with Egypt and Assyria- a blessing in the midst of the land, whom the Lord of hosts shall bless, saying, "Blessed is Egypt My people, and Assyria the work of my hands, and Israel My inheritance."* (Isaiah 19:24, 25)

It is likely to become that all people groups that historically hated Israel and their faith will eventually find acceptance and reconciliation through the works and love of Messiah. It may take numerous generations for the prophetic statement made by the prophet Isaiah to come to pass, but it eventually will. And He will in all His time as King fulfill this prophecy. *"His delight is in the fear of the Lord, And He shall not judge by the sight of His eyes, Nor decide by the hearing of His ears, But with righteousness He shall judge the poor, And decide with equity for the meek of the earth; He shall strike the earth with the rod of His mouth, And with the breath of His lips He shall slay the wicked. Righteousness shall be the belt of His loins, and faithfulness the belt of His waist."* (Isaiah 11:3-5)

Messiah will restore the Kingdom of God on Earth which is built upon the ruins of its past judgments and death. Just as in the vision that He gave to His prophet, He will resurrect the dry dead bones of Israel and make it alive once again. (Ezekiel 37:11-14) to become the Kingdom of Priests God had called them to be back in the days of Moses, according to God's Master Plan.

That Messiah will not bear the rod of iron in vain is clear but, He will do so with compassion and mercy where it is possible, whenever possible that *"mercy triumphs over judgment."* (James 2:13) In His compassion He will love His enemies and call on His subjects to do the same. To forgive and accept one another in their preparation for the New

Heaven and New Earth. The godless people that lived through judgment He has come to save, He knows their name. Their bitterness, heartbreak, and separation from God. He knows the thoughts of their heart, both the good and the bad. He will know of and endure their sins as their High Priest. Holy God will live among sinners and their sins but not forever. His desire will be to give them new hearts of peace, a new hope, love, and redemption and to see them align their will freely to His own and become Children of God, to the glory of God!

There are many specific unanswered questions about when and where will He be physically present and at what times will He interact with people physically; He will not rule by limiting Himself to only a physical presence or rely on His physical presence or upon other people to rule either. However, it is clear from what the Scriptures have already revealed, that He will continue to use people in the work of the Kingdom, both the glorified resurrected people like the Immortals and the redeemed sinners such as those of "The Way" in the revealing of the elect people of God.

In the spiritual realm, the angels are under the authority of Messiah and will participate in His Kingdom work to some degree as the Scriptures have shown, but to what level and impact throughout the millennial centuries is not known. The angels can transfer great numbers of people from any place in the world and bring them to the King. (Matthew 25:31) or execute His judgments. What their role will be in the transcendence of the Kingdom of God from the Earth into the New Heaven and New Earth is unknown as well.

Much of the mystery of "How will Messiah do all those things that are in the Master Plan will be settled by the end of the Millennium Age and with that, an end to what is physical of the Kingdom of God will come. We can be sure that the worldly work of Messiah throughout every generation during the Millennium will bring great numbers of people into the eternal inheritance of God. And bring eternal "Glory to Messiah" for His worldwide Kingdom and the spiritual fruit of humanity God has raised up out of a would-be dead world. A Millennial harvest of people that will join the heavenly saints from all the ages that have been prepared for the New Heaven and New Earth to come with a Lord and King who has proven to be worthy of all honor, glory, and praise, forever. Amen!

Added note: The following verses are pieces to the Millennial story puzzle and contribute to the narrative message above: Ezekiel 28:25,26, Isaiah 2:1-6, Zechariah 14:6-9, Micah 7:18-20, Micah 4:1-4, Micah 5:4-7, Psalm 2:5-12, Ezekiel 36:6-11, Ezekiel 36:33-38, Isaiah 60:10,11, Isaiah 43:9-12, Zechariah 9:9,10, Psalm 9:7-10, Isaiah 40:15-31, Isaiah 41:21-29, Isaiah 49:3-13, Isaiah 55:1-13, Isaiah 60:12-18, Isaiah 17:2-8, Isaiah 54:16,17, Isaiah 31:8,9, Isaiah 28:16, Zephaniah 3::19,20, Isaiah 49:3-6, Psalm 89:20-23, Psalm 72:1-11, Psalm 51:18,19, Psalm 86:8-13, Psalm 98:1-3, Psalm 145:10-13, Isaiah 52:1-12, Isaiah 65:10-16, Jeremiah 31:38-40,

11.3 The Covenant Keeping God

By the end of the Millennial Age, the Abrahamic and Davidic covenants will have been fully executed. Keeping all of His promises is one of the objectives in God's Master Plan. Their fulfillment can be attributed to only Jesus Messiah, the Son of God, who is both the "Seed of Abraham" (Galatians 3:16) and the "Son of David." (Matthew 1:1)

In Genesis, chapter 12, God calls on Abram to put his trust in Him and in doing so, God will covenant with Abram; later changing the man's name to Abraham. In a brief review, the covenant has four components that God offers to Abraham, which He has promised will come true. These promises are: One: God would bless those who bless Abraham, and curse those who curse Abraham. This promise was later clarified to include all of Abraham's descendants. Two: In Abraham, all the families of the Earth shall be blessed. Abraham knew that salvation had come to his family but now He understands that it is the revealed plan of God to extend the family blessing to all families, who by faith, are made righteous before God. Three: God will make Abraham's name great through a great nation that originates with Abraham and Sarah. Four: God will give all the land which He shows to Abraham and it is to be his descendant's possession forever. These covenant promises are repeated by God in Genesis chapters 13, 17, and 22.

Abraham never saw any of these promises fulfilled. God did however, show him the land that will belong to his offspring and He gave Abraham and Sarah the heir of the promise, his son Isaac, who was miraculously born of Sarah in her old age. God did have Abraham experience the blessing and cursing of God that came upon those around him. Abraham lived the rest of his life in a relationship with God, living by faith in the hope given to him, believing God would keep His promises to their fullness. He lived a life of wandering as an alien in a foreign land that would one day belong to his children. Yet, he believed God had another place for Him to call home, a spiritual city in Heaven with God and with others. (Hebrews 11:13-16)

It is the "Seed" of Abraham, Jesus, who is promised to be the blessing to all the families of the Earth and will experience the fulfillment of those promises. He, *"has become a servant to the circumcision for the truth of God, to confirm the promises made to the fathers."* (Romans 15:8) Jesus came to be born of Israel for their benefit that He would validate the promises of God made to them and their fathers many hundreds of years ago. Jesus alone is the fulfiller of the covenants of God. None are left up to man to fulfill none are left to chance. As a result of His first coming Jesus becomes a blessing to all the families of the world, having accomplished for them something that they could never do on their own, that is to have access to God the Father. At the death of His Son, the Father tears the temple veil that separates God from man. He is now accessible to all who repent and put their trust in the Lamb of God, who died for their sins.

The greatest blessing of all has come down from Heaven and reached the most foundational social structure of humanity, the family. Blessed redemption has been in the Master Plan of God from the beginning and its most common form of transference is generationally through the family. In the Millennium, Jesus Messiah will likely see to it that at some point after His return, every family and person on the Earth in every generation will be given the opportunity to embrace the Gospel of salvation in fulfillment of the covenant promise given to Abraham.

There is also the promise of God, of a people who will be great and bring greatness to the name of Abraham around the world. The descendants of Israel are to be that great nation. Over the centuries, the Jews have made notable contributions to humanity and they have prospered through much of their history despite not having a homeland of their own. They have managed to survive as a people group while many of the ancient nations in their region did not. However, their survival and prosperity among other nations in other lands, and the contributions made to humanity by its individuals do not make for a nation of people or their country to be great. When reviewing their kingdom history even with their 80-plus years of a golden age, it is hard to think that this relatively small nation of people, who gained political control over a relatively small area of the world for a short period, as being named among the great nations of history, Israel does not even make the top ten list.

Rather, the people of Israel are as the Scriptures say, under a curse from God, and they have profaned His name before the Gentiles. The world has responded to the Jews with anti-Semitism, death at a massive scale, and nationalistic vows that calls for their complete eradication. Regardless of the forces behind the world's rejection and oppression. Israel clings to survive as a nation of people. Today, by God's gracious hand alone, many Jews live in their homeland once again, given to them through the political efforts of leaders of the world's empires.

The promise of a great nation and the promise of the land that God describes to Abraham will be fulfilled by the "Seed" of Abraham in the Millennial Kingdom, in the person of Jesus Messiah. To the delight of God, the Messiah will see to it that Israel will once again be married into the land given to them by God, according to the promises and the plan of God. *"For Zion's sake, I will not hold my peace, and for Jerusalem's sake, I will not rest, until her righteousness goes forth as brightness, and her salvation as a lamp that burns. The Gentiles shall see your righteousness, and all the kings your glory. You shall be called by a new name, which the mouth of the Lord will name. You shall be a crown of glory in the hand of the Lord. And a royal diadem, in the hand of your God. You shall no longer be termed Forsaken, nor shall your land any more be termed Desolate; But you shall be called Hephzibah and your land Beulah..."* (Isaiah 62:1-4)

The nation of Israel will one day be "great" in the eyes of the nations of the Earth because of Jesus Messiah, who is the source of all fulfillment for Israel, including the covenant promises that God made to Abraham. He will call on Israel to be a Kingdom of Priests once again and they will do the work of a worldwide priesthood. They will bring God to the people and the people to God. The hearts and minds of the Gentile world will change from disdain and hatred of the children of Israel because of

Messiah and their priestly ministry. It will be the first of its kind in world history, a uniquely great nation that is not achieved by war and conquest, but by love and the Spirit.

And the nations will respond, *"Thus says the Lord of hosts: People shall yet come, Inhabitants of many cities; the inhabitants of one city shall go to another, saying, "Let us continue to go and pray before the Lord, and seek the Lord of hosts. 'I myself will go also. "Yes, many peoples and strong nations, Shall come to seek the Lord of hosts in Jerusalem, and pray before the Lord.' Thus says the Lord of hosts: 'In those days ten men from every language of the nations shall grasp the sleeve of a Jewish man, saying, "Let us go with you. For we have heard that God is with you."* (Zechariah 8:20-23)

This kind of Gentile attraction has never occurred in Israel's history although there were instances of individuals such as the Queen of Sheba, who was drawn to Solomon and the temple, a foretaste of the things to come in the Millennium Kingdom.

The promises made to Israel include a reciprocal for nations and individuals, who receive God's blessings and cursing for their treatment of Israel. Accounts of people being blessed and cursed for their treatment of Abraham and his children are seen in history and accounts scattered throughout the Scriptures. One particular blessing and curse event that stands out in the Scriptures is the discourse and actions between Balaam, son of Beor who was a seer, and Balak, son of Zippor, the king of Moab, found in Numbers, 22- 24, and Joshua, 24:9,10 having been written for our edification. Balaam, as much as He desired to and would personally gain riches from, could not curse Israel for king Balak's gain but rather, blessed Israel.

The fulfillment of all the covenant promises God gave to Abraham have never been fully executed in ages past, it was never promised to be so. The promise of fulfillment does not reside in a time, but in the "Seed" to whom it was promised. Jesus Messiah will bring the Abrahamic Covenant to its finality by the end of the Millennial Kingdom, exactly as determined in the Master Plan of God.

King David, started going forward with his plans to build a temple for His God, like so many of the other kingdoms had for their gods. He wanted to honor the Lord by building a place for God to dwell among

His people. A beautifully designed and elaborate House of God that replaces the portable tabernacle made of skins, fabric, and tent poles. A tent-like structure that served as Israel's meeting place with God for hundreds of years, since the days of Moses and Aaron.

In response to David's desires, God tells David through the prophet Nathan, that He, and not David, decides what kind of a place God will meet with His people Israel. He not so subtly tells David, *"Moreover, I will appoint a place for my people Israel, and will plant them, that they may dwell in a place of their own and move no more; nor shall the sons of wickedness oppress them anymore, as previously...* (2 Samuel 7:10) here the Lord tells David a little bit about the future of Israel. For even in David's day, God is not yet done moving Israel around and the continual uprooting that comes from their enemies is not over. As said, God will in His own timing "plant" Israel in its final place and where His temple will be built. David doesn't know it, but that time when God finally plants Israel and ends their enemy's oppression, will be at the time of the Millennial Kingdom. (Psalm 14:7) Then God turns the tables on David and tells him that, God will build the House of David, and his kingdom and throne shall be established forever. (2 Samuel 7:11-17) This is the essence of the Davidic Covenant: That God has chosen the lineage of David to rule over the physical Kingdom of God. That Messiah, He is the Son of God and the Son of David, the one who will hold the office of High Priest, King, and Prophet, God's choice in the fulfillment of the covenant.

The people of Israel, in the days of Samuel, demanded that they have a man rule over them as their king rather than God, so God gave them what they always wanted, a human king. Israel's history tells us the consequences of what happens when men rule over the Physical Kingdom of God. It becomes clear to see, that sinful men are not capable of ruling over the Kingdom of God on Earth. The position as King over all the kingdoms of Earth is a position that Satan claims for himself. But in the Millennium Age, it will be revealed that only the Son of David, the Messiah can be King. The Davidic Covenant was set up by God, as the means to take rightful control over all the kingdoms of mankind that exist on Earth and to put an end to man's rebellion against Him. Starting with Israel, Messiah will bring them under His subjection, and in doing so He will advance the plan of God according to His will, *"Then comes the end, when He delivers the kingdom to God the Father, when He has put an end to all rule and all authority and power."* (1Corinthians 15:24) This is as required in the Master Plan of God and will be accomplished by the close of the Millennial Age.

In the days of the Millennium, Messiah the God/ Man, will restore the physical Kingdom of God, (Isaiah 9:1-7) to be an extension of His Spiritual Kingdom of God. (John 18:36, 37) With the two forms of His kingdom together, the transformation of the Kingdom of God in the New Heaven and New Earth enters into the last age. When the Millennium has ended and the transcendence of all that is redeemed from the Earth completed, Jesus Messiah will be King of the supernatural everlasting Kingdom of God. (2 Peter 1:11)

There will be a story to tell among the Millennial generations about how Jesus Messiah came to save sinners, (Hebrews 9:28) and renew the Kingdom of God. A story about Jews and Gentiles who come out of a world in judgment to become the first fruits of the great Kingdom of the Messiah and be redeemed for citizenship in a New Heaven and New Earth for the Glory of God.

Added note: The following verses are pieces to the Millennial story puzzle and contribute to the narrative message above: Micah 7:18-20, Ezekiel 37:24-28, Isaiah 2:2-4, Zechariah 8:20-23, Isaiah 45:22-25, Isaiah 11:10, Micah 4:2-7, Psalm 67:1-7, Psalm 22:27-31, Amos 9:11,12, Micah 4:1-4, Isaiah 42:6-13, Isaiah 49:8-13, Isaiah 55:1-13, Psalm 25:14, Ezekiel 36:22-28, Isaiah 28:16, Isaiah 44:6-8, Zephaniah 3:11-15, Isaiah 61:1-11, Jeremiah 33:14,21, 1 Chronicles 17:12-16, 1 Chronicles 16:17-36, 2 Chronicles 21:7, Psalm 89: 1-52, Ezekiel 16:60-62, 17-28, Isaiah 56:7,8, Zechariah 14:6, 17-21, Exodus 19:5,6, Isaiah 61:8-11, Psalm 105:6-11, Isaiah 66:18-21, Jeremiah 32:40,41,

11.4 Living In The Millennial Age

When the early days of the Millennium have transitioned into years, this Kingdom millennial story has to transition as well, from being a Scripture driven account of the future about God's creation into another kind of story. What life will be like during the 1000 years of the Millennium Age cannot be answered definitively. A thousand years is a long time for everyone but God. A lot can happen with humanity in a thousand years. We can look back at just the last one hundred years and we are amazed at how much the world has changed, look back three hundred years and it is hardly recognizable as being the same world. What can be expected of life five years into the Millennial Age, five hundred years into the Millennial Age, what life will be like after 999 years into the Millennial Kingdom? From what we already know we can put together pieces of the puzzle that will reasonably complete this Millennial Kingdom story.

God gives us very little in the way of prophecy about what life is like in the future and for good reason. This is because prophecy about life, society, and His creation, during the Millennium will become reality for those who are going to live in it. God does not reveal much about how people will live in the future. He did not allow prophecy to reveal to Abraham what living in Israeli societies will be like, or to Moses what life will be like during or after the Church Age and He does not allow prophecy about life or societies in the Millennial Age. However, God has revealed both, the Church Age and Millennial Age and their transition from the one into the other.

Once the Scriptures get beyond the early days of the Millennium, we hear absolutely nothing about the remainder of the Millennium years until it ends 1000 years later. (Revelation 20:7) We have no more Scripture-formed pieces to the puzzle left to put into place. However, we can still add to the millennial picture puzzle, by adding in pieces of what we have come to know about God, His character, and what we have learned about His Master Plan. We can also insert pieces of what we know about ourselves as the image of God, human nature, and the sinful failings of people. We can add to the puzzle, pieces of what we have come to know about Messiah and those who returned to the Earth with Him. We also add in the pieces about the impact made upon humanity when considering that Satan is no longer present on Earth and neither is a demonic force to deceive humanity into believing it is something other than what we have been created to be. We will endeavor to take all we have been given, and what we understand, and prepare a scenario that will essentially capture life in the Millennial Age and then after it.

Any Millennial scenario story, whether it be this story or another, must reconcile their story with two major points that do come out from the Scriptures. The first point: the Kingdom of God on Earth will not be a sinless utopia. As long as people are born on this Earth, sin, the consequences of sinning, free will, our limited knowledge of good and evil, and our inconsistent ability to judge the difference continues. Death will remain both physically and spiritually. Sin, and corruption that has plagued mankind since the Fall… the lust of the eyes, the lust of the flesh, and the pride of life, continue to live on in every generation born to mankind; until that time when the last generation of people ceases to exist on the Earth. The King who has conquered the grave and broke the chains of death will reign over a sinful world with a Kingdom of sinners and of the redeemed for 1000 years that is followed by a world that will pass away and take its sin and death with it. (Revelation 21:1-5)

The second point: A plausible explanation is required as to why after 1000 years of the Kingdom of God a final rebellion occurs and why it is connected to Satan's release. The explanation will need to be consistent with what God has already revealed in the Scriptures. The world-wide rebellion ends poorly for most of the inhabitants of the Earth, who are deceived by the devil himself. This rebellion will need to make sense when considering what the Kingdom of God will likely accomplish over 1000 years and also what Messiah the King will have meant to His subjects over the generations. We are told in the Scriptures that it is a final rebellion targeted toward the saints and the beloved city, those who are in support of the rebellion come to experience a fiery end. (Revelation 20:7-9) We can be sure that the release of Satan and the rebellion that follows has a purpose other than just harassing the saints of God but what is that purpose, must be explained in the story.

There are many questions about the mystery of the Millennial Age. We cannot respond to them with absolute confidence that the answers we come up with are always the correct ones. We can only attempt to come up with a story that is reasonable, logical, realistic in its context, and in keeping with what we know about human character, God's character, and His Master Plan. We can form a puzzle that seems to fit together the many pieces that give us a picture.

It is reasonable to look at the Millennial Age as three distinct time periods; The Early Years, the Middle Years, and the Pre-Rebellion

Years. Each period brings in its own unique factors that are essential to the Millennial Kingdom story.

The Early Years:

These are the years and the generations of people who survived the Tribulation. They experienced the supernatural and natural judgments of God. They saw the end of the Antichrist and His attempt at creating a world kingdom. They saw the rapture and the resurrection of the dead occur. These generations witnessed the Messiah's return to Earth and saw a New World Kingdom emerge from the ruins of man's wars and God's judgment. They witnessed the death of all the world's religions and the futility of worshipping any god but that of the Christians, who were taken from the Earth by whom they call the Lamb of God. And now He has returned and has gathered the people of Israel to Himself, He is Jesus Messiah.

Eventually, when the fear of additional judgments has passed, people will begin to see that Messiah is benevolent, and a source of sustenance and security. As the basics for civilized life return, most people will seek to rebuild their lives and their way of life much like it was before the judgments. A return to modernity, in all aspects of society will likely be the goal worldwide and this return will most likely be allowed under the authority of Messiah. The certainty of supernatural interventions by Messiah are very likely as well. Certainly, the Scriptures suggest that the land of Israel and its agricultural industry will prosper in ways that may be supernatural in order to get food grown, harvested, and distributed out to the nations who need it before they are fully self-sustaining once again. This restored world will be influenced by the presence of the supernatural work that God will do in the inanimate, animate, and angelic realms that will be experienced by humanity. The presence of the Immortals, the Temple, even the appearances of Messiah Himself will eventually become normal for people.

At first, fear and distrust of God and His Messiah will be commonplace and will be somewhat slow to change. Those who openly stood against the Kingdom of God or who continued to be openly hostile to the people of Israel will be dealt with quickly.

The groundwork for rebuilding the nations and countries of the Earth will certainly be laid early in the Millennium and likely be led by the Immortals and those of The Way, who have been appointed to co-rule and execute powers at all governing levels. They will oversee all Kingdom development activities that require approval under the authority of the King. These glorified saints will work with a public that rejected their testimonies as witnesses to the truth during the Tribulation, now they will be compelled to listen. It is very probable that under Messiah, supernatural activities will be kept to a minimum and not overtake or control the rebuilding of the broken world of mankind. It would be a mistake to think that people will be able to rest in their afflictions and watch God do His thing for them by making life bearable once again. Rather, the pattern shown by God is that He desires people to work with Him in doing His will and the rebuilding of societies would be included.

It is very likely that all societies will model a new way of life, a life that is productive and personably satisfying, a life with dignity and value for themselves; yet without harm or loss to others. Lifestyles where self-worth and benevolence towards others is balanced and socially accepted in a still sinful world. It is life for the redeemed and unredeemed together just as it is today with no outward advantages for the redeemed. As the Scriptures say, the rain falls onto the just and the unjust alike. It will be the individual's responsibility to govern their life as they wish to, according to their own free will. Making choices in life, knowing right from wrong and accept the consequences of their decisions. Life will be very difficult for the early generations until the basics for living day to day have been met and a new normal for daily life emerges.

Commerce will return with the reconstruction of roads, airports and buildings, jobs, and the traditional institutions of societies. Governments, at the local and national levels, will return or be established. All boundary disputes and sovereignty issues will be resolved to the satisfaction of the new worldwide Kingdom ruler. Each country will likely pay taxes to the Kingdom of God, to raise the funding needed for rebuilding a decimated world. The country's budgets and human resources normally used for military expansion and security, would likely be used for peace-building enterprises. Communications, Education, Health Care, and Public Safety would be high on the list of the rebuilding of societies, with their agendas groomed for life in the Kingdom of God. The Immortals and the believers in The Way will have such a major impact on the daily lives of many people, that they will become much like Jesus to people and mentors for life in the Kingdom.

Crime, at all levels, would also be present, but will not be accepted in societies as it has been in the past. All forms of sin and social vices will continue to be high in the early years, but it is reasonable to expect that they will experience sharp reductions as the world's societies respond to a new normal, under the authority of the King. The work of reconciling lost people who come out of the Tribulation will border on the impossible but for the power in God's love and mercy. How sweet will these words of Scripture sound to those who put their life in Messiah's hands, *"For if when we were enemies we were reconciled to God through the death of His Son, much more, having been reconciled, we shall be saved by His life? And not only that, but we also rejoice in God through our Lord Jesus Christ, through whom we have now received the reconciliation."* (Romans 5:10, 11) Messiah, the Immortals, and the Apostles will demonstrate to all the world to see what it means to, *"Love your enemies, do good to those who hate you, bless those who curse you, and pray for those who spitefully use. You."* (Luke 6:27, 28) The love of God to be given to those who He called to survive the Tribulation's judgments, will be the only possible reason for their future in the Kingdom of God. The perfect King, lovingly longsuffering in an imperfect Kingdom. But will they be willing to love Him in return without reservation?

The Middle Years:

The Middle Years would be those centuries and generations that run from a time when humanity has recovered from the disastrous effects of the Tribulation, up until the last years of the Millennium, those years of the last generations before Satan's return to the Earth. Scripturally, we know very little at all about these Middle Years. It will certainly be the longest period of the millennium. And it will without any doubt be the very best years in the history of Humankind, and the greatest years of the physical Kingdom of God for many reasons.

During the Middle Years, humanity will have recovered from the effects of world war and the Tribulation judgments. Cities and cultures will have been rebuilt and prospering along with the growing populations of the world. For hundreds of years, there will have been no wars or attempts to eradicate ethnic groups. Catastrophic fears will become a thing of the past, and security for all countries and people groups will be assured by Messiah the King.

Governments at all levels will serve the people and be monitored for corruption and held to the ruling standards under the authority of the Immortals. The supernatural nature of these holy people is there for all to see and experience. The public's familiarity with them will likely result in taking them for granted among the populations, as the miraculous becomes commonplace day after day and year after year generation after generation. Yet they will serve to be society's guard rails as sinful humanity moves forward towards its destiny. They will be deeply involved in the general welfare of all people in their region, striving to meet the needs of people, helping the helpless, and intentionally bringing people together in the public square in the towns and cities. They will likely work together with the local leadership and the faith community of Jews and Gentiles, working to bring sinful people into the faithful service of their Lord and King and co-workers in the Spiritual Kingdom.

Another factor that makes sense is that humanity will prosper in all areas of its societies because of the absence of Satan and the demonic influences upon people. Worldly religions will not resume and evil regimes and oppressive governments will not be empowered by the great deceiver of mankind. Sin alone will be mankind's enemy. It is their sinful nature that causes unredeemed people to be overcome by their temptations and fall into the slavery of sin. Sin will live on in every person born into the world and throughout all the years of the Millennium Kingdom.

During this period in time, the Abrahamic Covenant and Davidic Covenant will be in full execution mode. Messiah will have had the people of Israel fulfilling their call as a nation of priests and a light to the Gentile nations, God will bless families of the Earth and the Son of David will reign unchallenged as King. The power of the Holy Spirit will be moving among the redeemed, both Jews and Gentiles. He will form one people in one Lord, under one God of Heaven and Earth. Unity, rather than division, will be commonplace among the redeemed who participate in the Everlasting Covenant.

That is not to say that the faithful will live life in a sinful existence, problem-free. There will still be problems and issues, even among the redeemed people of God just as it is today. Yet, the removal of satanic and religious barriers that prevented people from coming into a saving faith in the past, has been removed, resulting in a flourishing gospel. It is very possible that during the Millennium Age, reconciliation with God will likely result in more people entering into the spiritual Kingdom of God than at any other time in world history. In the Middle Years, the Messiah is executing the Master Plan of God to the glory of God. *"Therefore, if anyone is in Christ, he is a new creation; old things have passed away; behold, all things have become new. Now all things are of God, who has reconciled us to Himself through Jesus Christ, and has given us the ministry of reconciliation, that is God was in Christ reconciling the world to Himself, not imputing their trespasses to them, and has committed to us the word of reconciliation."* (2 Corinthians 5:17-19)

The Pre-Rebellion Years

We should expect that during the 1000 years under the eternal King, there will occur some things that humanity has never experienced before. Possibly some things that humanity always dreamed about, but was never able to achieve on its own, no matter how hard societies tried. The desire to live in a utopian world, something that has been relegated to science fiction by most of us today.

The Millennial story scenario speaks about a world better than our own today and in every way imaginable. A world where humanity has been generally at peace with one another for hundreds of years. There hasn't been a war since before the Tribulation. No riots, racial division, political oppression, genocide or unchecked exploitation of the masses. By the end or near end of the Millennium, the Kingdom of God will have long ago subdued major hostilities, and the glory of the Kingdom of God on the Earth will bring humanity to the very apex of its glory. The world will be a place that has prospered beyond imagination because of the perfect King behind all that is good in the Kingdom of God.

Starvation, epidemics, and urban decay will have become a thing of the past. Over time, the environment will be in complete harmony with the progress of human development and growth. Creation will thrive in natural splendor, where people are finally performing as the good stewards of the creation that God originally called them to be. With no wars, reduced disease, famines, etc. it is possible that the human population will increase to its highest numbers ever. While social acceptance and concern for the welfare of all people will never be higher. The number of people redeemed by the work of the cross has never been greater.

Human achievements will likely be magnanimous in those 1000 years, with the aid of the supernatural presence that exists. Mankind will likely discover new energy sources, medicines, and cures for most chronic afflictions. The quality of life will blossom for all people worldwide rather than for just the fortunate. Suicides, drug abuse, and mental illnesses will become rare. Even the possibility that the average age of death will reach what was at one time a rarity among people. The need for Messiah to wield the rod of iron will likely have been idle for hundreds of years. However, the products of sin such as abuse, theft, assault, and all moral failures remain throughout all humanity but are subdued in every society and rejected by all cultures. Generations of people blaming the previous generations for their world's woes will end and become springboards of confidence in believing that better days are ahead.

Humanity will have reached the pinnacle of its glory because of life in the Kingdom of God and with the King of Glory. Here on Earth under His authority and power, Messiah allows, even inspires the sons of Adam to achieve all that it possibly can achieve for good and He is pleased to do so. Yet, there remains the specter of sin for all to see and its grip upon humanity, who is always willing to accept it. As wondrous and as humanly satisfying life on Earth will become, the effects of sin and death continue to contaminate the human condition. Knowing that there is a God and that He reigns as their King does not overcome sin, but like the Mosaic Law of old, that only tempts the heart.

In every person of every generation born of Adam's race, the unredeemed heart and mind live in silent rebellion to God, and seeks for ways to be heard. In the Millennial Kingdom, great numbers of people will love their Lord and King and be in complete submission to Him, according to the Master Plan of God. However, the majority will listen to the corrupted nature within them because people love the darkness rather than the light. In their various forms, nations, and countries will have "tolerated" being in submission to the King. All people will be humbled before the Almighty King, but not all are willful subjects of His. Certainly, the Messiah knows these things about them, just as He knew the heart of the disciple named Judas. Many group leaders who are not of the administration of Messiah, would choose to be the sovereign ruler over their own people, rather than be accountable to the Kingdom of Messiah. Strong desires to do what is right in their own eyes will run deep, even if prohibited by their King. The seeds of their discontentment continue to sprout up out of free will. So is the nature of sin in the last days of the Millennium.

For all the lofty aspirations that mankind can achieve, each person will pay the wages for their sin. Although sin in its societies will not run with an evil abandon that makes life on Earth a living hell, but it will still lead the evil life into hell. These are people who have not entered into the spiritual Kingdom of God, doing life in the physical Kingdom of God will not eternally save people from hell. Living the good life in a near-utopic world will cause many people to seek nothing more from God. As long as there is a Son of Adam on the Earth alive and breathing, the lusts of the eyes, the lust of the flesh, and the pride of life, will be alive and well by the end of the Millennium.

PART THREE: LAST THINGS

CHAPTER 12:
The Last Rebellion

When reading the Book of Revelation, chapter 20, we can understand that Messiah has Satan incarcerated in the bottomless pit (a supernatural abyss) and then He reigns as the King of kings and Lord of lords over all the Earth.

The story goes that healing and recovery from the Tribulation occurs and eventually over time, things are looking pretty good for the Earth and its inhabitants. The world will likely find itself in the best place ever in its history, due to Messiah and His Kingdom. But then something shocking and perplexing at the same time happens. After 1000 years of Messiah's reign in the physical Kingdom of God comes to an end, He takes what is redeemed with Him into the supernatural realm in preparation for the Eternal Kingdom. (Revelation 20:2-4) Then, Satan is released upon the Earth to once again to deceive the nations of the world. After a short period of time, Gog and Magog rise up to lead the nations of the world in rebellion against God. The nations of the world gather together for battle in such vast numbers, that they surround Jerusalem and those faithful people who have encamped around the city.

This is the last rebellion of mankind and for Satan as well.

"Now when the thousand years have expired, Satan will be released from his prison and will go out and deceive the nations which are in the four corners of the earth., Gog and Magog, to gather them together to battle, whose number is as the sand of the sea. They went up on the breadth of the earth and surrounded the camp of the saints and the beloved city. And fire came down from God out of Heaven and devoured them. The devil who deceived them was cast into the lake of fire and brimstone where the beast and the false prophet are. And they will be tormented day and night forever and ever." (Revelation 20:7-10)

To best understand this portion of the story we must remember that it has always been in the Master Plan of God to have our physical realm be temporary, there are several Scripture references that make this clear. We are told that one day this world will pass away and that a new supernatural realm will be created, a New Heaven and New Earth.

(Revelation 21:1, 2) *"But the Heavens and the earth which are now preserved by the same word, are reserved for fire until the Day of Judgment and perdition of ungodly men. But beloved, do not forget this one thing, with the Lord one day is as a thousand years and a thousand years as one day. The Lord is not slack concerning His promise, as some count slackness, but He is long suffering towards us, not willing that any should perish but that all should come to repentance. But the day of the Lord will come as a thief in the night, in which the Heavens will pass away with a great noise, and the elements will melt with fervent heat; both the earth and the works that are in it will burn up."* (2 Peter 3:7-10) The events in Revelation chapter 20: 9-11 and the events in 2 Peter 3:7-10 describe the end to come.

From the days of Adam until the start of the Millennium Age, nobody had any idea what year the end of the world would come. For as many who predicted the end, only proved that they were wrong. People who live during the Millennial Age will know from Revelation, Chapter 20 that God has set an expiration date for the end of the physical Kingdom of God. It is to remain on the Earth for 1000 years, from start to expiration. The only question about its end on Earth will be the month and day. In the early days of the Millennial Kingdom, people will likely give little to no thought about this end to a Kingdom that has just formed; or about the end of the world, they had just gone through something much like it. Yet, concerns about the end of both will steadily grow over the generations. Certainly, the generations of people who are living out the last few years of the Millennial Kingdom will be greatly impacted by the ramifications. They will have to come to terms with the reality of a world that will no longer have the supreme governmental structure that they have had throughout the centuries. Kingdom authority, with the power in place to preserve social order and life as they know it. This will become terrifying to some, not believed by some, and a call to others to make preparations to take control and preserve worldwide order after the Messiah and His Kingdom's departure. As terrifying as these challenges are, a greater terror is to come upon all the nations of the Earth, the end of the world.

After 1000 years expire, the Kingdom will no longer be on Earth and Satan will be released "for a little while." (Revelation 20:1-3) This "little while" is an undisclosed amount of time between the end of the

Kingdom and the end to the Earth. (Revelation 20:7, 11, Revelation 21:1) With the expiration of the Millennial Age, Messiah, would have demonstrated for 1000 years that He has been the righteous and just King of kings and Lord of lords on Earth, just as He is in Heaven, and will be forever King in the New Heaven and New Earth. He has validated that He is the Alpha and Omega, the Beginning and the End, even when the created order of God is at its best and when it was at its worst. (Revelation 22:13) He will have put all kingdoms, all Earthly rule, and authorities under His subjection, according to the Master Plan of God. (1 Corinthians 15: 24, 25) During His reign on the Earth, Messiah will have completed the execution of the Abrahamic and Davidic covenants for humanity. For nearly 1000 years He will have successfully prevented the cancerous effects of sinful human desires that when fully conceived give birth to the destructive activities of war, institutional corruption, governmental tyranny, and social decay.

God has directed the course of humanity from its start to its destiny without ever taking their free will away from them. Allowing fallen humanity in the last 1000 years to rise to utopic heights while they exist within the earthly Kingdom of God. Every person ever born into this earthly Kingdom of God is burdened down with a sin nature within that must be overcome. Corrupted humanity will have advanced in its own glory as far as it can go as the image of God. At the apex of its achievement, humanity will demonstrate to all who are in Heaven and on Earth the inability to become fully complete in His likeness. And although humanity has always strived to be a god of its own making, it never can be. Now the time has come for it to end, now the work of the Messiah on Earth is completed, to be followed by the time when the physical to be replaced with a supernatural world. God has restored the world, He has made it good, better than it has ever been since the Garden of Eden but collective humanity has not changed since the Fall. Not even after everything that God could do for them has been done. If left unchanged, there will be no glory for God in that.

When this end comes, aspects of the physical Kingdom of God will complete its transcendence from the physical into the supernatural realm. Certainly, the righteous will become incorruptible, made into the likeness of Messiah, and leave with Him., but also, animate things, and inanimate things that God will redeem from this physical creation, will become new once again in the New Heaven and New Earth. Yet He will leave some saints to remain behind up until the end for a special purpose. (Revelation 20:9)

How Messiah leaves, details of how the Kingdom leaves, and who will leave with Him remain a mystery but leave it will. Jesus will not likely leave the Earth without giving instructions for facing their time of testing. Either through the Scriptures or possibly a new personal message from Jesus, given to a world that is fearful for its future and confused about His leaving it. What He might say to this world is not known, but He will likely speak with compassion and call on all people on the Earth to seek His Father's Heavenly Kingdom and leave with Him to live in it eternally. *"But, seek first the kingdom of God and His righteousness, and all these things shall be added on to you. Therefore, do not worry about tomorrow, for tomorrow will have worry about its own things. Sufficient for the day is its own trouble."* (Matthew 7:33, 34) He will make it clear that now is the time for salvation, now is the time to choose life in His name. His will likely offer messages of hope and peace for those who choose to forsake their world and the things of this world and choose to trust Him as the Lord of life. *"Peace, I leave with you, my peace I give to you; not as the world gives do I give to you. Let your heart not be troubled, neither let it be afraid."* (John 14:27) His messages will also demand that every person who is alive to make their choice, put your life in His hands or deny His offer.

How will people respond knowing that the end of the Millennial Kingdom and the end of the world will come in their lifetime, or the lifetime of their children or grandchildren? Those people who live near the end will see their life's clock ticking away the months and years. At some point, as the days look to be winding down to the last generations, people will be forced to face their end in this world. Life will take on a new perspective and with it, an urgency for every person to respond to the situation. For many who refuse to believe it, the end will come catching them unprepared, *"as a thief in the night"* (2 Peter 3:10)

This will be a time when these ancient words of the apostle Peter will speak once more to every individual who cares to hear from God about the end to come. *"Therefore, since all these things will be dissolved, what manner of persons ought you to be in holy conduct and godliness, looking for and hastening the coming day of God, because of which the Heavens will be dissolved, being on fire, and the elements will melt with fervent heat?"* (2 Peter 3:11, 12) It is God's word that calls out to all people for a response. "Will you choose to live in righteous faith, willingly, giving up this life, in this world, and all that it offers, in exchange for a life in a New Heaven and New Earth with me?" It is reasonable to think that the call to salvation is responded too much like it was responded to in the days when Jesus first walked among people.

Despite the miracles and words of Jesus that had to come from God, most people reject the gift of salvation. Not because they believed in another god, not because they thought that they were already righteous, but because the sin of the human heart insists on its own way and not God's way. They will reject His offer because they love this world and the things of this world. Corrupted hearts that love darkness rather than the light of redemption.

Unfortunately, most of the unsaved world will not respond to Peter's exhortation well. As pointed out previously, people will likely be living in a world that is at the apex of human achievement and glory, people who are not willing to become overcomers of the world. It is reasonable for us to think that most people who live in this time, will not be willing to give it all up. That kind of thinking among people will grow stronger as the world approaches the *"coming day of God"* and with it, the end of Earth. People will begin to reveal that they really do prefer their world and the things of this world over God. They will prefer to have life their way, rather than God's way! In their heart of hearts, they choose their own corrupted free will over what God graciously offers them. In the end, they do not want God to be all in all as in the final outcome to God's Master Plan, no, they want all they can get to be theirs for as long as they can hold on to it!

While the Kingdom still remains on the Earth, those who received a new heart and spirit, will heed the message of Peter and prepare for the end of the world. They will respond in righteousness and conduct their lives in holiness. Many from around the world will go to Jerusalem to gather with their fellow saints for the end, trusting God with the results. There is very likely to be a renewed sense of urgency among the redeemed to reach out to others with the saving faith in Jesus Messiah, to those who face an uncertain future. Their efforts will be the last acts of the Abrahamic Covenant promises to be kept, of which after there is no more blessings and no more grace from God. Unbelievers at that time will likely look with distain at the gift of salvation by faith through grace as nothing more than a form of spiritual blackmail, where we must choose to "Turn or Burn" along with the world. They may even twist the Scriptures to obtain a favorable outcome, they may claim additional revelations from God, or deceptions from Satan when he returns. In Revelation, Chapters 21 and 22. In John 22, the apostle writes a warning to everyone, saying, *"If anyone adds to these things, God will add to him the plagues that are written in this book; and if anyone takes away from the words of the book of this prophecy, God shall take away his part from the Book of Life, from the holy city, and from the things that are written in this book."* (Revelation 22:19). Adding or removing any prophecy from any of God's words is a clear warning for all generations, including those of the Millennium Age, but John is specifically talking about the book of Revelation.

The generations at the end of the Millennium will reveal that in spite of every good thing that God has done for them, and the bountiful blessings of Messiah's love given to them, they will defy His will and reject His love, and turn away from His offers for life, just as their ancestors did in the days of their Tribulation.

With the transcendence of the Kingdom from the Earth complete, people's thoughts will likely begin to develop into attitudes, a growing consensus among people develops on what they believe to be true and right, and these beliefs eventually lead people to express their displeasure and self-justification. "Humanity has advanced so much, but now God wants to stop us from going any further, why, what is God afraid of?" "Is God really going to end the world and kill us all, even the children?" "We don't want to die, and we won't just sit still and watch our children and their future, perish with them." "This is just not fair of God!" "We aren't bad people who deserve this!" "It would be evil of God to destroy this world, the plants, animals, and all its beauty and glory." "I don't think He will do that, it's just a test of some kind!" With a growing rebelliousness that spreads across all nations of the world, their utopian levels of living begin to show stress cracks in the social fabric. A new worldview emerges for the first time in one thousand years, one that is opposed to God. And with that new worldview, a new world leader eventually emerges. Not Satan himself, but Gog of Magog. However, humanity at this moment of revelation once again finds itself agreeing with Satan and rejecting God before all the witness of Heaven. Once again as in the days of the Tribulation, humanity's love for God will grow cold.

With the last of the 1000 years expired, Jesus and the Kingdom of God transcended the physical and into the eternal realm, taking with Him all things of the creation to be redeemed. Leaving behind the saints in Jerusalem to remain as His earthly witnesses to the truth to come. Then Satan is released back into the world and he, *"will go out to deceive the nations which are in the four corners of the world, Gog and Magog"* (Revelation 20:7, 8) Satan has had a thousand years to think about what he has done to humanity and about his failure to stop the Kingdom of God from coming. He had time to think about how Messiah took the scepter of rule over mankind out of his grip. He has had time to think twice about ever approaching mankind again, but Satan has the free will to do as he pleases and he is pleased to do evil.

When the Serpent is released from his prison, he engages humanity and begins the deception once again. Like the days of Adam and Eve, Satan will again convince people that if they choose to do things their way, *"their eyes will be opened and be like God."* (Genesis 3:4) And once again, even after the judgments of the Tribulation, even after God's Word has told them what will happen in the end, the sinful nature of people will choose self-deception and the lies of Satan over God's Word. Satan will help much of mankind become convinced that this world they have rebuilt is theirs as much as it is God's. They may come to believe that they have outgrown the need for Messiah, that they can do just as well without His Kingdom They choose to be in command of their own destiny, one without God's interference.

Satan will cast doubts and fear into people about God and His plan for ending the physical realm, ending all the good mankind has done, and ending their lives and the lives of their loved ones. Belief in God's Word and trust in Messiah's promises will quickly waver to such great extents that all the unredeemed of mankind will once again join Satan in rebellion against God. Blame for their crisis will be pointed one last time at the saints in the land of Israel who God left behind. Instead of joining the world in their rage, these saints live in holy conduct and are looking for the end of days, trusting that they are in God's hand.

With the expiration of the physical Kingdom, most believers are able to leave the Earth. They transform into their immortal glorified state and leave their corrupt nature behind, but we are not told how. It seems reasonable for the remaining witnesses of God that stay, to go to Israel and gather in Jerusalem, causing an overflow of people who will encamp around its perimeter. (Revelation 20:9) We don't know who these people are, but they occupy Jerusalem and a portion of the Holy District. This worldwide gathering of the faithful will likely include the Priests and Levites of the temple, the Prince of the District, and the support staff. They will wait upon God to do according to His will and will likely celebrate with a final feast. To celebrate in worship what the Lord has spoken of and wait for His salvation! (Isaiah 25:6-9) These saints will be the last people to enter into the eternal state of the Kingdom of God.

Hostilities will build throughout the world and with Satan's manipulations he will cause Gog and the Kingdom Magog, to gather people from around the world and prepare them for battle with the intent of taking over the Promised Land and the city of Jerusalem. Claiming the City of God and the throne for their own, and making all the world humanity's domain. The world's replacement governments will create a vast army for the first time in almost one thousand years and prepare it for war. It is to be a worldwide effort, with people making weapons, providing logistical support, communications, transportation, food and all provisions. All nations are included among those who prepare for the final act of rebellion, *"whose number is as the sand of the sea."* (Revelation 20:8)

The names Gog and Magog, are likely metaphors taken from a previous chief prince, and a country found in the ancient writings of the prophet Ezekiel, chapters 38 and 39. In that time, a would-be conqueror of the Promised Land that Ezekiel writes about, is swiftly and utterly destroyed by God in a fury of supernatural judgment. The Gog and Magog in Revelation, chapter 20 is likely a "type" of a rebirth of the spirit of Gog and Magog found in Tribulation history. There are many similarities, but clearly not one and the same. This hatred of God's saints grows out of a wicked heart, that is unchecked by the Spirit of God. Gog and Magog desire to plunder the Promised Land, Jerusalem, and especially the temple. With the Almighty King gone, there is no fear of the Lord God.

On the last day on Earth, massive armies of the new world system come to invade Israel. God will act to keep His promise to the children of Israel. He will not allow His people to be put into bondage again or allow the Promised Land to be put into the hands of their enemies once again. In their final act of rebellion, Satan and the nations of the world come to Jerusalem to destroy God's people, God in turn beckons His enemies to come. He will destroy them and bring upon them an all-consuming fire that engulfs all of the world, in a judgment of fire that also sends Satan into the lake of fire. (Revelation 20:9, 10) *"Come near, you nations, to hear; and heed, you people! Let the Earth hear, and all things that come forth from it. For the indignation of the Lord is against all nations, And His fury against all their armies; He has utterly destroyed them, He has given them over to slaughter, Also their slain shall be thrown out; their stench shall rise from the corpses, and the mountains shall be melted with their blood. All the host of Heavens will be dissolved, and the Heavens shall be rolled up like a scroll all their host shall fall down, as the leaf falls from the vine, And as fruit falling from a fig tree."* (Isaiah 34:1-4)

What follows is that all of the created physical realm is consumed in a melting fire, just as foretold by the apostle, in 2 Peter, chapter 3. It is possible that every atom ever created in the universe will likely lose its mass and energy in some kind of event involving a loud bang and intense heat. Possibly a universal chain reaction that will likely dissolve all time and space. It was by God's word alone that out of nothingness, all things came into being, now at His word, all things return to nothingness.

With Messiah gathering the last of His saints to Himself, the collective Kingdom of God is complete with its people and its angels. Every soul that was born to be saved for life in the Kingdom of God will be saved and gathered together, according to the Master Plan of God. Jews, Gentiles, and people from every tribe, nation, and tongue, and out of every generation of humanity; redeemed and prepared for eternal life in a New Heaven and Earth. All of God's enemies have been destroyed.

Every earthly promise that God has ever made to Humanity has been kept. Yet, there remain still more promises to keep and the fulfillment of the Master Plan.

233

CHAPTER 13:
The End Of Death And Its Dead

With the temporary physical realm having passed away sometime shortly after the millennial age, there remains one more event in the Master Plan of God which will occur before the Spiritual Kingdom realm completes its transformation into a newly created supernatural Heaven and Earth. The event occurs in an unknown place in the presence of God, often referred to as the Great White Throne of Judgment. The apostle John writes saying, *"Then I saw a white throne and Him who sat on it, from whose face the earth and heaven fled away. And there was found no place for them. And I saw the dead, small and great, standing before God, and the books were opened. And another book was opened which is the Book of Life. And the dead were judged according to their works, by the things which were written in the books. The sea gave up the dead who were in it, and Death and Hades delivered up the dead who were in them. And they were judged each according to their works. Then Death and Hades were cast into the lake of fire. This is the second death. And anyone not found written in the Book of Life was cast into the lake of fire."* (Revelation 20:11-15)

After the end of the Millennium in that final rebellion, Satan will join the Beast and the False Prophet, in the Lake of Fire and will be tormented forever. This lake of fire is the gathering place created by God for the unredeemed to exist, first for angels and then later for humans. It is something like an opposite creation to the New Heaven and New Earth. Both of these realms will bring glory to God, for all things are created by Him, and for Him, for His glory and nothing made can prevent God from having glory in all things. *"Hell from beneath is excited about you, to meet you at your coming: It stirs up the dead for you. ... How you are fallen from heaven, O Lucifer, son of the morning! How you are cut down to the ground, you who weakened the nations! For you have said in your heart: I will ascend into heaven, I will exalt my throne above the stars of God; I will be like the Most High. Yet you shall be brought down to Sheol, to the lowest depths of the Pit."* (Isaiah 14:9-15)

Jesus has authority over the resurrection of the righteous, those who trust Jesus, believing that in Him they will have everlasting life, *"and shall not come into judgment but has passed from death to life."* (John

5:24) On the day when the redeemed are raised from the dead, these faithful people are given resurrected bodies that are incorruptible and made in the likeness of Jesus and are prepared for the New Heaven and New Earth. That which God has restored, He has also made better than its original, and God receives greater glory.

All who have died unredeemed have been taken into Hades; that place for spirits that we call Hell. Many will have performed good works and believe they have earned a place in the New Heaven and Earth. However, all they have done with their life has been recorded in the books that are opened before them at the white throne. (Revelation 20:12). They will have their day in court and stand before God and make their case.

At the end of time, God will have completed what He began to do in the days of Cain and Abel that is to form a complete separation of all of humanity that ever existed into two groups, the righteous and the unrighteous. Each person in each group will have experienced a bodily resurrection of the two types but they will experience very different destinies. God will have redeemed all the righteous, who will experience one type of resurrection, a resurrection of life to live eternally with God. And the unrighteous will experience another type of resurrection, one of condemnation, to live eternally without God. Jesus the Son of God has authority over the resurrection of the unrighteous as well as the righteous. Speaking of Himself, being the Son of Man, he says *"Do not marvel at this; for the hour is coming in which all who are in the graves will hear His voice and come forth- those who have done good, to the resurrection of life, and those who have done evil, to the resurrection of condemnation. As I hear, I judge; and my judgment is righteous because I do not seek my own will but the will of the Father who sent me."* (John 5:28-30)

Jesus makes it clear that there will be no righteous people found standing before Him, while He sits upon the great white throne. There will be no people who have been resurrected in the likeness of their redeemer present to be judged for their crimes against God. Those offenses have already been paid for and the sentence had been carried out on the cross on Golgotha's hill. However, the saints will be present at the court proceedings and in great numbers, to sit in judgment of and issue verdicts upon, the ungodly who rejected their Savior. (Jude 14, 15, 1 Corinthians 6:2, Luke 11:31, 32)

God the Son, will be sitting on the throne of judgment, (Acts 10:42, Romans 2:16) and all the resurrected people who stand before Him will be those who have not "passed from death to life." These people are those who in some way, are unrighteous. Their body and spirit reunited once again in a supernatural resurrection of the dead. Assembled, then called individually to make their case before their judge and a jury, who will hear them and judge them with a righteous judgment, according to the will of His Father who sent Him.

Their life becomes an open book and Jesus will allow them to speak to their defense, allowing each person to claim all the good works that they have done with their life. Even for some, claiming to do their good works in His name. But Jesus has already shared in the Scriptures what He will say to them on judgment day, *"Not everyone who says to me, Lord, Lord, shall enter into the kingdom of Heaven, but he who does the will of My Father in Heaven. Many will say to Me Lord, Lord, have we not prophesied in your name, cast out demons in your name, and done many wonders in your name? And I will declare to them, I never knew you; depart from me, you who practice lawlessness!"* (Matthew 7:21, 23) It was Jesus who also said, *"But I say to you that for every idle word men may speak, they will give an account of it in the Day of Judgment. For by your words, you will be justified, and by your words, you will be condemned."* (Matthew 12:36, 37) What people who are justified understand is there are no words that they can say that would justify themselves before God. Rather they, while in life repented of their sinful life and confessed to God that they deserve His righteous condemnation. The righteous will have expressed by faith that they have put their trust in the hands of a redeemer who saves them from their sins. The Savior, who paid for their sins with His own sacrificial death. A Lamb of God, who takes away the sins of the world. Claiming these things as God's gift to us, His grace spares all the righteous a trip before the White Throne of Judgment.

What those people who stand before the white throne do not understand is that all their own righteous good will not save them. They do not understand that it is the Master Plan of God, to save sinful mankind by the placing of a personal faith in a personal redeemer, who died in their place. It was to be a simple matter of a person trusting that it is the Lamb's righteousness that is sufficient to pay the price, not theirs, that it is His efforts that are rewarded and not theirs.

Before the sentence is given out, the Judge will make it clear that there will be no last-minute appeals for mercy and a change of heart, the times for repentance have all passed them by. The book that each person has written with their life will certainly reveal all their crimes against God and against people, which must be paid for. But it will also reveal the truth that in their heart of hearts, they never wanted God to have control over their life. In their own words and deeds, their book will reveal the moments in life when they rejected the words of God and the presence of the Spirit of God among them.

The books will reveal all the rejected testimonies and witnesses of God's righteousness, believing them to be foolishness, imaginary, or weakness. They will have called what was holy useless, and what was true, lies. Every day, they were confronted with the attributes of God which are clearly visible to them by the created physical realm they lived in; choosing to suppress the knowledge they already possess about God. They will be seen pushing away any thoughts of what they owe Him for their life. Like many people, they believe God is out there, but they find no time for Him. Still, others believe that God is too kind to judge them. They abuse the image of God by which they were made, preferring to pursue the lusts of the eyes, the lusts of the flesh, and the pride that can come with a life that takes what it wants. Others will be seen in their moments of rejecting the painful truths of God and settling for the comfort of a lie.

At the end of their story no words can be said, no defense can be made. Every mouth is stopped.

The Judge has a book as well, it is the Lamb's Book of Life, Jesus the Lamb of God who takes away all the sins of the world (John 1:29) In the Book of Life is the name of every person who has lived, from the days of Adam until the last day of the Earth, who have been granted eternal life through the righteousness of God's sacrifice. Jesus died for the sins of the world, but only those who place their faith in what Jesus did for them have their name written in the Book of Life.

Those people standing before the Judge at the White Throne will have their condemnation validated when their name is not found in the Lamb's Book of Life. These resurrected from the dead are judged according to their works, for they do not possess God's righteousness. No one escapes from taking their turn before the Judge. The sea gave up the dead who were in it, and Death and Hades gave up all their dead, no one is left in spirit only. They all are once again as a resurrected body and spirit together when they are cast into the lake of fire. (Revelation 20:15)

The lake of fire and brimstone is described by Jesus as a place where that person's "worm" does not die. The individual will experience an unending fire that burns both body and spirit that cannot be quenched. (Mark 9:43-48) We cannot be sure what the "worm" of that person is, but it is a negative expression, possibly of the corrupted soul of a person that has been stripped of all that is good that comes with the image of God. A life that was at one time a living image of God and able to commune with his creator is now left only with a singular purpose in living and that is to bear the wrath of God in a display of His holiness, justice, and power, that brings fear of God and glory for who He is, for all eternity. Evil has in its finality been thoroughly and appropriately judged. The just righteousness of God has been validated according to the Master Plan of God. Now the condemned exist in separation outside of the presence of God, all who had willingly cut ties with God are beyond the reach of both humans and angels, the second death is not an end to existence any more than the first death was. It is a person's final experience that lasts eternally.

After all the sentences are carried out and the unrighteous are in their final state in the lake of fire, we are told in Revelation 20:14 that both Death and Hades will also be cast into the lake of fire. After the white throne of judgment event, there is nobody left spiritually in Hell, neither angels nor humans. All people from the first to the last have been accounted for. The sting of Death and its power over all of the redeemed people had been broken by the Son of God. Yet its power over the flesh remained. But now, after the physical realm has passed away and final judgments sentenced, Death no longer has any authority or power. Death itself, along with its dead, will be cast into the lake of fire forever. Final justice will have been executed with the separation of the just and unjust along with an eternal end to Death. Now all things are made subject to God the Son, according to the Master Plan of God, that God may be all in all.

"Then comes the end, when He puts an end to all rule and all authority and power. For He must reign till He has put all things under His feet. The last enemy that will be destroyed is death. For 'He has put all things under His feet.' But when He says "all things are put under Him," it is evident that He who puts all things under Him is accepted. Now when all things are made subject to Him, then the Son Himself will also be subject to Him who put all things under Him that God may be all in all." (1 Corinthians 15:24-28)

CHAPTER 14:
He Makes All Things New

The Master Plan of God begins for us with the creation story, with the words *"In the beginning God created the heavens and the earth."* (Genesis 1:1) And it ends with the closing statement, *"Now I saw a New Heaven and a New Earth for the first earth and the first heaven had passed away."* (Revelation 21:1) This is followed by the statement, *"Then He who sat on the throne said, "Behold, I make all things new."* (Revelation 21:5) We read that God creates a new supernatural order, a New Heaven and Earth. We can say with confidence that at this time the ultimate outcome,*" that God may be all in all,"* (1 Corinthians 15:28) will have become a reality. The plan for a New Heaven and New Earth was revealed to the prophet Isaiah and should be of no surprise to Israel or to the Church as well. (Isaiah 65:17, 66:22, 23) And with a new supernatural realm, God will have completed all that He has revealed to humanity about His Master Plan.

In this newly created realm; the four parts of creation, the realm of "Inanimate Things," the Animate "Plant and Animal" realm, the "Angelic" realm, and "Humanity" will have all be made "new," each as God intended. He restores all things to their "good" origin, but He also restores them by making them better than they were originally. He prepares the four parts of creation that we have identified, for the supernatural, eternal realm where God will dwell with us.

The inanimate things of the spiritual and physical worlds that exist separately today, in the New Heaven and Earth, will be made compatible with one another as a part of the new supernatural realm. Physical things that have always been subject to the laws of physics and matter itself as we understand them, May or may not, have a place in the construction of the New Heaven and New Earth. Our experiences and interactions with the inanimate things of the in the physical realm may or may not be transferrable in a supernatural realm. Things like gates and walls and cities and streets in the supernatural may take on different qualities and compositions yet function as described. For example, a large gate made of pearl (Revelation 21:21) is still a gate, a sun is still a star and a moon is still a satellite that revolves around the Earth. Inanimate things such as seasons, weather conditions, atmosphere, oceans and landscapes of the

New Earth are all very likely components of the New Heaven and Earth but it is very probable that there will be more, much more to them. Time itself is certain to have a place in this eternal realm and will likely be tracked. The trees at the River of Life we are told, will bear its fruits "monthly." (Revelation 22:2) But time will likely lose its control and influence in an eternal realm. How is that possible? It is a mystery that we cannot understand for now.

As to any changes that impact the inanimate spiritual realm that exists now, we have nothing to say. We can contemplate changes that could possibly occur in the spiritual Kingdom but God has kept that door closed for now. It is probably safe to say that any thoughts about cloud sitting and playing golden harps will have to come to an end.

Inanimate things in the New Heavens and New Earth will be free from the curse brought upon them because of mankind's sins. It will not experience entropy or those "gaps" that plagued the physical realm after the "fall". Rather, the new inanimate things will function according to the perfect will of God and serve as intended.

All though we are exposed to very little about the animated part of creation, that of plants and animals in the New Heaven and New Earth, it is very probable that plant and animal life will be prolific in the supernatural realm. There will be two significant changes made in plant and animal creation. First, God will remove the futility and corrupt bondage that plagues all creation and a glorious liberty will come to it with the revealing of all of God's children. (Romans 8:19-22) Like the children of God, the animate creation will be delivered from the bondage brought about by humanity's sin. Second, God promises a day when He will covenant with nature. *"In that day I will make a covenant for them. With the beasts of the field, with the birds of the air, and with the creeping things of the ground. Bow and sword of battle I will shatter from the earth. To make them lie down safely."* (Hosea 2:18) There will be no curse. That warfare among nature, we know as the survival of the fittest, will give way to safety and peace. With the end of Death which was thrown into the Lake of Fire, the supernatural plant and animal world will be freed from the pestilence and the brutally violent natural order of things. The food chain will be broken and nature's life will be freed to live in peace. God will provide all creatures great and small with a new natural order, just what that will looks like, we can only imagine for now.

How this covenant and the absence of the curse impact the plant does and animal world we cannot be sure. Will the wolf dwell with the lamb, the leopard lay down with the young goat, and the lion eat straw like an ox, just as the prophet Isaiah speaks of? Or should we see these as only images representing an unnatural peace to come that brings harmony and safety for people and all living things? (Isaiah 12:6-9) The New Earth will likely take on a restored Garden of Eden kind of quality, which God said was good. However, God's pattern is that He not only restores things to their original intent, but He makes them better; never again vulnerable to the things that diminished His glory, but in a newness that will bring greater glory to God.

In the New Heaven and New Earth realm, the angels of the spiritual realm will continue to be the servants of God. They will continue to be His morning stars of a new creation, serving God as, *"His ministering spirits to humans, sent forth to minister to those who have inherited salvation."* (Hebrews 1:14) It is very likely that this directive from God to angels to be in holy service to humans will remain in His will. Providing service to humans is most likely what moved Satan and the demonic forces to take hostile opposition to God's Master Plan. Seeking rather a means of corrupting humanity that would result in their destruction by God. Angels will no longer serve over corrupted sinful people but rather serve with those who were called by God to be the inheritors of the Kingdom and made to be the glorified children of God.

With the eternal destruction of Satan and the dark angel forces that rebelled, angels will have changes in their roles in serving God. The Satanic rebellion, the war in Heaven, and the countless skirmishes between the demonic and the Heavenly sons of God have ended forever with Messiah, as King of kings and Lord of lords over humanity and the angels.

Their role as guardians and instructors for people will be over with as well. It is not revealed to humanity what if any personal transformation occurs or not, for the tens of thousands, the myriads of God's spiritual servants. It is very probable however that with the transformation that occurs to the redeemed of humanity, the relationship between people and angels will become a strong one. Angels and humans together in co-service to God just as the angel speaking to the apostle

John states, that he is John's *"fellow servant"* (Revelation 22:9) One highly probable thing is that all the mysteries that mankind has always had to awkwardly accept about angels, will likely no longer remain a mystery.

It is likely that each person among the redeemed will hear from angels themselves, stories and personal accounts of how they intervened in critical moments in time. Or how they acted on behalf of that man or woman while living in the flesh. Such will be the building up of a new relationship of humble appreciation and trust of angels.

Messiah will have fulfilled the Plan of God that includes the angels, *"that in the dispensation of the fullness of the times He might gather together in one all things in Christ, both which are in heaven and which are on the earth- in Him."* (Ephesians 1:10) and *"let all the angels of God worship Him."* (Hebrews 1:6) Now the King of kings and Lord of lords who reigns over the Kingdom of Heaven is no longer made a little lower than the angels. Jesus Messiah reigns as King of all and has been set by God over all the works of God, who has put all things, including the angels, in subjection to Him. Leaving nothing that is not put under him, but the Godhead. (Hebrews 2:7-9, 1 Corinthians 15:27)

Humanity, the fourth part of God's creation has arrived in its place in the New Heaven and New Earth. *"But the meek shall inherit the earth, and shall delight themselves in the abundance of peace."* (Psalm 37:11)

In the story of Humanity from start to finish, we see God progressively revealing Himself and His character to people over the generations of time. And in the revealing of Himself to people, He reveals some things about what He is going to specifically do for people. And with that added revelation, there becomes another entry into the Scriptures, another declaration that comes with promises, that people trust God for another new ordinance to be executed in the Master Plan of God.

The story of Humanity's place in God's will has always been front and center in the revealed Master Plan of God. Mankind's good and glorious start and then their fall into sin, is the cause for the other three parts of creation to fall into their own corruption as well. But God has a Plan, one that existed before the creation of the world. Central to the Plan, is that God will come into the world as a man and save humanity from its corruption. He will cause many people from every tribe, nation, peoples, and tongue, from every generation that ever lived until the end of the world to be saved by this Redeemer. He will cause them to become overcomers of a world that is enslaved to sin and evil and He will bring each overcomer into the Kingdom of God. He will take them into His Father's house to live face-to face with God into eternity. This God/Man, our Deliverer, who redeems us is front and center to the execution of the Master Plan of God and as King, will remain so going into eternity.

When the God/Man, Jesus Messiah, has fulfilled all the promises and declarations of God ever made to humanity, then God cannot be denied to be all things attributed to His character. When Jesus Messiah has executed all the judgments in the presence of the Heavenly witnesses, His judgments will be validated to be true and righteous and God can be said to be all-knowing and good for all eternity. With the execution of God's Master Plan completed, never again will angels or humans, out of their own free will, call into question the character of God or the extent of His authority. When Jesus Messiah has brought all things into subjection and under His authority, then He becomes subject to the Godhead. Then it can be said, "That God is all in all." The all-present, all-powerful, all-knowing, all-majestic, all-sovereign, eternal God. To His Glory forever!

We can know some things about what life will be like in the New Heavens and New Earth. The last two chapters in the Book of Revelation speak about this in some detail. The apostle Paul reminds us that it has always been God's intention to bring us into this new supernatural realm to be with Him. *"But God who is rich in mercy, because of His great love with which He loved us, even when we were dead in trespasses, made alive together in Christ (by grace you have been saved) and raised up together, and made to sit together in the heavenly places in Christ Jesus, that in the ages to come He might show the exceeding riches of His grace in His kindness towards us in Christ Jesus."* (Ephesians 2:4-7)

All the redeemed in the Kingdom are saved by God's grace, out of His love for us. But also, God also has another plan for the redeemed which appears to be for a future time, but that goes beyond speculation. For now, we know that the redeemed will be seated together with the

King of Heaven and Earth. This is a place of reigning with Christ and most likely involves having a place of regal authority in some capacity. Who they are reigning over and what are the limits of rule are is not made known to us in the Scriptures. Titles of authority and an assumed hierarchy of power are referred to but they are not identifiable. There are kings of the New Earth who enter into the New Jerusalem, bringing glory and honor to the Lord God. (Revelation 21:26) Because these are kings, we must assume by their titles that they have some role of authority over their people, but that is all we know. The whole matter of authority over others grows more complicated in that Jesus taught us clearly in the gospels that in His Kingdom, those who sit at His right hand and left hand in glory are not those who would desire to be great, but rather willing servants to all. Kingdom greatness will be in serving, not in being served as it was in the kingdoms of men. It will not be until the New Heaven and New Earth when people will experience a perfect Kingdom with its' perfect King.

All of the redeemed in the Kingdom of God will include people throughout the ages of humanity who have overcome the world. *"For whatever is born of God overcomes the world. And this is the victory that has overcome the world- our faith."* (1 John 5:4) The New Heaven and New Earth will be populated only by those who trusted in the Lord for salvation from the days of Adam to the last person to be redeemed on the last day of the Earth. The writer of Hebrews gives us many examples of people who by faith were overcomers. *"Therefore, God is not ashamed to be called their God, for He has prepared a city for them."* (Hebrews 11:16)

In Revelation, chapter 21, the apostle John is approached by an angel who talks to John and says to him, *"Come, I will show you the bride, the Lamb's wife." 'And he carried me away in the Spirit to a great and high mountain, and he showed me the great city, the holy Jerusalem, descending out of heaven from God, having the glory of God.* This fascinating revelation of the New Jerusalem, the Bride of the Lamb, and all that occurs within it is not clearly revealed. It remains obscured in a mystery that will one day be revealed to us. It can reasonably be understood as follows, by relying mostly on the information given to us in Revelation chapters 21 and 22.

In the account found in these two chapters, the redeemed people of the nations of the world are people groups from every tribe, nation, and tongue. All people from the kings on down will be able to approach the city as children of the inheritance. It is their city and it is their Heavenly Father's house. All who enter into the city are redeemed Children of God. To enter, people will approach the walls with gates that surround the city. There are twelve walls that are about two hundred feet high. (Revelation 21:17) Engraved on the foundation base of these walls are the names of the apostles. In these walls are massive pearled gates that always remain open; each with the name of each tribe of Israel engraved upon them. The streets that led from the gates to an incredibly massive city will be of a glassy-like gold.

The people groups who come into the city find themselves illuminated by God in the Lamb's glorious light. Again, the details are a mystery. People will see that there is no temple structure, we are told that the Lord God Almighty and the Lamb, are the temple, another mystery. (Revelation 21:22, 23) The people are taken to the River of Life that flows out from the throne of God and the Lamb but where to is unknown, possibly around the entire New Earth. (Revelation 22:1) People drink of the living water and eat the fruit from the Tree of Life, the same tree which Adam and Eve and all of humanity were denied. Every person of every nation partakes and eats from it. They pick the leaves from the trees, which will bring "healing" to their wounds and remove the scars experienced at the hands of one another who are there among them, while they lived in the flesh. No animosity, no regrets, nothing to hold back on, nothing needing to be let go or to get over. Harm's effects done to one another and to oneself are willfully removed though not forgotten. There along the river, healing comes to the nations from the River of Life that flows from God and sustains all who partake of His goodness. (Revelation 22:1-2)

After their healings, Jew and Gentile alike will enter into the throne room and stand together as one people, as the Bride of the Lamb, presented before God and the Lamb, dressed in the pure white linen of holiness, standing in the presence of the entire angelic host. There they will see their Heavenly Father face to face, with the Lamb standing with them as the bridegroom surrounded by a great assembly of witnesses, the four living creatures, and the twenty-four elders. Possibly, it is at this time that the words of the writer of Hebrews come to life for every person present, *"But you have come to Mount Zion and to the city of the living God, the heavenly Jerusalem, to an innumerable company of angels, to the general assembly and church of the firstborn who are registered in heaven, to God the Judge of all, to the spirits of just men made perfect, to Jesus the Mediator of the new covenant, and the blood of sprinkling that speaks better things than that of Abel."* (Hebrews 12:22-24)

There in the city, before the throne of God, is a convocation that includes all God's people. It is a formal ceremony, a timeless event that is likely the consummation of the marriage between God and the redeemed; in the ceremony, each individual will stand before the Father and Jesus. It is likely that Jesus will confess each person's name before His Father and the angels (Revelation 3:5) and a new name is written on a white stone, a name that only Jesus and that person whom He gives it to know; (Revelation 2:17) much like a bride taking on her husband's name. Each represents the new person in the Lord, a name that identifies with who they are in the Kingdom. There also, in the presence of all witnesses, God will put His name upon each person's forehead, to mark that person as His own for all to see. A mark that signifies that person as God's holy possession. Now that person is His priest, prepared to reign with God forever into eternity. (Revelation 22:3-5) With their inheritance now made complete, never again will His people be separated from the God who is all in all.

In our Father's house all people will come to experience Him, *"Behold the tabernacle of God is with men and He will dwell with them, and they shall be His people. God Himself will dwell with them and be their God."* (Revelation 21:3) And so, the story we are given in the Scriptures comes to its end, only to find that there at its end, a start of a new untold story to come emerges. A story that we cannot even conceive of, a story from the heart of the Father, Son and Holy Spirit for us to participate in. A story that is also part of the Master Plan of God.

AFTERWORD:
Framework For The Millennial Story

Questions and their answers about the Millennium Age come with the study of the Scriptures and our understanding of what they say and what they mean. Of course, Scripture alone is not the sole source for an understanding of all that is in the millennial story events. As previously stated, the formation of events and ultimately a story is similar to assembling a jigsaw puzzle. In order to connect the dominant images of the puzzle you have to infill between these images with many non-descript pieces. These nondescript pieces are necessary to align the images and properly place them within the context of the bigger picture and fall within the borders. Many of the pieces in the story are not verses of Scripture but are needed to bring continuity to the connecting of words written by multiple men, each having different lives, visions, and experiences with God. Also, external resources such as history, chronology, simple logic, and rational thought were factored in to make reasonable speculations where the word of God did not speak. Speculations formed and expressed in the story were guided by what the Scriptures reveal in general revelations about God, Man, sin, relationships, prophecy, glory etc.

Scripture guides the speculation in the direction that expose truths that we on Earth have never experienced before. Such as a world without Satanic influence and a world with Christ-like immortal people, who walk around leading and helping mortals just like you and I. Using a guided speculation helps us recognize that life will take on new values and purpose for many in the Millennium Age. There will be physical experiences for people with their Savior and King much like what the Apostles experienced. But it is also likely that as the centuries roll forward, faith remains the place for confidence in the unseen. Blessed, are those who have not seen and yet believe; obviously, many people in the Millennium will likely never actually see Messiah standing on the Earth among them.

Framework For The Millennial Story

Because the story narrative is about future experiences, speculation must play a part in its formation. With that in mind, the depth of speculation would need to be limited to just what is necessary, to what is pertinent to the story, without writing unnecessary embellishments, rabbit holes that would take us away from the story's direction, just as a historian might do. I have said myself many times, that if a person wants to, they can get the Bible to say anything they want it to say, by simply taking the words out of their context. In the preparation of the millennial story, I have endeavored to make sure that all Scripture references are given in their proper context, I will leave my critics to identify otherwise.

It is important to always ask, "What makes a story true when facts do not tell the entire story told?" It is important to emphasize that assumptions, embellishments, and logical conclusions must be distinguished from the truth of the Scriptures. If Scripture is contradicted intentionally, or not, it causes cracks to form in the story that the writer wants to tell. The same can be true for the writer who fails to include Scripture that sheds the light of truth and offers direction to the writer's story. Historical writings do not stray far from the perspective of their writer and will usually reveal the writer's intent for producing the narrative. Unlike doctrine, a historical narrative story can be put into a context that directs the reader to look at certain facts of history in a particular way or viewpoint that helps these facts become better understood. The writer's narrative must uphold the doctrinal truths and facts already known or be guilty of neglect or worse, deceit.

It should be obvious that God has intentionally allowed His story to be re-told in different ways. To be shared with people over the ages, a story spoken through the eyes of a storyteller whoever that may be. A person stirred up by the Holy Spirit to tell it, whether it be a Pastor, Theologian, Educator, Pipefitter, or someone like myself. The degree of information that God has revealed to us is documented in His Scriptures. The storyteller has no right to intentionally contradict, omit, or change the meaning of the intended message of the words that God has given to us. To be clear about this point, I will give this example. There is some commentary around these days which we often hear around Christmas time about what we know of the Nativity facts, as opposed to the conjecture found in Nativity stories. For example, it is pointed out that the Bible does not say that Mary rode a donkey to Bethlehem while Joseph walked alongside her like so many Christmas cards. Or that there were Three Wise men, or that the innkeeper told them that he had no room at the inn for them. And that the baby who was placed in a manger was not born with animals around them. Concerns that the story's teller is intending to replace some of the facts with conjecture is always to be a concern.

However, is it wrong for a story, to having being told from logical or reasonable postulations formed from the facts in the telling of a story? No, it is only wrong when the intent is to change the truth or to deceive the reader into believing a lie. Is it a reasonable to think that pregnant Mary didn't have to walk 90 plus miles to Bethlehem that she likely rode on a donkey or rode in a cart? Or that there were three Wise men because there were three gifts mentioned, frankincense, gold, and myrrh? Did someone not bring a gift? Even the little drummer boy thought it was needful to bring baby Jesus a gift? (No, there was no drummer boy, that is not reasonable, but is an example of an unreasonable embellishment to the story's message) And should we reject the idea of a stable occupied by sheep and goats? Or that Joseph never inquired at the inn, but was told by someone other than the innkeeper? Do we limit our thinking to just what is said in the scriptural text? Do all we dare to think about is that there was an animal stall somewhere and Mary and Joseph placed the baby in that? I believe God is not concerned about what perspective the story is taken from as long as His words and actions are not exchanged for our own. What God is concerned about and we as well should be, is that those things which He means to reveal will be changed to words that the storyteller has put into His mouth, and into actions that God did not take.

I propose that the same can be said of future events. God has told us about future events in the Scriptures. That all prophecy that has not come true, will be fulfilled and be a part of the story. Should we develop reasonable, logical scenarios about the future that hold to the doctrinal truths and specific words of Scripture? Would it be helpful to understand a story behind the words given to us from God? I believe so. To make this point clear I give the example of the doctrine of the Rapture. It is a hot subject of discussion and many people have prepared scenarios and lines of thought that differ from others who have reasoned out a Pre-Tribulation, Mid Tribulation, or Post-Tribulation story. Logic tells us that they cannot all be true but they could all be wrong. Yet, if the doctrine of the Rapture itself is preserved and honored in them, they make for stories with plausible scenarios. A Rapture according to Scripture will occur, but we cannot be sure of when or the details of how it will occur because God has not given us that piece to the puzzle.

The same can be said of the Millennial Kingdom, New Heaven and New Earth, and the Second Coming of Christ. Each has a doctrinal truth and each with a limited amount of revelation that is revealed to us in the Scripture. To be sure, when considering the Millennium Age and the Kingdom of the Messiah, all prophetic revelation needs to be recognized as authoritative, none of its details can be ignored simply because it doesn't fit into the scenario that the writer wishes to reach others with in communicating their story.

How will we view the writings of the Prophets as it relates to prophecy? There are patterns to take note of in the study of the Prophets. **First**: The Millennial Age is spoken of by almost every Prophetic book in the Old Testament. Only the two books, Jonah and Nahum, which are focused on God's work among the Gentiles of Nineveh, lack any word concerning the Millennium. **Second**: God's message about the Millennial Kingdom to come, is almost always given from God after He has pronounced judgment on the nation of Israel. This makes sense, God makes known the fact that just because He was shutting down the Kingdom and the Throne of David, it was not to be permanent. **Third**: The Millennial messages from God are true. Just as sure to be true as the prophetic judgments and punishments that were going to come to pass, so would the restoration and glory of Israel. Not by human effort and decision, but always done by the hands of the God who remembers them and His promises.

Four: The prophecies concerning millennial times are recorded by multiple Prophets in multiple revelations, there is no lasting chronological order that helps to make the story come together from start to finish. Their purpose was not to write about the order of events and their durations like a story. Their purpose in writing is to reveal in short postcard-types of messages, a single picture of what is to take place in the continued Master Plan of God, and how it will impact His people and the world they live in. These prophetic postcards brought hope to the faithful who followed the days of the prophet. They revealed God's compassion in times of despair and in the doom to come. These words from the Prophets reveal the loving heart of God, even in a time of pronouncing His judgment upon the faithless. The prophetic messages about the Millennium offered hope, acceptance, and blessing, to those who desire to see a better day ahead for the generations that follow their own. There is to be confidence that even in the "later years," God will be there for Israel with His Plan of redemption, reconciliation, and glory. Just as you gathered a handful of postcards on your last vacation which are intended to capture key experiences of your vacation story, so God, has produced these prophetic writings intending to capture Millennial Kingdom experiences that when brought together form a future story of hope to be told.

The Prophets wrote about their contemporaries, people in the not-so-distant future, and also about people far into the future. They also wrote concerning current events and issues, near-future events that will impact their contemporaries, and they wrote of events of the "later days."

Who the prophet was writing about presents a challenge for us. To which people of which time in history is the prophet writing about? Several tools can be used to help identify how to place the prophet's writing into its proper context. God doesn't do this for us, not to confuse us but to cause us to seek understanding in the work of the Holy Spirit. He will glorify Jesus in doing this, taking what is Jesus' and declaring it to you and I. (John 16:14)

The prophet does help us with context by frequently using key phrases such as, "in the latter days", "after those days", "in that day" or "in those days" to establish an undetermined milestone point in a time to come. These statements setup a future event or occurrence that is to be expected, not occurring now, but one that the reader may be familiar with or should take note of as something to be looking for, and He often uses words that bring sequencing to events, words like, "then", "afterward", "before", "after these things", and "in a little while."

Understanding the text within the context in which it is being delivered is crucial. We cannot make it say what we want it to say, as the Apostle Peter said, *"No prophecy of Scripture is of any private interpretation. For no prophecy came by the will of man, but holy men spoke as they were moved by the Holy Spirit."* (2 Peter 1:21). Attempting to force a text to fit into a particular event will likely cause problems with the overall integrity of the larger message or event. Generally, loosely hold any text that did not naturally fit into place.

Another important tool is the use of internal Biblical history to determine if specific events or claims made by the prophet, have already come to pass at some point in time, or if their fulfillment remains in the future. An example of this would be the manifested glory of the Lord. This presence of God left the temple built under Solomon as recorded in the early chapters of Ezekiel, and returns once again to a new temple built by the Branch, at the end of the Ezekiel. How can we know that this new temple in Ezekiel chapter 40 is to be the one built in the Millennium Age? Because of the internal Biblical history included in the story found in Chapter, 11.5.

External historical sources can be used in similar ways. A review of the history of Israel and the surrounding region is very useful in understanding the historical context in which the Prophets wrote. Does the external history point to a fulfillment of a prophecy at a specific time and event, or is it yet to be fulfilled as a potential prophecy for the Millennium? Another understanding of a text is to examine if the statement in question applies to multiple events of different time frames. In other words, is God limited to the use of prophetic words that apply to only one specific time and one specific event? I don't think so. Patterns, copies, and repetition are frequently observed in the movements of God's work.

Another observation about the story is that some of the words of a prophet or apostle are not prophetic in the normal sense, but are statements general enough, but intentionally applicable multiple times. Reoccurring truths that were applicable at one time, but also applicable again in the future are common. Words given by God, for all His people, for all times.

When reviewing all prophetic writings in both of the Testaments, we can determine what is believed to be specific prophecies, generalized truths, and prophecies that speak of two different times or events that apply to the Millennial Kingdom, by applying the use of the following tools:

1. Is the prophetic text in question symbolic of something else and not to be taken literally or as defined in Scripture?

2. Is the prophetic text in question an expression of poetry that cannot be taken literally?

3. Is the prophetic text in question something that the people of the prophet's day would understand differently than we would today?

4. Has the prophetic text been fulfilled in a specific past event, if so, is there a valid reason why the prophetic text should be denied being applicable to a second event that it fulfills?

5. Does the prophetic text clearly belong only to a different event or situation, rather than the one being considered?

If the answer to all these questions for each text in question is "no" then the text is likely a legitimate puzzle piece to be considered for the millennial story.

MEASURES OF SUCCESS

Without a doubt, writing about future events will generate differences of opinion from what has been stated in this writing. Rejection and criticisms are expected but such responses are not an indicator of a reduced measure of success. Success is in hand when:

1. A clearer understanding of how the Millennial Kingdom holds a key place in God's Master Plan.

2. An unshakeable understanding of how pertinent Old Testament covenants and prophets are in forming our understanding of the Millennial Kingdom and the fulfillment of God's plans for His creation and our future.

3. Those of the Church determine that they need to commit to being a blessing to the covenant people of Israel, by sharing the hope they can find in Messiah. And in return, be blessed by God according to His promises.

4. A renewed commitment to being witnesses of Jesus as Lord and Savior and living in this world as one among His Holy Priesthood. Bringing their people to God and God to their people.

5. Recognize the reality that there are people who are around them, Jew and Gentile alike, who reject salvation now but maybe only seven years away from becoming survivors of the Great Tribulation and find themselves to be among the first citizens of the Millennial Kingdom of God. Pray that they will live to see that day should their salvation tarry.

6. People will read and understand the Word of God as diligently as the Bereans did in the days of Paul.

7. A renewed wonder of how great God is, that He has a Plan that He may be all in all.

For Jesus is Lord and King over every age of humanity, that He alone is the fulfiller of God's Master Plan. *"That at the name of Jesus, every knee should bow, of those in Heaven, and on those on earth, and those under the earth, and that every tongue should confess that Jesus Christ is Lord, to the glory of God the Father."* (Philippians 2:10, 11) AMEN.

In an effort to limit the story of the Millennial Kingdom to a high-level commentary much like many historical writings. Numerous details and thoughts of both the author and reader could not be addressed. If you have enjoyed this book and wish to pursue more details concerning the Millennial Kingdom.

Please reach out to me at: **donaldcurwick3@gmail.com**

ACKNOWLEDGMENTS AND REFERENCES

Holy Bible New King James Version by Thomas Nelson 1982 (Used by permission. All rights reserved)

The Zondervan Greek and Interlinear New Testament by William Mounce 2008

Mickelson Clarified Dictionary of Old Testament Hebrew, MCT by Johnathan K. Mickelson 2019

The Interlinear Bible Hebrew-Greek-English by Hendrickson Publishing 2022

Israel and the Nations by F.F. Bruce revised by David F. Payne An Intervarsity Press Publication 1983

A History of Israel Revised Edition by Walter C. Kaiser Jr. and Paul D. Wegner 2016

A History of the Jewish People by Max L. Margolis and Alexander Marx Re-Published 2023

Unger's Bible Dictionary by Merrill F. Unger The Moody Bible Institute 1966

* 9 7 9 8 3 4 8 1 8 4 7 6 6 *